New Racial Missions of Policing

This book identifies new formations of race, racism and ethnicity at the intersection of neoliberalism, security, urban governance and the law through a comparative, international analysis of police organizations and practices. It pushes analytical and theoretical boundaries by examining racialization and ethnicization in locations where the topic is politically taboo, such as in China, India and France, and where racial and ethnic hierarchies have supposedly been banished to the past, as in Bosnia and South Africa.

This book also examines police and security services not as mere artefacts of state authority or the prerogatives of capitalist development, but as relatively autonomous and uniquely productive intersections of new kinds of state, social and cultural formations that are remaking race, embodiment, fear and control on their own terms.

This book was published as a special issue of *Ethnic and Racial Studies*.

Paul Amar is Associate Professor in the Global & International Studies Program, with appointments in Sociology, Feminist Studies, Latin American Studies and Middle East Studies, at the University of California, Santa Barbara.

New Racial Missions
of Policing

International Perspectives on Evolving
Law-Enforcement Politics

Edited by Paul Amar

Routledge
Taylor & Francis Group

LONDON AND NEW YORK

First published 2011 by Routledge
2 Park Square, Milton Park, Abingdon, Oxon, OX14 4RN

Simultaneously published in the USA and Canada
by Routledge
270 Madison Avenue, New York, NY 10016

Routledge is an imprint of the Taylor & Francis Group, an informa business

This book is a reproduction of *Ethnic and Racial Studies*, vol. 33, issue 4. The Publisher
requests to those authors who may be citing this book to state, also, the bibliographical
details of the special issue on which the book was based

Typeset in Times New Roman by Value Chain, India
Printed and bound in Great Britain by MPG Books Group, UK

British Library Cataloguing in Publication Data
A catalogue record for this book is available from the British Library

ISBN13: 978-0-415-54978-3

Contents

Notes on Contributors

Paul Amar is Associate Professor in the Global & International Studies Program, with appointments in Sociology, Feminist Studies, Latin American Studies and Middle East Studies, at the University of California, Santa Barbara.

Jaime Amparo Alves is a PhD candidate in social anthropology at the University of Texas at Austin.

Sophie Body-Gendrot is Professor at the University of Paris IV (La Sorbonne), and serves as Director of the Center for Urban Studies.

Dong Han is a doctoral candidate at the Institute of Communications Research, University of Illinois at Urbana-Champaign.

Eduardo Moncada is a PhD candidate in the Department of Political Science and a Graduate Program in Development Fellow at the Watson Institute for International Studies, both at Brown University.

AnnJanette Rosga, PhD, is a sociologist specializing in gender, ethnicity and security sector reform. She serves as Director of the UN Office at the Women's International League for Peace and Freedom.

Tony Roshan Samara is Assistant Professor in the Departments of Sociology and Anthropology at George Mason University.

Anasuya Sengupta is completing her D.Phil in Politics from the University of Oxford, and is the Regional Program Director for Asia and Oceania at the Global Fund for Women.

João Costa Vargas is Associate Professor of Anthropology at the University of Texas at Austin.

Abstracts

Introduction: New Racial Missions of Policing
PAUL AMAR

Why do police worldwide continue to reproduce race, racism and ethnic conflicts even as more members from historically stigmatized groups participate in policing, and as states adopt explicitly post-colonial, antiracist policy agendas? Why do new policing practices and technologies affirm racial, caste and ethnic distinctions even as diversity and antiracial profiling campaigns become central to defining norms of police professionalism in every world region? In this introduction to this collection, I will begin by acknowledging how the intersections of policing and race have returned to the forefront of public and academic concern in the US and UK. I then provide context by highlighting the gaps in the literature that this set of contributions addresses. I conclude by sketching the outline of a comparative, international framework for studies of race and ethnicity that aims to offer fresh avenues for scholarship and policy-making.

Policing and racialization of rural migrant workers in Chinese cities
DONG HAN

This article examines policing practices that produce forms of race-like status for rural migrants in Chinese cities. I analyse new forms of 'natural attributes'-based discrimination and regulation of the rural-urban divide based on hukou, the body of laws that control household registration and movement of workers within China's developing urban industrial order. I argue that rural migrant workers are policed in cities through a process by which new disadvantageous racializing identifications take shape, reinforcing stereotypes of rural migrants' bodily features. This research applies critical race theory to issues generally analysed through the lens of class. Contextualized within China's market-oriented reform, economic growth and social transformations, this approach to racialization endeavours to understand the intricate cultural and material aspects of rural–urban migration in China.

Geographies of death: an intersectional analysis of police lethality and the racialized regimes of citizenship in São Paulo
JOÃO COSTA VARGAS AND JAIME AMPARO ALVES

This paper presents an intersectional analysis of police lethality in the city of São Paulo. We deploy the concept of geography of death to investigate the multi-layered aspects of state-sanctioned lethal violence perpetrated by, but not limited to, the police force. This entails a consideration of at least three types of factor: actual violent acts, their symbolic dimensions and the historical and structural conditions within which violence emerges. Based on official data from the Brazilian state we argue that there is a perverse correlation between vulnerability to death and new racial formations, as they intersect with social class, age, gender, and place. Thus, the distinctive social geographies of São Paulo not only provide the context, but also define the very nature, frequency and experience of police violence. Ultimately, we argue, police lethality is a manifestation of the police and the state's complicity in reproducing boundaries of privilege and exclusion.

Order and security in the city: producing race and policing neoliberal spaces in South Africa
TONY ROSHAN SAMARA

This paper examines the reproduction of racialized urban spaces in post-apartheid South Africa through a case study of the Central City Improvement District in Cape Town. Urban neoliberalism provides mechanisms of governance that reproduce spaces generated by apartheid under conditions of democracy. My focus is on private policing and the regulation of the central city through the socio-spatial ordering of downtown in ways that secure the interests of property owners and more affluent consumers. Private policing in this context produces a form of social ordering based on emerging conceptions of racialized citizenship linked to market access. It works to exclude or tightly regulate the black urban poor, who are unable to participate freely in this quasi-public neoliberal space, and to remove these 'undesirable' elements back into the townships. In doing so, it contributes to reproducing the spatial segregation and the racial identities of the apartheid period.

Police marginality, racial logics and discrimination in the banlieues of France
SOPHIE BODY-GENDROT

Youth in 'high-risk' urban zones in France see police discrimination and brutality as a fundamental problem in their relationship to the state, but the state insists on marginalizing or silencing issues of racism and police impunity. At first glance, it seems that mainstream society and its political representatives are indifferent to the racial and ethnic dimension of violence that takes place in marginalized minority neighbourhoods. This paper takes a closer look at how the strength of entrenched French institutions and of police unions play a large role in institutionalized racism. This paper argues that a lack of institutional accountability within the French culture of governance also helps us to understand why the French national police are so reluctant to embrace the community policing model or to register the persistent histories and geographies of intersecting racial, post-colonial and class hierarchies.

The Bosnian police, multi-ethnic democracy, and the race of 'European civilization'
ANNJANETTE ROSGA

In many social science accounts of the role of law enforcement organizations in relation to race and racism, police are positioned as the agents of racialization projects, directly or indirectly carrying out the state's work of demarcating insiders from outsiders along racial or ethnic lines. This paper will argue that in post-war Bosnia-Herzegovina the Bosnian police themselves have been the targets of a massive racialization project — one undertaken by police reformers from the international community. Furthermore, by entering the fray with Anglo-American paradigms of ethnicity and identity, and by imposing reforms governed by such paradigms, they only differently 'ethnicized' the Bosnian police rather than helping them to heal extant divisions. In turn, these imposed solutions trapped internationals and Bosnians alike in a situation in which the presence or absence of appropriate ethnic demographics became, for too long, one of the main proxy measures for democratic policing practice.

Counting bodies: crime mapping, policing and race in Colombia
EDUARDO MONCADA

How do internationally informed, technology-driven efforts to democratize the police and citizen security policies in developing countries intersect with pre-existing racial dynamics and discourses? This question is relevant to scholars of both race and security in developing countries, given the current global diffusion of US policing reforms into distinct racial and political contexts. I analyse the intersection between the adoption of crime-mapping technology in urban Colombia and dynamics and discourses regarding the Afro-Colombian population. I find that efforts to democratize the police can paradoxically displace important questions about race from citizen security policy discussions and generate seemingly 'objective' findings that fuse with subjective assumptions regarding the links between criminality, violence and race.

Concept, category and claim: insights on caste and ethnicity from the police in India
ANASUYA SENGUPTA

Drawing upon contemporary conceptual understandings of race and ethnicity, this essay examines their relevance to ways in which the meaning and effects of caste are transformed within the everyday Indian state. Ethnographic insights from the police in Karnataka demonstrate the continuum of analytical concept, social category and political claim: different moments along this continuum allow for specific individual and institutional constructions of identity. Analysing caste and ethnicity in this fashion pushes further the porous boundaries of affinity and identification with concept, category and claim, i.e. with the politics of participation, representation and inter-relations. 'Training' processes to engender change and lessen discrimination by the police, therefore, need to use this complexity as a starting point, and root their methodologies in the notions of 'dignity', rather than 'diversity', critiqued for being flawed in its assumptions of difference and multiculturalism, and its inability to invoke a sense of social justice.

Introduction
New racial missions of policing: comparative studies of state authority, urban governance, and security technology in the twenty-first century

Paul Amar

Abstract

Why do police worldwide continue to reproduce race, racism and ethnic conflicts even as more members from historically stigmatized groups participate in policing, and as states adopt explicitly post-colonial, anti-racist policy agendas? Why do new policing practices and technologies affirm racial, caste and ethnic distinctions even as diversity and anti-racial profiling campaigns become central to defining norms of police professionalism in every world region? In this introduction to this collection, I will begin by acknowledging how the intersections of policing and race have returned to the forefront of public and academic concern in the US and UK. I then provide context by highlighting the gaps in the literature that this set of contributions addresses. I conclude by sketching the outline of a comparative, international framework for studies of race and ethnicity that aims to offer fresh avenues for scholarship and policy-making.

On the 16 of July 2009, Cambridge, Massachusetts police Sergeant James Crowley arrested Harvard professor Henry Louis Gates Jr, a prominent African-American scholar of race, literature and history who serves as Director of the W.E.B. Du Bois Institute for African and African-American Research. Sergeant Crowley, although white and named after an Irish militant nationalist, identified strongly with new post-racial professional norms and was described as a leader in implementing anti-racist reforms within a racially integrated police department. In fact, Sgt Crowley had been promoted by a black mayor of Cambridge; and a black police chief of Lowell chose the sergeant to lead a training course on ending practices of racial profiling within the police, which he had done since 2004. But at Professor Gates' front door, the achievements of decades of police reforms around race seemed to evaporate.

In an emergency call to the police, a neighbour had reported seeing two men possibly attempting to open the door to Gates' house. In fact, the men in question were Gates and his driver, who were simply prying loose a screen door that was stuck. The cautious neighbour had not reported the men as black and had underlined that they might, in fact, be residents of the home. But when the police operator relayed the message to the officers on duty, the operator raised the urgency level by mis-stating that the neighbour had reported two black men breaking in. When Sgt Crowley arrived, Gates was already inside and settled in his own home. The officer demanded to enter and ordered Gates to produce his identification. Gates complied, but also angrily demanded to see Crowley's identification and badge number. Crowley refused to comply and decided to punish Gates for his pride. Crowley did not, it would seem, draw upon his own sensitivity training and the new values of anti-racist professionalism that he had taught others for so long. Crowley arrested the professor in Gates' own home, charging him with a baseless disorderly conduct charge that was dropped after Gates spent a few hours in jail

Meanwhile, in the United Kingdom, another model police service, known for its world-standard, race-conscious reforms was also redefining itself around issues of pride, fear and insecurity rather than legal accountability or racial justice. A few months earlier, on 12 December 2008, a jury in the United Kingdom had found that police had acted 'unlawfully' when they shot dead the mixed-race, 27-year-old Brazilian electrician Jean Charles de Menezes. But this was an 'open ruling' which held no specific officers or police administrators accountable. The London Metropolitan Police had killed the young man in the London underground in July 2005 in the days following the terrorist attacks on subway trains, carried out by young British Muslims.[1] Ten years earlier, following the police mishandling of the investigation of the racially motivated murder of black teenager Stephen Lawrence, Judge Sir William Macpherson released a report on the London Metropolitan Police that included seventy recommendations for how to change police cultures, institutional practices and accountability structures in order to root out institutional racism. This report became a template for police reform around the world.

As in the Gates case above, interpretations of the Menezes case split into two irreconcilable camps. Some focused on the persistence of racism in a police force that had served as a world model. Others refused all engagements with questions of race and, instead, asserted the authority of police as heroes whose security and pride must be bolstered as they struggle to defend the city from the new threat of suicide bombers. In July 2009, the Metropolitan Black Police Association said they would not advise black and Asian officers to join the force, as they may face intimidation and violence within the institution.[2]

These recent police controversies in the US and UK allow us to glimpse changing patterns of governance and social structure, and to identify trends and paradoxes of interest to students of race, ethnicity and modernity. The cases above reveal the tensions that arise when new industries of security, which equate high degrees of social difference with dangerous levels of risk, are married to new forms of publically-minded professionalism that champion diversity (Bolton 2004). Also, we see how outward-looking reformist governments, whose leadership now includes members of historically stigmatized groups, have reached out to tutor the world and export 'progressive' models (Weitzer and Tuch 2006), all while seeming to reproduce or intensify racial logics at home (Phillips 2007). And we witness how city spaces have become repressive zones of surveillance and racialized fear (Keith 2005; Wacquant 2007), riddled with cameras and civilian informants, just as law enforcement consolidates an international consensus on the need to ensure community trust and provide equal protection to each individual. But what can we learn about these seemingly incompatible trends in police and security agendas by leaving behind the much explored cases of the US and UK to adopt a more global, comparative approach to these issues?

This research taken as a whole, represents a comparative project that tracks country-by-country distinctions in national legal norms, security technologies and discourses of state authority that converge around changing policing systems. We argue that intersections and contradictions between these trends are often managed through agendas that continue to essentialize and reproduce race and ethnic identities and hierarchies, even as law-enforcement professionals insist on the eradication or denial of racial and ethnic discrimination.

Anti-racial policing in a world of diversity

Police services in racially hierarchical and ethnically conflictual societies increasingly incorporate citizens from historically stigmatized groups as officers or administrators. But, paradoxically, in many of these same societies, levels of police violence and racial targeting of ethnic and caste groups are increasing just as police are implementing diversity and desegregation goals. What mechanisms allow these two trends to coincide and sometimes to reinforce each other? Why do new policing practices and technologies affirm racial, caste and ethnic distinctions, even as diversity and anti-racial profiling campaigns become central to defining norms of police professionalism in every world region?

Part of the answer to these questions lies in the ways that contradictory agendas – between intensive state-driven development and market-oriented neoliberalism, as well as between militarized humanitarianism and anti-militarist human rights politics – have been forged together locally and transmitted internationally by expanding the moral charges and civilizing undertakings of policing. The title of this collection highlights the increasing resemblance of police operations to travelling 'mission' organizations – their increasing links to humanitarian rescue missions, their historical relationship to colonial civilizing missions, their interest in exporting and inculcating morals and values, and their increasing tendency to operate as 'missionaries of modernization', carrying new forms of social control, urban spatial order and security technology into urban and international zones represented as 'savage' or 'at-risk'. Although the new missions of policing appear, in the frameworks of liberal and humanitarian understandings, as neutral, secular, techno-professional innovations, we argue that the symbolic and social power of these new missions of policing is not fully comprehensible without recognition of their embededdness within racial, ethnic and/or caste orders, and the illiberal economic, religious and governance structures that draw power from them.

This book brings together interdisciplinary and international work by social scientists to probe shifts and patterns in racialized practices of policing and related security and justice systems in Africa, Latin America, North America, Europe and Asia. The range of work in this collection addresses certain gaps in race studies literature, which I will discuss briefly below. Together, these essays also provide a new framework for a comparative analysis of race and policing. In the remainder of this introduction, I detail this new framework by drawing directly upon the contributors and their convergence around three objects of analysis: (1) new forms of authority deployed by the neoliberal state; (2) projects that remake urban space, territory and class; and (3) technologies and professional norms linked to globalizing security industries. Rather than walk through the authors' contributions in the order they appear, this introductory essay traces how these contributions converse with each other around these three themes.

Methods for analyzing police and race

This collection builds a bridge between critical race scholarship and the more public-policy-oriented fields of criminology and police studies. Since the 1960s, empirical studies and policy reforms in the law enforcement arena have been concerned with questions of race relations and racial prejudice. But many of the recent innovations in comparative race/ethnicity scholarship (Twine 2000; Goldberg 2002; Gunaratman 2003; Bulmer and Solomos 2004) have not been integrated by police/crime/justice studies. Likewise, some scholars of race have missed out on police studies work on political-economic structures, training regimes, professional cultures and the growing influence of private sector military companies (Shearing 1983; Bayley 1996, 2005; Amar and Schneider 2003; Andreas and Nadelmann 2006). What is lacking is an interrogation of how new forms of criminal-justice racism in the North relate to or diverge from forms of ethnic reification and racial formation in conflict zones of the Middle East and Southern Africa, and globalizing patterns and technologies of racialization and ethnicizing power (Banton 2002; Olzak 2002). Police studies and race theory can also work together to grapple with the social implications of changing security technologies deployed in the new populist states of Latin America or the booming cities of China. These disciplines can also collaborate on issues of multiculturalism and diversity taken up by police forces in the heterogeneous societies of South Asia and South-Eastern Europe.

In the North American and European academies, social science work in the area of race and policing has tended to focus on psychological dispositions and personal attitudes and prejudices. Studies of the cognitive or psychological aspects of race (Brubaker et al. 2004; Brubaker 2006; Holdaway and O'Neill 2007) have seen ethnic identities and racial attitudes, among groups like the police, operating as an epistemological framing device that both preserves and masks institutional 'prejudice'. But these analyses have not specified how these cognitive states relate to broader power relations and state governance logics, and cannot explain patterns of change beyond the level of the individual mind or collective psyche. On the other hand, rational-choice methodologies offer close measurements of the strategic choices of ethnic 'identity entrepreneurs' or they examine the accumulation of social capital by unions, police or other public actors as they incorporate racialized or ethnic groups (Woolcock 1998; Szayna 2000, p. 48). Rationalistic methods are best at highlighting questions of agency and competition, but are less adept at situating racial questions in relation to broader systems of power and histories of hierarchy. Taking a much broader view, historiographers of post-coloniality (Gilroy 2002; Hesse 2004) have connected race with

European projects of colonialism and fascism, offering a deconstruction of white supremacy. These perspectives could be enhanced by engaging more broadly with comparative and international work in the global south, where European models and colonial legacies interact today with changing class orders, developmentalist governance frameworks, security agendas and patterns of transnational technological innovation and financial circulation.

This collection develops a comparative framework that builds on new work in critical race theory and political philosophy that examines the racialization of the governance state in the context of globalization, and that takes the challenges of international comparative analysis of the 'racial state' seriously (Goldberg 2002; Sayyid 2004; Winant 2004; Gilmore 2007; Simon 2007; Goldberg 2009). The book interrogates how racial projects of the state, operating at its margins and at the street level, struggle to redeploy, naturalize and re-configure police identities and criminal justice practices under pressure from reform movements, legal changes, explosive conflict and neoliberal restructuring. These contributions trace fault lines, mapping where states in different world regions are shaken by the productive contentions and counter-hegemonic effects of disciplining and re-ordering racial categories through affirmative, inclusive and (at least rhetorically) emancipatory socio-legal policies. We draw upon the innovations of critical human geography and social movement specialists (Winant 1994, 2001; M. P. Smith 2000; Puar 2007; M. P. Smith and Bakker 2008) and their emphasis on participatory action, urban racial-political subject-formation, pragmatic interactions, and on the specificity and autonomy of state social-control agencies. These scholars' case studies reveal how race and ethnic formations are produced or transformed in specific places, and particularly in urban or national border zones where collective agencies meet. Certain contributions also incorporate the insights of those who study race, law, fear politics and security through the lens of gender and sexuality (A. M. Smith, 1994; Alexander and Mohanty 2003; A. M. Smith 2007).

Neoliberal authority and new state formations

The contributions in this collection examine new forms of neoliberal authority in relation to institutions of law enforcement as they participate in the roll-back of the state through privatization, as well as the roll-out of new forms of interventionism. These interventions can be repressive or humanitarian, or mixtures of both. They can be deployed in the interests of human rights or dehumanization. This book examines the concept of neoliberalism, not primarily in connection with processes of market formation but as a state-building ideology in Latin America, Africa, Asia and in post-colonial and post-socialist

Europe. By examining neoliberal globalization in a comparative light, we explore how the policing of race and ethnicity sustains (and masks) new extensions of state authority, all while enhancing the forms of expropriation and labour regulation that sustain models of a market-based society. Our collection extends the work of Stuart Hall in *Policing the Crisis* (1978) which analyses how the neoliberal state reduces the regulation of markets while it intensifies the targeting and regulation of social bodies. Hall argues that neoliberal forms of state authority broaden policing functions that aim for the punitive regulation of class and space, masking this shift by sparking race and ethnic panics which are then used as justification for repressive intervention. This work on governance through panic has grown into a sophisticated debate that utilizes the tools of political economy and political sociology to examine the production racialized insecurity as an essential tool of modern control (Balibar 1991; Parenti 2000; Garland 2003; Lee 2007; Lentin 2007).

In this book, Dong Han's analysis of policing in China explores the state's massive drive to promote export-oriented industrialization, build massive urban concentrations of infrastructure and cultivate a neoliberal class of entrepreneurs and consumers. His study argues that police practices that racialize rural workers are central to China's contemporary efforts to marry state power and market globalization. These rural groups' status, movements, culture and physiognomy are identified and reconfigured by police as they enforce internal migration-control regimes in China. 'Contemporary China's economic growth took place when neoliberal capitalism swept through the West, and China's growth model incorporated substantial elements of neoliberalism, in ways that enhanced rather than suspended authoritarian politics .... [T]he second-class status of rural migrants in the cities, are in line with the interests of both state and capital. The "temporary" status of rural migrants deprives them of state welfare and protection, and discourages them from self-organizing' (Han 2009).

The jointly authored chapter by João Vargas and Jaime Amparo-Alvez gathers together new empirical findings to produce an integrated mapping of distributions of violent death in neoliberal São Paulo. They develop a provocative analysis of the racial state in Brazil, focusing on how impunity and violence have come to dominate certain territories under processes associated with neoliberalization. More conventional statistical analyses that locate high rates of murder and crime in black and mixed-race neighbourhoods could reproduce old Chicago School-type models – 'ecologies of violence' or 'cultures of poverty' – that re-identify black behaviour or culture as implicitly or explicitly the cause of crime. Instead, compiling a vast register of new data on violent death and state violence, and drawing upon work on police cultures and racialized state violence (Huggins 1991, 2002; Amar 2003), this analysis maps the 'geography of death' back onto specific policing practices and institutionalized forms of state violence. They generate an illuminating reading of racialized violence that re-centres the actions and responsibilities of the state, which too often hides behind the racial myths of 'black markets,' gang masculinity and narco-trafficker power.

Neoliberalism as a vehicle for state extension and assertion also serves as a central focus of Tony Samara's analysis of the racial character of corporate-managed security in Cape Town, South Africa. Samara draws upon the African Studies literature on the 'privatized state' in Africa and the 'global cities' literature on urban business development and 'quality of life' projects, challenging us to reconsider the growth of private-sector police powers in contemporary South Africa. Some scholars have even suggested that urban neoliberalism constitutes a new racial project under conditions of democracy (Hetzler, Medina and Overfelt 2006), one in which the regulatory functions of the state are transferred to the market, or to the heralded 'public-private partnership'. Samara suggests that this type of neoliberal governance continues practices of the apartheid state under the guise of democracy, 'in ways that secure the interests of property owners and more affluent consumers. Private policing in this context produces a form of social ordering based on emerging conceptions of racialized citizenship linked to market access' (Samara 2009).

In AnnJanette Rosga's analysis of policing in Bosnia, 'globalization' and 'neoliberalism' become identified with agents of international humanitarian intervention. In a fascinating divergence from the other cases presented here, the law-enforcement sphere of the state in Bosnia does not justify the extension of its repressive power by focusing on the deviance of local racialized or ethnically identified groups, as one might expect. Instead, a racialized image of globalization is projected onto international forces who are charged with implementing peacekeeping and state-building missions (Wheeler 2002). From the perspective of the Bosnian police, it is not the Serbian militias or ethnic Croats that stand as the ethnic 'other.' Instead, NATO and European Union peacekeepers are seen as white, effeminate and alien 'civilizing missions'. And UN peacekeepers, often drawn from the police and military forces of India and Brazil, are seen as imposing a despised form of 'black internationalism' on the Balkans. Referring to Indian and Pakistani UN police trainers, 'a fifty-year-old male officer who had been on the force some twenty-five years said: "This might sound hard, maybe I shouldn't say this, but I feel [the] need to say it. Someone who's coming from a country where they hit people with a stick cannot come in front of me and teach me about human rights .... Many who came to Bosnia were having opinions about us that we are totally uncivilised. I think that you could see for yourself that we are after all people with a high level of civilisation"' (Rosga 2009).

Assembling class and territory in urban space

Many of the studies included in this book draw upon original fieldwork in the urban context, in spaces where national-, local- and global-scale phenomena intersect. In the spaces of globalizing cities, patterns of deindustrialization and reindustrialization, migration and segregation, consent and coercion, intersect. Research presented here emphasizes the mutually constitutive relationships between issues of class, territory and race as these formations are interpreted and impacted by police organizations. Here we examine how police attempt to control the economic, symbolic and political status of rural or peripheral populations in the city, and to root out the symbolic and social residues of colonial domination or neo-colonial types of racial and ethnic segregation.

Working through the urban frame, this set of studies offers new empirical data and theoretical models for bringing together analyses of class, caste and race. Han's paper on the policing of rural migrants in China's rapidly developing cities carefully weaves together questions of race and class: 'By "racialization", I do not assert that a new ethnicity is taking shape, but that there is a "racial" aspect to the oppression and exploitation of rural migrant workers, which is usually analysed using a class framework. While rural migrants lack generally recognized "ethnic" features, I emphasize the importance of trans-cending existing racial and ethnical classifications and endeavour to contextualize forms of embodied control within specific social, political and economic circumstances (Bulmer and Solomos 2004; Virdee 2006). The "racialization" approach does not exclude or deny class-based approaches' (Han 2009). The contemporary Chinese city, in Han's study, also operates through a system of permit controls regulating internal migration from country to cities, called *hukou* (Florence 2006; Pils 2008). Through stops, searches and detentions within this *hukou* system, the police generate a spatially specific, race-like order that facilitates economic extraction and exploitation, reminiscent of apartheid systems or societies that depend upon racialized non-citizen labouring groups to create wealth: 'Researchers have pointed out the de facto "immigrant" status of rural migrant workers in Chinese cities. Chinese law explicitly prescribes discrimi-natory treatment on the basis of *hukou*, and rural migrants are in a condition parallel to "illegal" Mexican immigrants to the US (He 2009). Through this system, rural migrants are deemed as 'visitors' in their own country, 'strangers in the city' (Zhang 2001), 'second class' citizens in urban China (Solinger 1999)'.

Samara's analysis of new post-apartheid racialisms in South Africa integrates the literature on 'race blindness' discourse with the critical urban studies literature on privatization. He argues that neoliberal urban redevelopment programmes, ubiquitous in the cities, 'are powerful examples of "colour blind" discourse and public policy that are deeply implicated in the reproduction of racial inequalities' (Omi and Winant 1994; Bonilla-Silva 2006) (Samara 2009). In the paper on São Paulo, Brazil, Vargas and Amparo-Alvez draw upon Henri Lefebvre's neo-Marxist's work on the production of space to generate a radical rereading of how police forces embed racialized violence in the operation and meaning of city space: 'All urban spaces, all human geographies are the product of historical power struggles, and the social relations deriving from such struggles become spatialized according to the hegemonic political order: "Every mode of production ... produces a space, its own space" (Lefebvre 1991, p. 53). While the resulting spatial relationships expressing degrees of subordination and privilege are normally maintained through consensus, there is often a need for explicit coercion. Police presence in general, but police lethality in particular, is a key element in the coercive apparatus as it enacts, to the limit, shared and normalized understandings about those it affects' (Samara 2009).

In Body-Gendrot's contribution on policing in France, the assemblage of class and race is interpreted as a territorializing dynamic based on how the nation space was transformed after Algerian independence, and the changing ethnic profile of urban working-class spaces during more recent processes of deindustrialization: 'After the second oil shock, a new law passed at the end of the 1970s focused on access to home ownership rather than on subsidizing public housing. Numerous large households belonging to unskilled or semi-skilled families – a majority of those were of immigrant origin – were then invited to occupy the vacant public units deserted by upwardly mobile employees and workers'. In this study, we learn that it's not the racialized populations who are identified as rural aliens, but the police. In the insecure peripheries of French cities, police are caught between the rigid apparatus of their state and the populations that the police, recruited in the provinces, have no capacity to engage or understand: 'Police recruits are almost never selected from within similar communities as the high-risk urban zones. Ninety per cent of those coming from provincial localities have their first assignments in the Parisian suburbs. They are influenced by what they see continuously on television and are not familiar with the urban culture of the high risk zones. It is difficult for them to distinguish among youth, most of whom wear hooded sweatshirts and hip-hop style clothes, and to separate out actual offenders (Bellot and Thibau 2008)' (Body-Gendrot 2009).

New security technologies and professional norms

This collection offers a comparative analysis of transnationally circulating professional norms and technologies of policing – from the 'soft' techniques of community policing, diversity promotion, gender mainstreaming and 'access to justice' promotion, to the hardware of crime mapping, closed-circuit surveillance and census-taking. These shifting sets of norms and technologies have been reconfigured, imposed or disposed differently in distinct urban settings. This is not only because of the influence of local legal, cultural and institutional dynamics, but also a result of conflicts within and between contradictory and irreconcilable policing norms and trends. These contributions share a commitment to analyzing how race, ethnicity and caste serve as the material that fuses incompatible professional trends and technologies (and embeds the social power that lies behind them).

How can one unite the police value of 'community interaction and trust' that has become the global 'gold standard' of police professionalism with the consolidation of a multibillion-dollar economy that funds the development and globalization of repressive counterinsurgency policing technologies? How do the police regularly pose as models for diversity and affirmative-action projects, while also elaborating crime-mapping and surveillance technologies that place entire communities into suspect status, thus cementing their racial status in the optic of the state as they are detained within exceptional curfew dictates, movement restrictions and punitive 'quality of life' codes? Our comparative, international analyses do not show that the circulation of these policing technologies and norms leads to a global homogenization of policing, nor to the integration of regimes of accountability or regulation (Walker 2005). Nor do we catalogue forms of 'local' resistance to these international policing trends. Instead, we utilize the lens of racialization/ethnicization to examine how these police norms and technologies justify themselves by generating fear, alterity and subjectivity in bodies and urban spaces.

In the study here based on fieldwork in India, Anasuya Sengupta offers an analysis of new police training techniques that identify and manage explicitly marked gender, caste and 'ethnicized religious' identities within the police service of Karnataka. She traces how the threadbare doctrine of 'diversity promotion' has become revived within the specific local context. In Karnataka, a long-term socialist provincial government has been working to remake its police within a national context shaken by triumphant neoliberalism and resurgent populism, and divided between Congress multiculturalism and Hindu nationalist chauvinism. In its focus on caste instead of race, this case offers a uniquely creative example of the value of comparative work that examines the contradictions of diversity projects used as a technology of reform and accommodation by professional organizations (Ahmed 2006). Sengupta identifies processes by which diversity projects reclassify Muslim citizens as a caste group or ethnic category, but fail to address the violence of Hindu nationalism or the persistent forms of structural inequality faced by Muslim Indians. The study also examines how police advocate the advancement of women without undermining certain 'masculinist' cultures or prerogatives, as has often been the result in gender-integrated police forces worldwide (Westmarland 2003). On a more positive note, this piece traces mobilizations within the police that offer an alternative framework of 'dignity' to substitute for the identity politics of 'diversity' that has become identified with governance technologies of patronage, cultural reductionism and racketeering rather than empowerment and citizenship: 'We soon recognised that "dignity" was a powerful entry point, precisely because it was, as one woman police officer put it, experientially potent: "I know when my dignity is violated, though I may not know what my rights are"' (Sengupta 2009).

Eduardo Moncada's study is based on fieldwork in Colombia, and upon new Latin American studies' comparative race work (Applebaum and Rosemblatt 2007). He also focuses on how a self-consciously innovative local administration takes on international policing technologies and remakes them in the interests of local class, race and power relations. Moncada's analysis of crime mapping in Cali challenges the reader to rethink this technology, which has become the holy grail of modern, reformed urban policing (Weisburd and Braga 2006). These computer-based data collection and visualization platforms plot and predict crimes by tracking them on maps of poor urban areas. Moncada explores how crime mapping redeploys and extends new forms of racialization even as the tool explicitly distances itself from the paramilitary and para-policing tactics of the war on narco-traffic: 'In the absence of a broader political project that explicitly recognizes racial discrimination's potential contribution to violence, crime mapping can both displace important questions about race from citizen security policy-making and generate seemingly "objective" findings that fuse with subjective assumptions regarding the links between criminality, violence and race' (Moncada 2009). We see how crime mapping operates in ways that appear blind to the more 'obvious' racial hierarchies and attitudes that once governed this Afro-Colombian capital, but end in justifying the containment and symbolic and political disenfranchisement of black Colombians.

Vargas and Amparo-Alvez's analysis, by generating visualizations of structural violence, offers what we might interpret as a progressive 'inside-out' version of 'crime mapping': 'Such maps suggest a geography of death that is constituted by not only the actual police and civil society's lethal violence, but also a social climate that can be accessed when we analyse various social indicators defining specific locations. This methodology allows us to gain entry into the perception of violence, including lethal police violence, graspable as socially shared and socially constructed knowledge that draws on the multiple, overlapping historical and contemporary forces affecting a particular geographical area' (Vargas and Amparo-Alves 2009).

In the 1970s, critical criminologists, in their analysis of the emergence of uniformed policing and carceral prisons during the industrial revolution, and subsequently Michel Foucault, in his work on the origins of modern governmentality and biopolitics in the early modern 'police state', focused on how the gathering of statistics has always been intertwined with the racial missions of policing. As Body-Gendrot writes, in France 'tools like ethnic statistics, which other countries use to fight racial discrimination, have not been gathered by the state, as this practice, itself, is still taboo (Body-Gendrot and De Wenden 2003). For example, after the GIA, a radical Algerian Islamist group, carried out terrorist attacks in 1995 and 1996 on French soil, the Commission monitoring the processing of personal data [CNIL] agreed that "objective, unalterable distinguishing physical marks" could be included in the police database. This was done despite loud protests by both civil rights advocates and right-wing conservatives.' However, Body-Gendrot points out that when the police later referred to the skin colour of people suspected of participating in collective urban violence, the Socialist Minister of Interior said such racial identification was 'against "the values of the Republic" ... and the practice was discontinued' (Body-Gendrot 2009).

Every case presented here is one where 'race' is taboo and where the political prohibition of race as a governance category is a cornerstone or 'founding myth' of the modern or post-colonial state. In some cases, race (in South Africa), ethnicity (in Bosnia) or caste (in India) are identified with past forms of unjust governance that the state must banish into history in order to achieve local and international legitimacy. In other cases, states see present-day racialization processes as 'national security threats', as alien ways of categorizing the population, or as external attempts to challenge the state. For example, France defends its Republican race-blind position against 'Anglo-Saxon'-style multiculturalists who, by tracking race in their censuses and surveys are seen as generating racial divisions. China insists on the inclusive mission of its coercive nation-building project and links racial studies to attempts to stir subversion and introduce recolonizing interests. Brazil and Colombia identify strongly with post-racial nationalism of *mestiçagem/ mestizaje* and 'Racial Democracy' ideologies. Although they are increasingly amenable to affirmative action and racial identity politics, they are careful to adapt the policies to their own national frameworks.

Conclusion

The group of studies included in this collection demonstrate that police are not reducible to artefacts of global capitalism, nor do they serve blindly as instruments for reproducing national or urban race, class, ethnic or caste hierarchies. Police services are complex assemblages of agencies, histories, class identities, masculinities and femininities, institutional and legal cultures. They are torn by internal class, gender and ethno-racial conflicts, not to mention the tensions imposed by jurisdictional limitations and, increasingly, by divergent corporate and municipal agendas imposed by privatization and decentralization processes. As the more ethnographically oriented studies here demonstrate, police officers themselves can also provide uniquely lucid analyses of the inner workings of these patterns of conflict and race and ethnic orders in the contemporary context, and can offer visions for radical change. There is a utopian dimension to some moments in these papers, demonstrating the subversive possibilities offered by fine-grained studies of the police. The edges of governance and constructions of racial and ethnic categories, and the violence that sustains them, are brought into relief. And as many of the police interviews reveal here, law-enforcement officers, at moments, can offer remarkable perspectives of clarity in how state processes, global forces and racial orderings materialize when they hit the street and are apprehended by the force of law. The studies presented here aim to encourage the development of new comparative approaches for the analysis of changing patterns of racialization in the global context. They contribute to a more nuanced reading of the coercive, symbolic and cultural-political power of the police services as state agencies and social formations.

The findings presented in this volume come together to generate a set of general conclusions or recommendations to be considered by those working on policy reforms, as well as by theorists of race and ethnicity. We find that: (1) Diversity promotion and social integration projects within the police cannot substitute for more rigorous, structural efforts that would ensure economic, cultural and legal equality and human dignity in the justice sector, and in the state. (2) New crime-mapping technologies will only intensify racial and ethnic animosities if they do not broaden their methodologies to cultivate measurement of the structural and institutional factors that drive racialization and ethnic stratification and that lie behind patterns of crime and violence. (3) The privatization of security and the militarization of policing in the urban context tend to escalate polarization rather than resolve race, class and territorial tensions in globalizing cities; for this reason, law enforcement needs to be folded into publicly administered, civilian-run, citizen-monitored organizations. (4) Forms of neoliberal state authority that designate large groups of citizens primarily as targets of enforcement – as problems for the police rather than as subjects of justice or as agents of participation – will inevitably generate increasingly repressive 'missions' for policing that racialize and dehumanize. And, (5) international peacekeeping organizations or transnational police-training industries can import and export race and ethnic identities and hierarchies, even as they train police to be anti-racist and to pacify ethnic and caste conflicts; so critical race and ethnic consciousness and scholarship need to be integrated with these reformist international interventions. These problems illuminated by the findings compiled in this group of studies can be best addressed not by suppressing questions of race and racialization, but by expanding international, comparative analysis of these formations.

Notes

1.   United Press International 'Jury: London police shooting not lawful', 12 December 2008.
2.   BBC News Online 'Delay in Met Police race report', 8 July 2009, http://news.bbc.co.uk/2/hi/uk_news/england/london/8140064.stm

References

AHMED, SARAH 2006 *Queer Phenomenology: Orientations, Objects, Others*, Durham, NC: Duke University Press
———— 2007 'The language of diversity', *Ethnic and Racial Studies*, vol. 30, no. 2, pp. 235–56
ALEXANDER, JACQUI and MOHANTY, C. T. 2003 *Feminism without Borders: Decolonizing Theory, Practicing Solidarity*, Durham, NC: Duke University Press
AMAR, PAUL 2003 'Reform in Rio: reconsidering the myths of crime and violence' *NACLA Report*, vol. 37, no. 2, pp. 36–40
AMAR, PAUL with SCHNEIDER, C. 2003 'The rise of crime, disorder and authoritarian policing', *NACLA Report*, vol. 37, no. 2, pp. 12–16
ANDREAS, PETER and NADELMANN, ETHAN 2006 *Policing the Globe: Globalization and Crime Control*, Oxford: Oxford University Press
APPELBAUM, NANCY and ROSEMBLATT, KARIM (eds) 2007 *Race and Nation in Modern Latin America*, Chapel Hill, NC: University of North Carolina Press
BALIBAR, ETIENNE 1991 'Racism and crisis', in E. Balibar and I. Wallerstein, *Race, Nation, Class: Ambiguous Identities*, London: Verso, pp. 217–227
BANTON, MICHEL 2002 *The International Politics of Race*, Cambridge: Polity Press
BAYLEY, DAVID 1996 *Police for the Future*, Oxford, UK: Oxford University Press
BAYLEY, DAVID 2005 *Changing the Guard: Developing Democratic Police Abroad*, Oxford: Oxford University Press
BELLOT, MARRIANICK and THIBAU, ANGELIQUE 2008 'Police and discrimination, an investigation by Radio Program Surpris par la nuit', *France Culture*, June 25
BODY-GENDROT, SOPHIE 2009 'Police marginality, racial logics, and discrimination in the *banlieues* of France', *Ethnic Racial Studies*, vol. 33, no. 4, pp. 656–674; 2010 *New Racial Missions of Policing*, London: Routledge
BODY-GENDROT, SOPHIE and WIHTOL DE WENDEN, CATHERINE 2003 *Police et Discriminations Raciales: le tabou francais*, Paris: Editions d'Atelier
BOLTON JR, KEN 2004 *Black in Blue: African-American Police Officers and Racism*, New York: Routledge

BONILLA-SILVA, EDUARDO 2006 *Racism without Racists: Color-Blind Racism and the Persistence of Racial Inequality in the United States*, Lanham, MD: Rowman & Littlefield Publishers

BRUBAKER, ROGERS 2006 *Ethnicity without Groups*, Cambridge, MA: Harvard University Press

BRUBAKER, ROGERS *et al*. 2004 'Ethnicity as Cognition', *Theory and Society*, vol. 33, pp. 31–64

BULMER, MARTIN and SOLOMOS, JOHN 2004 *Researching Race and Racism*, London: Routledge

FLORENCE, ERIC 2006 'Debates and classification struggles regarding the representation of migrants workers', *China Perspectives*, vol. 65, http://chinaperspectives.revues.org/document629.html (accessed 10 January 2008)

GARLAND, DAVID 2003 *The Culture of Control*, Chicago, IL: University of Chicago Press

GILMORE, RUTH WILSON 2007 *The Golden Gulag: Prisons, Surplus, Crisis, and Opposition in Globalizing California*, Berkeley, CA: University of California Press

GILROY, PAUL 2002 *Against Race: Imagining Political Culture Beyond the Color Line*, Cambridge, MA: Belknap Press

GOLDBERG, DAVID THEO 2002 *The Racial State*, London: Blackwell

—— 2009 *The Threat of Race: Reflections on Racial Neoliberalism*, Oxford: Wiley-Blackwell

GUNARATMAN, YASMIN 2003 *Researching Race and Ethnicity: Methods, Knowledge, and Power*, Thousand Oaks, CA: Sage Publications

HALL, STUART *et al.* 1978 *Policing the Crisis: Mugging, the State, and Law and Order*, New York, NY: Holmes and Meier Publishing

HAN, DONG 2009 'Policing and racialization of rural migrant workers in Chinese cities', *Ethnic and Racial Studies*, vol. 33, no. 4, pp. 593–610; 2010 *New Racial Missions of Policing*, London: Routledge

HE, LIDAN 2009 'Chongqing Gaokao Jiafen Luanxiang [Cheating in college entrance exam in Chongqing]', *Xinmin Weekly*, http://edu.qq.com/a/20090723/000095.htm (accessed 21 July 2009)

HETZLER, OLIVIA, MEDINA, VERONICA E. and OVERFELT, DAVID 2006 'Gentrification, displacement and new urbanism: the next racial project', *Sociation Today*, vol. 4, no. 2, http://www.ncsociology.org/sociationtoday/gent-htm. (Accessed 5 June 2009)

HESSE, BARNOR 2004 'Racialized modernity: an analytics of white mythologies', *Ethnic and Racial Studies*, vol. 30, no. 4, pp. 643–63

HOLDAWAY, S. and O'NEILL, M. 2007 'Where has all the racism gone? Views of racism within constabularies after Macpherson', *Ethnic and Racial Studies*, vol. 30, no. 3, pp. 397–415

HUGGINS, MARTHA, *et al.* (eds) 1991 *Vigilantism and the State in Modern Latin America: Essays on Extralegal Violence*, Westport, CT: Praeger

—— 2002 *Violence Workers: Police Torturers and Murderers Reconstruct Brazilian Atrocities*, Berkeley, CA: University of California Press

KEITH, MICHAEL 2005 *After the Cosmopolitan? Multicultural Cities and the Future of Racism*, New York: Routledge

LEE, MURRAY 2007 *Inventing Fear of Crime: Criminology and the Politics of Anxiety*, Portland, OR: Willan

LEFEBVRE, HENRI 1991 *The Production of Space*, Oxford: Blackwell

LEINEN, STEPHEN 1985 *Black Police, White Society*, New York: New York University Press

LENTIN, RONIT 2007 'Ireland: Racial State and Crisis Racism', *Ethnic and Racial Studies*, vol. 30, no. 4, pp. 610–27

MAC AN GHAILL, MAIRTIN 1999 *Contemporary Racisms and Ethnicities: Contemporary Transformations*, Buckingham, UK: Open University Press

MONCADA, EDUARDO 2009 'Counting bodies: crime mapping, policing and race in Colombia', *Ethnic and Racial Studies*, vol. 33, no. 4, pp. 696–716; 2010 *New Racial Missions of Policing*, London: Routledge

OLZAK, SUSAN 2002 *The Global Dynamics of Ethnic and Racial Mobilization*, Palo Alto, CA: Stanford University Press

OMI, MICHAEL and WINANT, HOWARD 1994 *Racial Formation in the United States: From the 1960s to the 1990s*, New York: Routledge

PARENTI, MICHEL 2000 *Lockdown America: Police and Prisons in Time of Crisis*, New York: Verso

PHILLIPS, CORETTA 2007 'The Re-emergence of the 'black spectre: minority professional associations in the post-Machpherson Era', *Ethnic and Racial Studies*, vol. 30, no. 3, pp. 375–96

PILS, EVA 2008 'Citizens? The legal and political status of peasants and peasant migrant workers in China', unpublished manuscript

PUAR, JASBIR 2007 *Terrorist Assemblages: Homonationalism in Queer Times*, Durham, NC: Duke University Press

ROSGA, ANNJANETTE 2009 'The Bosnian police, multi-ethnic democracy, and the race of "European civilisation" ', *Ethnic and Racial Studies*, vol. 33, no. 4, pp. 675–695; 2010 *New Racial Missions of Policing*, London: Routledge

ROWE, MICHAEL 2004 *Policing Race and Racism*, Portland, OR: Willan

SAMARA, TONY ROSHAN 2009 'Order and security in the city: Producing race and policing neoliberal spaces in South Africa', *Ethnic and Racial Studies*, vol. 33, no. 4, pp. 637–655; 2010 *New Racial Missions of Policing*, London: Routledge

SAYYID, S. 2004 'Slippery people: the immigrant imaginary and the grammar of colours', in Ian Law et al. (eds), *Institutional Racism in Higher Education*, Staffordshire, UK: Trentham Books, pp. 149–160

SENGUPTA, ANASUYA 2009 'Concept, category and claim: insights on caste and ethnicity from the police in India', *Ethnic and Racial Studies*, vol. 33, no. 4, pp. 717–736; 2010 *New Racial Missions of Policing*, London: Routledge

SHEARING, CLIFFORD D. and STENNING, PHILIP C. 1983 'Private security: implications for social control', *Social Problems*, vol. 30, no. 5, pp. 493–506

SIMON, JONATHAN 2007 *Governing through Crime: How the War on Crime Transformed American Democracy and Created a Culture of Fear*, Oxford: Oxford University Press

SMITH, ANNA MARIE 1994 *New Right Discourse on Race and Sexuality: Britain 1968–1990*, Cambridge, UK: Cambridge University Press

—— 2007 *Welfare and Sexual Regulation*, Cambridge, UK: Cambridge University Press

SMITH, MICHAEL PETER 2000 *Transnational Urbanism: Locating Globalization*, London: Blackwell

SMITH, MICHAEL PETER and BAKKER, MATT 2008 *Citizenship Across Borders: The Political Transnationalism of El Migrante*, Ithaca, NY: Cornell University Press

SOLINGER, DOROTHY J. 1999 *Contesting Citizenship in Urban China: Peasant Migrants, the State, and the Logic of the Market*, Berkeley, CA: University of California Press

SZAYNA, THOMAS S. 2000 *Identifying Potential Ethnic Conflict: Application of a Process Model*, Santa Monica, CA: RAND

TWINE, FRANCE WINDDANCE and WARREN, JONATHAN 2000 *Racing Research/ Researching Race: Methodological Dilemmas in Critical Race Studies*, New York: New York University Press

VARGAS, JOÃO COSTA and AMPARO-ALVES, JAIME 2009 'Geographies of Death: An intersectional analysis of police lethality and the racialized regime of citizenship in the city of São Paulo', *Ethnic and Racial Studies*, vol. 33, no. 4, pp. 611–636; 2010 *New Racial Missions of Policing*, London: Routledge

WACQUANT, LOIC 2007 *Urban Outcasts: A Comparative Sociology of Advanced Marginality*, Cambridge: Polity Press

WALKER, SAMUEL 2005 *The New World of Police Accountability*, Thousand Oaks, CA: Sage Publications

WEISBURD, DAVID and BRAGA, ANTHONY (eds) 2006 *Police Innovation: Contrasting Perspectives*, Cambridge: Cambridge University Press

WEITZER, RONALD and TUCH, STEVEN 2006 *Race and Policing in America: Conflict and Reform*, Cambridge: Cambridge University Press

WESTMARLAND, LOUISE 2003 *Gender and Policing: Sex, Power and Police Culture*, Porland, OR: Willan

WHEELER, NICHOLAS 2002 *Saving Strangers: Humanitarian Intervention in International Society*, Oxford, UK: Oxford University Press

WINANT, HOWARD 1994 *Racial Conditions: Politics, Theory and Comparisons*, Minneapolis, MN: University of Minnesota Press

―――― 2001 *The World is a Ghetto*, New York: Basic Books

―――― 2004 *The New Politics of Race: Globalism, Difference, Justice*, Minneapolis, MN: University of Minnesota Press

WOOLCOCK, MICHAEL 1998 'Social capital and economic development: toward a theoretical synthesis and policy framework', *Theory and Society*, vol. 27, no. 2, pp. 151–208

ZHANG, LI 2001 *Strangers in the City: Reconfigurations of Space, Power, and Social Networks within China's Floating Population*, Stanford, CA: Stanford University Press

Policing and racialization of rural migrant workers in Chinese cities

Dong Han

Abstract

This article examines policing practices that produce forms of race-like status for rural migrants in Chinese cities. I analyse new forms of 'natural attributes'-based discrimination and regulation of the rural-urban divide based on *hukou*, the body of laws that control household registration and movement of workers within China's developing urban industrial order. I argue that rural migrant workers are policed in cities through a process by which new disadvantageous racializing identifications take shape, reinforcing stereotypes of rural migrants' bodily features. This research applies critical race theory to issues generally analysed through the lens of class. Contextualized within China's market-oriented reform, economic growth and social transformations, this approach to racialization endeavours to understand the intricate cultural and material aspects of rural-urban migration in China.

Introduction

Studies of racial identity in China often focus on concepts constructed along with the rise of China as a modern nation-state or on the relationships between state-recognized ethno-national 'minority' identities within the country. The former tend to probe deep into Chinese history and to trace the formation of Chinese nationalism and the notion of Han Chinese as a 'race' (Dikötter 1992, 1997). The latter can cover a wide range of issues in relation to ethnic minority culture, politics and economy. According to the official account, there are 55 ethnic minority groups in China, with the majority of Han Chinese amounting to 90.56 per cent of the total population by the end of 2005 (National Bureau of Statistics of China 2006). Ethnic conflicts, issues of 'assimilation', Chinese state policy and construction and transformation of minority identities are frequently discussed topics. However, drawing on critical racial theories, this chapter takes a different approach.

Seen most broadly, 'race' is a concept that signifies and symbolizes social conflicts and interests (Omi and Winant 1994). Racial identities are constructed culturally and socio-historically, rather than based on any 'scientific' findings in human genes or biological traces. The idea of race evolves and is transformed through a process in which power and resources are distributed on the basis of fictional biological traits (Roediger 2008). In the US race is often perceived as a matter of skin colour, where differences can mark and regulate social status, pointing to different positions in the power relationship (Gómez 2007). A critical racial study needs to avoid prioritizing any particular system for classifying race or ethnicity, and, instead, can endeavour to develop comparative studies of racism with other social relations in order to understand how racialized identities are being articulated in particular social and political contexts (Bulmer and Solomos 2004). It is important to note that 'all social relationships have both material/economic aspects and cultural/meaningful aspects' and 'it is possible to develop an analysis of social identities round the notion of *multiple positioning*' (Fenton and Bradley 2002, emphasis in original). Although these arguments are mostly based in Western contexts, they figure significantly in this chapter and open up new spaces for researching racism in China.

It is in this sense that police practices and systematic stigmatization of rural migrants in Chinese cities become the focus of this research. I focus on a 'natural attributes'-based discrimination in China's developing urban industrial market economies, and on the rural-urban divide based on *hukou*, the body of laws that control household registration and movement of workers within the country. I argue that rural migrant workers (*mingong*) are policed in cities through a process by which disadvantageous new racial identities take shape. Solinger draws a parallel between migrant workers in China and racial groups in the West, stating that 'the Chinese peasants' lot in the city was much more akin to that of black people in South Africa before the 1990s or of blacks and Asians in the United States throughout the first half of the twentieth century' (1999, p. 5). This chapter seeks to test and explore this comparison by documenting the process in which migrant workers are not merely 'parallel to' victims of racism but can be seen as subject to processes of 'racialization' unique to the Chinese context.

The analysis of changing policing practices is central to new perspectives on racialization in contemporary China. Chinese police are the sole governmental organ to implement the system of *hukou* (similar to an internal passport regime made up of legal controls over one's right to reside and work in a particular area). Police manage *hukou* registration, transfer and book-keeping. In enforcing the rural-urban *hukou* divide, urban police use force to execute their duties, including locking up rural migrants and transporting them back to where their rural registration fixes them. In the process, the police rely on stereotyped physical features of *mingong* to identify the subjects of *hukou* enforcement, thus creating a situation in Chinese cities in which having particular visible features can subject one to a whole set of discriminatory legal restraints and policing treatments. I begin by discussing ethnicity and racism in China, then move on to discuss *hukou* as a segregation system and its enforcement through policing. Then I detail the case of Sun Zhigang, a *hukou*-less migrant worker victimized under racializing *hukou* enforcement and extra-legal brutality. I conclude by situating the racialization of rural migrant workers in the context of socioeconomic changes in contemporary China.

Locating racism in China

A discussion on racism in China needs to begin with a mapping of ethno-national identities. In the official account, there are 56 different ethnic groups in China. Han Chinese (*hanzu*) form the dominant majority and the other 55 groups are referred to as 'ethnic minorities (*shaoshu minzu*)'. This categorization is a recent product of the People's Republic, which conducted a lengthy process of 'ethnic identification (*minzu shibie*)', using the Stalinist formula of four criteria: common language, territory, economy and culture (Smith 2000; Wang 2000). Today, the Chinese government uses the narrower criterion of descent to establish ethnic identity. A person with one-eighth ethnic minority descent can claim minority identity, without proving cultural affiliation or language competency (Hoddie 1998, p. 124).

The Chinese government has always paid significant attention to managing ethnic relations, particularly the relation between ethnic minorities and Han people. State ethnic policy has two distinct features: 'politicizing' ethnic relations and preferential treatment for the minorities (Ma 2004, 2007). Ma coined the term 'politization *(zhengzhihua)*', which means to grant minorities institutionalized political power on the basis of state-recognized ethnic identities. In addition, the Chinese government offers significant preferential treatment and privileges to minority groups (Hoddie 1998; Pang 1998; Ma 2007). Such preferential treatment may include less tax, more governmental subsidies and suspension of one-child-per-family restrictions. As a result, Chinese people try to claim ethnic minority status whenever possible, motivated by the benefits of minority identities (Hoddie 1998).[1] One researcher parallels such preferential treatments to affirmative action in the USA, and maintains that they contribute to greater social equality (Sautman

1998), but street riots in Tibet and Xinjiang by 'ethnic minority nationalities' in recent years challenge the state's claim to affirmative treatment of minorities, asserting instead that the state is aiming to extinguish them through Han colonization of their 'home' communities and violent police repression of minority members when they migrate to cities.

Issues of ethno-national or racial prejudice in China are talked about in ways that are very different from in the west. First, in the west many understand racism as between whites and people of colour, but this concept of 'race' does not apply to systems of racial ordering in some non-western countries (Dikötter 1992). In addition, over the last few centuries China has not had significant immigration, which is an important focal point of racialization and stigma in many western countries. Different ethnic groups in China today have been living together for hundreds, sometime thousands, of years and had extensive interaction with, and influence upon, each other. Significant differences in history and socio-political circumstances highlight the importance of locating 'common features' of racism (Bulmer and Solomos 2004, p. 8), rather than looking for Chinese versions of manifestations of western racial logics.

This research focuses on the particular contemporary Chinese logic of racialization of rural migrant workers in cities undergoing rapid industrialization and socially polarizing development. 'Racialization' emphasizes that racial and ethnic identities are not static but are constantly undergoing transformation. The focus on rural migrant workers (in Chinese, *mingong*) does not seem to fit readily into ethnic and racial studies – *mingong* do not seem to possess any unique, formally recognized ethnic features that distinguish them from urban residents. However, through policing they are subject to a whole set of discriminatory regulations and practices, enforced largely by looking for visible/audible identity markers like hair, apparel, personal hygiene and dialect. This is a Chinese case of racism, which 'attempt[s] to fix human social groups in terms of natural properties of belonging within particular political and geographical context' (Bulmer and Solomos 2004, p. 8).

It is by no means novel to note the racial (for some, quasi-racial) aspect of discrimination against Chinese rural migrant workers. Solinger (1999) draws a parallel between *mingong*, black people in South Africa under Apartheid and blacks and Asians in the USA in early twentieth century. While the latter two are generally framed and understood in racial terms, by placing *mingong* side by side with them she implicitly points to the potential of applying racial analytical tools to migrant labour in China. Based on the fact that rural identities are determined by blood rather than place of birth, Pils (n.d.) points out that the status of *mingong* in China bears significant similarity to that of *pariah* in the Indian caste system. In addition, web forum postings and blogs in China tend to be more assertive in defining the discrimination against *mingong* in racial terms. A posting titled '*Hukou, the Chinese version of Apartheid*' argues that the Chinese rural population is faced with a segregation system comparable to, if not worse than, that of Apartheid in South Africa (Chinaworker.info 2008). A blogger argues that one of the consequences of *hukou* is racial discrimination (*zhongzu qishi*), that the segregation of *hukou* has resulted in the formation of two distinct *ethnic* groups, the urban and the rural (*cheng hanzu* and *xiang hanzu*), and that the gap between the two is deep-rooted and difficult to cross (Guancanghai 2008). When both institution-based researchers and individual bloggers use racial terms and analogies to describe rural migrant labour, generally analysed under a class-based framework, can we not argue that they have all perceived the inadequacy of a simple class perspective as well as the promise of racial analysis in this case?

Hukou, rural migrant workers and the police

Rural-urban migration and state intervention have a long history in the People's Republic of China. When the Communist Party came to power in 1949, China adopted the Soviet Union's developmental model that stressed industrialization and urbanization. This model drew a profound distinction between the urban and the rural, the former being the developmental front and the latter the supportive backstage. However, massive migration from country to city began immediately, when underemployment in the countryside drove many peasants to move to urban areas to make a living. During 1950s the Chinese state took measures to stop and to reverse the rural-urban population flow, including both 'soft' measures like incentives and persuasion and harsh actions including detention and 'deportation', sending them back to where they were from (Solinger 1999; Biddulph 2007). This was because, under a centrally planned economy, state welfare benefits were available only to city residents on the basis of a static, easy-to-calculate urban population. Rural-urban migration threatened the provision of welfare to the 'privileged' urban residents (Cheng and Selden 1994; Solinger 1999). This was when *hukou*, the household registration system that regulates domestic migration, came into being.

Contemporary Chinese society has undergone profound changes in the past three decades. Market-oriented reform (re)installed capitalistic relationships in a wide array of social sectors and significantly re-shaped social hierarchy. City-centred, industrialization-oriented developmental policy extracted rural surpluses to fuel urban growth (Meisner 1999). Cities became the centre and forefront of economic and cultural development. Rural residents, mostly peasants, went to cities to look for jobs and to seek fulfilment, when country life could promise neither a livelihood nor a future (Yan 2008). These processes resulted in large-scale rural-urban migration in contemporary China (Davin 1999), at a time when urban industrial sectors were hungering for 'free', cheap labour. The *hukou* (household registration) system, originally set up in the 1950s to bind peasants to the land they farmed, was no longer necessarily enforced to expel rural migrants from cities, but to mark their presence in the cities as forever 'temporary', taking advantage of their labour while denying them urban citizenship at the same time (Solinger 1999; Wang 2005; Florence 2006).

Researchers have pointed out the *de facto* 'immigrant' status of rural migrant workers in Chinese cities. Chinese law explicitly prescribes discriminatory treatment on the basis of *hukou*, and rural migrants are in a condition parallel to that of 'illegal' Mexican immigrants to the US (He 2004). Without *hukou*, rural migrants are deemed 'visitors' in their own country, 'strangers in the city' (Zhang 2001), 'second-class' citizens in urban China (Solinger 1999). In the prejudiced view of urban discourse, they are thought to be poor, greedy for money, having no good judgment and no education (Florence 2006), and they face intense contempt from the 'privileged' urban dwellers (Pils n.d.). The Chinese government, in many cases, also sees them as the cause of increased crime rates, worsening sanitary problems and deteriorating public order in the cities (Zhang 2001). Similar to some western cases in which new immigrants tend to be blamed for all social and community problems, *hukou*-less *mingong* in Chinese cities are always the target of social prejudice and intense police surveillance.

The police are the sole state organ to implement *hukou* in China. Different from the USA (and most western countries), where social security and other household-related administrative tasks are carried out by non-police governmental branches, Chinese *hukou* has always been managed by the police, which keep *hukou* books, register, transfer or change residential status and issue ID cards and temporary residence permits. In addition, it is the police who have the power to stop people in the streets, knock on doors, check ID cards and temporary permits, and detain people if they fail to show the required photo IDs. It makes the police overwhelmingly the most important and most frequently contacted state agency for rural migrant workers.

The police system in the People's Republic of China is deeply embedded in the history of political struggles. According to Dutton (2005), the Chinese policing system was born in response to a crisis in the history of the Communist Party, when its close ally, the Nationalist Party, suddenly turned against it and massacred huge numbers of Communists and sympathizers in late 1920s. From then on, the police force became a core organ in the party system, fighting against 'enemies' of the Party. This function persisted after the Communists came to power in 1949, and is a key feature of policing in China. Police in China have always enjoyed a wide range of power in investigation, interrogation and detention. The division of power between the police, the procuratorate[2] and the court is subject to the larger goal of fighting the enemies of the Party, spearheaded by the police. While the police are not free from supervision and checks from other party and governmental organs, their broad powers have deep historical and institutional origins.

One of the most significant powers of Chinese police is the ability to detain people as a form of administrative penalty. This is referred to as 'administrative detention (*xingzheng juliu*)', in that the police is deemed an administrative organ, with an almost unlimited discretion to detain people. Administrative detention is a widely used policing tactic. As early as the 1950s, the police detained rural migrants in urban areas so as to 'cleanse' streets in the cities (Biddulph 2007). The Administrative Penalty Law (*Xingzheng Chufa Fa*) in 1996 formally stipulated that administrative detention is a form of 'administrative penalty (*xingzheng chufa*)' for 'administrative offences (*xingzheng weifa*)', which are minor offences that are deemed less serious than 'crimes (*fanzui*)'. The power of administrative detention solely rests with the police, though judicial review may be invoked afterwards. In addition, being the state organ that enforces *hukou*, the police have the power to check anybody's ID cards and other identity documents at any time. Suspected vagrants and beggars, or basically anybody that fails to produce required documents, can be detained by the police for further investigation, and, if applicable, be sent back to where their *hukou* belongs.

This is tremendous power for the police. It means that a police station, if so inclined, can lock up (if only temporarily) anybody in the absence of a photo ID. However, if we take into consideration that policing in contemporary China emphasizes targeting particular groups of people, rather than treating the population as a homogenous whole (Dutton and Lee 1993), then excessive police power cannot be deemed as a threat to an abstracted 'citizen' but rather as an institution aiming to distinguish some 'citizens' from others. Many urban residents of the new middle classes in China tend to blame rural migrants for social problems and increased crimes, a situation not much different from that faced by immigrants in the USA (Solinger 1999). In the city of Beijing, Zhejiang Village (*Zhejiang Cun*), the community of migrants from the southern province of Zhejiang, was demolished by the police in the name of tackling crime (Dutton 1998; Zhang 2001). In another instance, a report from Beijing police argues that control over migrant workers is the primary strategy for maintaining social order and tackling crime, though their own statistics show that migrants commit less than a quarter of the total crimes in the city (Yang and Wang 1998). Indeed, rates of crime by rural migrants are generally overestimated. And most of these criminal activities, when they do occur, are petty, non-violent economic crimes – driven by extreme need and marginalization (Zhao and Kipnis 2000).

A new term, 'three withouts', was coined for rural migrant workers, beggars and the homeless, which compose a 'target group' for the police. 'Three withouts' means 'without ID card, without temporary residence permit and without proof of employment'. It depicts rural migrant workers as aimless (without jobs), lawless (without temporary residence permits) and faceless (without identity). Being an updated version of another derogatory label, '*mangliu* (blind, floating people)', widely used in the 1980s (Florence 2006), 'three withouts' not only demeans rural migrant workers, but also justifies arbitrary detention and abuse by the police.

As a matter of fact, nobody is really a 'three withouts'. Every Chinese citizen has a government-issued ID card. Many rural migrant workers do have jobs in the cities, and if they are willing to go through the lengthy procedure and to pay often over-charged fees, they can obtain temporary residence permits.[3] 'Three withouts' actually refers only to the moment one is stopped by the police in the streets – without the three in hand one will be detained at once. This poses a significant threat to rural migrant workers in the cities because, in order to protect them from theft, loss or damage at work, not many of them carry their documents with them all the time. If someone loses her/his ID card, the process of applying for a new card can be unpredictable and time-consuming, especially when the person lives away from where her/his *hukou* is. Also, migrant workers who toil on construction sites or collect scraps generally have very few belongings. It would be an excessive burden for them to carry their documents all the time. Through the case of Sun Zhigang, we will explore in detail what it is like to be a 'three withouts' caught by the police, how one's looks could trigger discriminatory policing and extra-legal brutality, and how racial identities are constructed through the process.

The detention and death of *hukou*-less Sun Zhigang

On 17 March 2003, Sun Zhigang, a 27-year-old young man, was walking in the streets of Guangzhou, one of the largest cities in the southern part of China. He had recently accepted a job offer from an apparel company, and had only just moved to the city. Sun was a migrant worker. The complexity and rigidity of the strict Chinese *hukou* system did not allow him to get a Guangzhou *hukou* although his employment was legal and a regular one. According to the law, he must obtain a 'temporary residence permit (*zanzhuzheng*)' in order to live and work legitimately in the city. In addition, he was supposed to carry all his identity documents with him all the time, because the police might stop him in the street and check. On that day it happened. Sun did not have a temporary residence permit, and he actually did not have any forms of ID on him at the time. He was detained by the police, who a few hours before had just held a 'mobilization conference (*dongyuan dahui*)' that called for more severe law enforcements against 'three withouts' in order to maintain social order and to tackle crime.[4]

Sun Zhigang's experience with the police could have ended shortly after. His friends and employer quickly learned about his detention and took his ID card and cash to the police station. Generally this could have led to an immediate release of the detained – it had been proved that he had an ID card and a regular employment and, since he just arrived in the city, it was excusable not to have a temporary residence permit. More importantly, Sun's friend brought cash to pay 'fines' to buy him out. As Pils (n.d.) points out, without any lawful justification, it is common practice for the police to detain 'three withouts' in order to levy 'tariffs'. It has become a lucrative business for the police and detention facility managers (Alexander and Chan 2004).[5] With the 'tariff' paid and documents produced, the detention of Sun could have ended here. However, the police flatly refused to release him. Two days later, Sun Zhigang died in a detention facility. The police at first claimed that he died of a heart attack, but an autopsy showed that he had been beaten to death.

The fate of Sun Zhigang, reported through newspapers and online, triggered outrage among media audiences and internet users all over the country. As a matter of fact, Sun's encounter with the detention and repatriation system reflected only routinized policing practice against rural migrant workers. Zhao (2008) points out that there had been many cases similar to that of Sun, though none of these stories reached the media or evoked any public reaction. Pils (n.d.) also notes that a number of similar cases, otherwise unreported, were brought to light only in the aftermath of Sun Zhigang. Sun's case stood out as a newsworthy story because he had a college degree, which made him 'atypical' as a rural migrant. If people like Sun, that is, people who should fall into a category entirely different from that of *mingong*, could be detained, then arbitrary policing is indeed a threat to urban dwellers, who compose the majority of media audience and internet users in China. Guangzhou authorities later stated that Sun was 'wrongly' detained. It directly addressed the anxieties of non-migrant urban residents over the detention of Sun. Indeed, how Sun was 'wrongly' picked up by detention police from the streets was an underlying concern in a number of media stories and online comments.

Although the police have the power to check ID cards in the streets, they cannot possibly stop everybody passing by – in a crowded city like

Guangzhou it would virtually block the streets. Rather, the police judge people from their looks – their apparel, hair, dialect. For biased city dwellers, rural migrants have a series of identifiable physical features, including shabby clothing, untidy hair, bad personal hygiene and unrefined (or just non-local) dialect. The police obviously adopt these demeaning labels and use them in their identification of 'three withouts'. As a college graduate, Sun Zhigang presumably should look different from a 'typical' *mingong* with little or no formal education. Therefore, whether Sun 'looked' like a rural migrant the night he was stopped by the police became a key question for worried non-migrant urban residents. The story by *China Newsweek* went like this:

> Walking on Huangcun Avenue, Tianhe District, Sun Zhigang was suddenly stopped by police officers from Huangcunjie Station of Guangzhou Public Security Bureau. After that night it was impossible to know what he wore at the time. Therefore, it is impossible to know whether the police stopped him because 'he did not take proper care of his looks [buxiu bianfu]'. (Tang 2003)

Some comments in the media, feeling less restrained by 'professional' principles that emphasized documented evidence, were more direct. One story went, in a sarcastic tone: 'What are the features of rural migrant workers? They generally have shabby clothing. Sun Zhigang has a poor family. Even in his office he "wears only one outfit day-to-day". ... Of course he must be checked' (Lao 2003). Another comment put it: 'You may not look like a city dweller that much, having rough skin and coarse flesh (*cupi caorou*); or you are just like Sun Zhigang, taking poor care of your looks, having untidy hair and unshaved beard, then you may be spotted by the "experienced" detainers on the first sight' (Chen 2003). The police never explained how they picked up Sun from the streets, but the correlation of visible 'rural' features and the probability of being detained was central to any attempts to rehearse the scene.

Through what Sun Zhigang went through, we could have a glimpse of a person's experience once identified by the police as a 'three withouts' *mingong*. Here again Sun's tragic death was 'atypical'. After all, not every detainee was beaten to death. Most of them would docilely produce some forms of ID, pay the fines and be freed. Sun Zhigang was an exception. And, again, the police never explained, but Sun's family, friends and media and online accounts all arrived at the same conclusion. From what his friends recalled, Sun quarrelled with the police. Different from an 'average' rural migrant worker, Sun apparently had some self-confidence and 'talked back' to the police, which was probably why he was killed (Pils n.d., p. 23). Several other accounts also related Sun's death with his 'talking back' (Lao 2003;

Hong 2009). For Sun's father and brother, Sun would not have died if he had not gone to college and developed the habit of (and confidence for) reasoning with people (Chen and Wang 2003). A posting online maintained that Sun died because he courageously questioned the 'detention and repatriation' system as a detainee. He did not die as a tragic victim, but as a forerunner challenging the injustice of policing practice against rural migrant workers (Chukuangge 2003).

We may never be able to know what Sun said to the police, who refused to disclose any details on Sun's detention. However, given Sun's temperament and the general experience of detained rural migrant workers, it is not difficult to imagine the encounter of Sun and the detention police. Sun's family and friends all knew that he liked to reason and to debate. His roommate in Guangzhou remembered talking to Sun and advising him to be 'more flexible and adaptive' (Li 2003), in other words, to know when to stop talking and to swallow it. His advice probably did not work when Sun was locked up. To be detained as a 'three withouts' was a very humiliating experience, and physical abuse and brutal beatings were daily routines (Chen 2003). In addition, if Sun took it that urban and rural residents were equal before the police, he might have seen his detention as outrageously unreasonable – if merely failing to produce an ID card resulted in detention, then the city was too dangerous to live in. Moreover, why should he pay 'fines' for his detention, which was unjust and unlawful in the first place? However, detained 'three withouts' were in no position to debate with the police over their situation. Instead, they were expected to behave in a docile, inferior manner and to fit into the stereotype that urban police had of them, but Sun Zhigang apparently did not understand this as well as his fellow detainees. As his brother put it, 'My brother ... always wants to reason with people. If he had done whatever he was asked to, if he had squatted when told to,[6] had obeyed the police's words, he for sure would not have died' (Li 2003). For the police, here was a rural-looking guy who tried to deal with them on an equal footing or, worse yet, tried to tell them that they were wrong. Sun was deemed 'too noisy' and must be taught a lesson. He was brutally beaten again and again, and died after two days at a detention facility.

Sun's case is only one more example of how the police select their targets from the streets by appearance (Alexander and Chan 2004). By relying on bodily features to identify subjects of *hukou* enforcement, policing sets up direct links between physical appearance and particular social, economic and political status. According to Hall (1996, quoting W. E. B. Du Bois), the essence of racism is to categorize people on the basis of 'differences of colour, hair and bone' and to distribute power unequally along racial lines. It is in this sense that policing against rural migrants in Chinese cities contributes to a process of 'racialization'. The case of Sun Zhigang exemplifies how categorization by physical features, followed by discriminatory law enforcement and extra-legal brutality, actually 'took place'. The *hukou* system, the stigmatizing labels attached to rural bodies and policing practices that construct social hierarchy in correlation with social bias constitute the racist facet of the oppression and disenfranchisement that China's rural population suffers.

Racialization of rural migrants under China's market reform and development

Contemporary China's economic growth took place when neoliberal capitalism swept through the west, and China's growth model incorporated substantial elements of neoliberalism, in ways that enhanced rather than suspended authoritarian politics (Harvey 2005). Deteriorating social and economic conditions in the countryside drove hundreds of millions of peasants in another wave of migration to cities to look for jobs, forming 'the largest mass migration the world has ever seen' (ibid., p. 127). Due to the *hukou* system, rural-urban migration in China is different from internal migration in many other countries in that rural migrants must keep close links to their home village and county, knowing that they will eventually return (by choice or force) (Davin 1999). The cities they work in do not grant them any social, political or economic rights and benefits except (meagre) monetary returns for their work. The vast rural areas are essentially being treated as a reservoir and a reproduction site for cheap labour for industrialization in the cities (Yan 2008).

Under China's present developmental policy, *hukou* and the second-class status of rural migrants in the cities are in line with the interests of both state and capital. The 'temporary' status of rural migrants deprives them of state welfare and protection, and discourages them from self-organizing, knowing that they may be leaving at any time. As a result, migrant workers' wages can be driven very low. Because of *hukou*, China's minimum wage is often lower than that of poorer countries like Vietnam and Cambodia, which makes China particularly competitive for transnational investments (Alexander and Chan 2004). As Loong-Yu and Shan put it, this helps the ruling elites to restore a 'barbaric capitalism' (2007, p. 79) and to enrich a few through the spatial and social apartheid of *hukou*. Moreover, *hukou* contributes to state control of a population undergoing rapid stratification and polarization. It is indispensable for China's concurrent economic growth and political stability, achieved largely 'through division and exclusion' (Wang 2005).

Along with the economic 'necessity' of exploiting cheap migrant labour is urban bias against the countryside, rural way of life and rural people, which is closely linked to China's modernization. Ancient China had long been an agrarian society, but clashes with western industrial capitalism in the mid-nineteenth century initiated a series of profound changes. The intrusion of imperialism, symbolized by foreign concessions in Chinese cities, re-configured urban-rural relationships. In the modernization discourse, the countryside represented backwardness, poverty and incivility, in contrast to economically, culturally and technologically advanced (westernized) cities.[7] The 'new' image of the countryside continues today. Yan (2008) maintains that contemporary urban bias against rural residents must be situated in the city-centred developmental path over the last three decades, when urban development was prioritized at the cost of the countryside. The dominant ideology places the city at the centre and forefront of national development, and China's backwardness is linked to its agrarian roots. It is in this context that 'peasant (*nongmin*)' becomes itself a derogatory term. Being rural becomes an identity decidedly different from the urban, and that difference can be conveniently summarized by the keyword '*suzhi*'.

Suzhi is a word central to contemporary China governance and society (Kipnis 2006). Sometimes translated as 'quality', *suzhi* is an inclusive and elusive term that can refer to one's morality, intelligence, education and many other elements in relation to character and ability. Yan (2008) draws an interesting parallel between '*suzhi*' in neoliberal developmental discourse and the term 'value' in Marxist analyses of commodification. According to her, *suzhi* refers to the essential qualities one must possess in order to be useful for, and to fit into, a developing society. The concept abstracts and reduces the heterogeneity of human beings, just like 'value' abstracts and reduces concrete and individual aspects of human labour. Kipnis points out that 'references to *suzhi* justify social and political hierarchies of all sorts, with those of "high" quality gaining more income, power and status than the "low"' (2006, p. 295). While the countryside is linked to backwardness, rural residents are defined by their lack of, or low levels of, *suzhi*. They are regarded by biased city dwellers as of 'low quality', including low 'physical quality', 'scientific and cultural quality' and 'quality of understanding notions' (Pils n.d., p. 31). Biased media depict them as being unqualified to live in the cities for both cultural and moral reasons (Florence 2006), implicating a certain standard of 'quality' that only city residents meet. Thus, the social divide drawn by *hukou* is directly associated with human subjectivity. *Hukou* no longer only determines where one can 'legitimately' live, but also connotes one's way of thinking and behaving.

Visible bodily features are key markers of one's *suzhi*, or quality. According to Kipnis, 'poorly dressed' is a sign of 'lacking quality' (2006, p. 296). In another instance, female rural migrants' *suzhi* is thought to be 'improved' when they have learned to appreciate and to follow fashion (Yan 2008). The most comprehensive account of *mingong*'s negative stereotype comes from a rude urban joke. According to that joke, for rural migrants to pass for urban residents, they need to be taught to take showers, brush teeth, manicure their nails, put on new clothes, refrain from talking in rural dialects, stop fighting and, most importantly, not to squat on chairs (Yan 2008, p. 178). These bodily features are widely adopted as the basis of discrimination not only by police but also non-governmental institutions. In 2005, a scenic area in Ningbo city put up a sign at its entrance forbidding rural migrant workers and scrap collectors to enter. According to the manager of the facility, this was because several thefts took place before, and the management believed that rural migrants were responsible. And how did they tell a rural migrant from a local? A security staff told the journalist that he identified them through clothing and dialect (*Beijing Youth Daily* 2005). The linkage between rural *hukou*, rural looks, low *suzhi* and discriminatory treatment is clear and straightforward.

In analysing Tibetan women weavers in a Lhasa carpet factory, Zhang argues that the deployment of labour policy and the embodiment of meaning-making practices always go hand-in-hand. To label weaver workers as 'deaf-mutes, illiterates, and women' works to '*reproduce* hegemonic relations' and to 'normalize and legitimize the exploitative labor relations in a profit-driven industry' (2007, p. 393, emphasis in original). In her account, class formation is intertwined with gender and ethnicity politics. Similarly, Ngai points out that migrant rural bodies in Chinese cities are usually imagined to be 'rough, dirty, rustic, or lazy' (2005, p. 14), and this construct of new identities is fully in line with disciplining in the workplace. Indeed, it could be so much easier to make migrant workers toil in sweatshops if they internalized the low-*suzhi* discourse and felt they justifiably belonged to an inferior group of people. It is in this context that *hukou* no longer really binds peasants to the land but binds stigma to their labouring, migrant bodies. Policing, through enforcement of *hukou* and the threat/exerting of violence, is an indispensable part in the process. To revisit the case of Sun Zhigang, was he not trying to resist the racialization and thus dehumanization of his identity imposed upon him when faced with extra-legal brutality of the police?

To study the 'racialization' of rural migrant workers in Chinese cities is an effort to add to existing research a cultural perspective drawing from critical racial studies in the west. By 'racialization', I do not assert that a new ethnicity is taking shape, but that there is a 'racial' aspect to the oppression and exploitation of rural migrant workers, which is usually analysed using a class framework. While rural migrants lack generally recognized 'ethnic' features, I emphasize the importance of transcending existing racial and ethnic classifications and endeavouring to contextualize forms of embodied control within specific social, political and economic circumstances (Bulmer and Solomos 2004;

Virdee 2006). The 'racialization' approach does not exclude or deny class-based approaches. Rather, by borrowing analytical tools from critical racial theories, I aim to address the cultural processes that always come along with class oppression. If ethnic and class issues intersect, and all social relations have both material and cultural aspects (Fenton and Bradley 2002), then racial and class approaches do not diverge, but supplement each other.

Acknowledgements

The author wants to thank Paul E. Amar. This paper would not have been possible without his warm support and help. In addition, the author thanks the anonymous reviewers as well as researchers with whom he communicated in relation to this piece. It repeatedly reminds the author that writing is not a private and proprietary process but a social and public one.

Notes

1. In a most recent case, the Chinese media covered a scandal in which a number of high school students in Chongqing forged minority ethic identities in order to receive priority in university/college admission (He 2009).
2. The procuratorate, or *jianchayuan*, is a judicial organ in China's legal system. It acts as the prosecutor on behalf of the state in criminal cases.
3. According to research on rural migrants to Shenzhen, it cost two months' salary to pay for various certificates and permits before a migrant worker could 'legitimately' start to look for a job (Alexander and Chan 2004). Indeed, not many rural migrant workers are willing to, or can afford to, obtain a temporary residence permit. In 2003, less than half of the migrant workers in China had the permit (Pils n.d.). In the aftermath of Sun Zhigang, many local governments reduced the fees they charged for the permit.
4. Newspaper stories on the case of Sun Zhigang abound, and most of them are reprinted on the internet. Information in this paper was collected through documentary and online research in March 2006 and November 2008. Most details are from two stories published in *Nanfang Metro News* (*Nanfang Dushi Bao*) and *Beijing Youth* (*Beijing Qingnian Bao*), at http://news.sina.com.cn/s/2003-04-25/09501015845.shtml and http://news.xinhuanet.com/newscenter/2003-04/28/content_851808.htm (accessed March 2006).
5. See also the story on *Southern Weekend*, 19 June 2003, by precisely the journalist who first reported on the case of Sun Zhigang. Available at http://news.sina.com.cn/c/2003-06-19/01551186977.shtml.
6. The tendency to 'squat', in the biased urban account, is a signature bodily feature for rural migrants. In this case, apparently Sun's brother knew that Sun would resist it, and that it could be of great importance in Sun's circumstances.
7. I thank Yan Yuan at the University of Westminster, UK, for this point.

References

ALEXANDER, PETER and CHAN, ANITA 2004 'Does China have an Apartheid pass system?', *Journal of Ethnic and Migration Studies*, vol. 30, no. 4, pp. 609–29

BEIJING YOUTH DAILY 2005 'Notice at scenic area forbidding *mingong* and scrap collector to enter' (Fengjingqu guachu jinrupai, mingong yu shoupolanzhe bude runei), http://news.xinhuanet.com/society/2005-10/18/content_3636364.htm (accessed 5 June 2009)

BIDDULPH, SARAH 2007 *Legal Reform and Administrative Detention Powers in China*, Cambridge: Cambridge University Press

BULMER, MARTIN and SOLOMOS, JOHN 2004 'Introduction: researching race and racism', in Martin Bulmer and John Solomos (eds), *Research Race and Racism*, London: Routledge, pp. 1–15

CHEN, FENG 2003 'We run detention and repatriation just to make money' (Women gao shourong qiansong jiushi yao gao qian), *Nanfang Metro Daily*, 19 June http://www.southcn.com/news/china/zgkx/200306190185.htm (accessed 3 March 2006)

CHEN, FENG and WANG, LEI 2003 'The abnormal death of a citizen' (Yige gongmin de fei zhengchang siwang), *Nanfang Metro News*, 25 April, http://news.sina.com.cn/s/2003-04-25/09501015845.shtml (accessed 3 March 2006)

CHEN, LUMIN 2003 'From priest Martin to Sun Zhigang' (Cong mading shenfu xiangdao Sun Zhigang), http://past.people.com.cn/GB/guandian/27/20030611/1014459.html (accessed 26 June 2009)

CHENG, TIEJUN and SELDEN, MARK 1994 'The origins and social consequences of China's hukou system', *The China Quarterly*, pp. 644–68

CHINAWORKER.INFO 2008 '*Hukou*: the Chinese version of Apartheid' (Hukou: zhongguo de geli zhidu), http://www.jincg.com/html/2008-08/24441.htm (accessed 2 June 2009)

CHUKUANGGE 2003 'A tribute to the victimized forerunner' (Xiang shouhai de xianxingzhe zhijing), http://www.tecn.cn/data/1693.html (accessed 26 June 2009)

DAVIN, DELIA 1999 *Internal Migration in Contemporary China*, London: Macmillan

DIKÖTTER, FRANK 1992 *The Discourse of Race in Modern China*, Hong Kong: Hong Kong University Press

—— 1997 *The Construction of Racial Identities in China and Japan: Historical and Contemporary Perspectives*, London: Hurst

DUTTON, MICHAEL R. 1998 'Zhejiang Village, Beijing: a visit' and 'Zhejiang village: a government tale', in Michael Robert Dutton (ed.), *Streetlife China*, Cambridge: Cambridge University Press, pp. 147–59

—— 2005 *Policing Chinese Politics: A History*, Durham, NC: Duke University Press

DUTTON, MICHAEL R. and LEE, TIANFU 1993 'Missing the target? Policing strategies in the period of economic reform', *Crime & Delinquency*, vol. 39, no. 3, pp. 316–36

FENTON, STEVE and BRADLEY, HARRIET 2002 'Ethnicity, economy and class: towards the middle ground', in Steve Fenton and Harriet Bradley (eds), *Ethnicity and Economy: 'Race and Class' Revisited*, New York: Palgrave Macmillan, pp. 9–30

FLORENCE, ERIC 2006 'Debates and classification struggles regarding the representation of migrant workers', *China Perspectives*, vol. 65, http://chinaperspectives.revues.org/document629.html

GÓMEZ, LAURA E. 2007 *Manifest Destinies: The Making of the Mexican American Race*, New York and London: New York University Press

GUANCANGHAI 2008 'The evil consequence of China's *hukou*: racial discrimination' (Zhongguo hukou zhidu zhongxia de erguo: zhongzu qishi), http://lwp8421.blog.163.com/blog/static/100825275200811103230124/ (accessed 3 June 2009)

HALL, STUART 1996 *Race: The Floating Signifier*, video-recording, Northampton, MA: Media Education Foundation

HARVEY, DAVID 2005 *A Brief History of Neoliberalism*, New York: Oxford University Press

HE, LIDAN 2009 'Chongqing Gaokao Jiafen Luanxiang' (Cheating in college entrance exam in Chongqing), *Xinmin Weekly*, http://edu.qq.com/a/20090723/000095.htm (accessed 21 July 2009)

HE, XIN FRANK 2004 'The stickiness of legal collusion: a difficulty of legal enforcement', *International Journal of the Sociology of Law*, vol. 32, pp. 103–17

HODDIE, MATTHEW 1998 'Ethnic identity change in the People's Republic of China: an explanation using data from the 1982 and 1990 census enumerations', *Nationalism and Ethnic Politics*, vol. 4, no. 1, pp. 119–41

HONG, HE 2009 'In memory of Sun Zhigang' (Jinian Sun Zhigang jun), *Business Watch Magazine*, http://www.businesswatch.com.cn/Mag/Cover/2009/0313/972.html (accessed 26 June 2009)

KIPNIS, ANDREW 2006 'Suzhi: a keyword approach', *The China Quarterly*, pp. 295–313

LAO, XIN 2003 'Questioning the case of Sun Zhigang' (Zhuiwen Sun Zhigang an), *Sanlian Life Week*, no. 244, http://www.lifeweek.com.cn/2003-06-18/000015708.shtml, (accessed 3 March 2006)

LI, JING 2003 'The unbearable lightness of being (without a) temporary residence permit' (Wu zhanzhuzheng de shengming zhi qing), *Sanlian Life Week*, no. 240, http://www.lifeweek.com.cn/2003-06-02/000535492.shtml (accessed 2 June 2009)

LOONG-YU, AU and SHAN, NAN 2007 'Chinese women migrants and the social apartheid', *Development*, vol. 50, no. 3, pp. 76–82

MA, RONG 2004 'The "de-politicization" of ethnic minority issues' (Shaoshu minzu wenti de qu zhengzhihua), *Journal of Peking University (Philosophy and Social Sciences)*, no. 11.

—— 2007 'A new perspective in guiding ethnic relations in the twenty-first century: "de-politization" of ethnicity in China', *Asian Ethnicity*, vol. 8, no. 3, pp. 199–217

EISNER, MAURICE 1999 *Mao's China and After: A History of the People's Republic*, New York: The Free Press

NATIONAL BUREAU OF STATISTICS OF CHINA 2006 'Statistical report on 1% sampled national population survey in 2005', http://www.stats.gov.cn/tjgb/rkpcgb/qgrkpcgb/t20060316_402310923.htm

NGAI, PUN 2005 *Made in China: Women Factory Workers in a Global Workplace*, Durham, NC, and London: Duke University Press

OMI, MICHAEL and WINANT, HOWARD 1994 *Racial Formation in the United States: from the 1960s to the 1990s*, 2nd edn, New York: Routledge

PANG, KENG-FONG 1998 'Unforgiven and remembered: the impact of conflicts on everyday Muslim-Han social relations on Hainan Island', *Nationalism and Ethnic Politics*, vol. 4, no. 1, pp. 142–62

PILS, EVA n.d. 'Citizens? The legal and political status of peasants and peasant migrant workers in China', unpublished manuscript

ROEDIGER, DAVID R. 2008 *How Race Survived US History: From Settlement and Slavery to the Obama Phenomenon*, London and New York: Verso

SAUTMAN, BARRY 1998 'Preferential policies for ethnic minorities in China: the case of Xinjiang', *Nationalism and Ethnic Politics*, vol. 4, no. 1, pp. 86–118

SMITH, CHRISTOPHER J. 2000 *China in the Post-Utopian Age*, Boulder, CO: Westview Press

SOLINGER, DOROTHY J. 1999 *Contesting Citizenship in Urban China: Peasant Migrants, the State, and the Logic of the Market*, Berkeley: University of California Press

TANG, JIANGUANG 2003 'The truth of the death of a twenty-seven year old citizen Sun Zhigang' (Er shi qi sui gongmin Sun Zhigang siwang zhenxiang), *China Newsweek*

VIRDEE, SATNAM 2006 '"Race", employment and social change: a critique of current orthodoxies', *Ethnic and Racial Studies*, vol. 29, no. 4, pp. 605–28

WANG, FEI-LING 2005 *Organizing through Division and Exclusion: China's Hukou System*, Stanford, CA: Stanford University Press

WANG, HOMGMEI 2000 'Woguo Minzu Shibie Gongzuo de Lilun Yiju he Shijian Biaozhun' (The theoretical basis and practical criteria for China's ethnicity identification), *Xizang Minzu Xueyuan Xuebao (Tibetan University of Ethnicity Journal)*, 200003, pp. 6–10

YAN, HAIRONG 2008 *New Masters, New Servants: Migration, Development, and Women Workers in China*, Durham, NC, and London: Duke University Press

YANG, WENZHONG and WANG, GONGFAN 1998 'Peasant movement: a police perspective', in Michael R. Dutton (ed.), *Streetlife China*, Cambridge: Cambridge University Press, pp. 89–92

ZHANG, LI 2001 *Strangers in the City: Reconfigurations of Space, Power, and Social Networks within China's Floating Population*, Stanford, CA: Stanford University Press

ZHANG, TRACI Y. 2007 'Deaf-mutes, illiterates, and women', *Feminist Media Studies*, vol. 7, no. 4, pp. 381–96

ZHAO, SHUKAI and KIPNIS, ANDREW 2000 'Criminality and the policing of migrant workers', *The China Journal*, no. 43, pp. 101–10

ZHAO, YUEZHI 2008 *Communication in China: Political Economy, Power, and Conflict*, Lanham, MD: Rowman & Littlefield

Geographies of death: an intersectional analysis of police lethality and the racialized regimes of citizenship in São Paulo

João Costa Vargas and Jaime Amparo Alves

Abstract

This paper presents an intersectional analysis of police lethality in the city of São Paulo. We deploy the concept of geography of death to investigate the multi-layered aspects of state-sanctioned lethal violence perpetrated by, but not limited to, the police force. This entails a consideration of at least three types of factor: actual violent acts, their symbolic dimensions and the historical and structural conditions within which violence emerges. Based on official data from the Brazilian state we argue that there is a perverse correlation between vulnerability to death and new racial formations, as they intersect with social class, age, gender, and place. Thus, the distinctive social geographies of São Paulo not only provide the context, but also define the very nature, frequency and experience of police violence. Ultimately, we argue, police lethality is a manifestation of the police and the state's complicity in reproducing boundaries of privilege and exclusion.

In the period between 1997 and 2007, the state of São Paulo's Civil and Military Police killed 5,331 people. The data on the identity of those killed and the circumstances under which they met their fate, including location and short narratives describing the facts leading up to the deaths, when made available by non-governmental Brazilian and international watchdog groups, are neither comprehensive nor systematized.[1] Given the relatively reduced number of cases catalogued, and the absence of reliable comparative information across time, the patterns that can be extracted from such non-governmental data leave much to be desired.

Such statistical absence should not erase the obvious: state-sanctioned lethal violence feeds from, at the same time as it energizes, social environments marked by frequent death. Still, for the sake of specificity, and taking into account Brazil's long and continuing historical patterns marked by deep social inequalities, we must ask: if vulnerability to violent death, including death perpetrated by the police, is not distributed evenly across society, then is it possible to show correlations between vulnerability to violent death and social class, age, gender and race? In which ways, if any, are such correlations distributed in urban space? We recognize the incisive yet still relatively marginalized scholarship that seeks connections between police action and race (Khan 1998, 2002; Silva 1998; Mitchell and Wood 1999; Reis 2005), while we link this research on race to explorations of the gender and age implications of such connections as they are expressed in and shaped by urban space.

This paper is an intersectional analysis of police lethality in the city of São Paulo. In spite of the absence of deaths perpetrated by the police in official lethal violence data – homicide, for example – we consider the use of lethal force by the police a significant and indissociable aspect of the particular forms and frequency of violence experienced by differently situated populations. Specific collective experiences of state-sanctioned lethal violence are thus derived from a composite of at least three types of factor: first, the actual manifestation of violent acts, which include, but are not restricted to, lethal events and those perpetrated by the police; second, the symbolic, but no less important, acts of violence that, while not necessarily accompanied by factual violence, nevertheless constitute the cultural understandings that, in the realm of social representations, negatively impact on individuals and communities (e.g. Bourdieu 1977); and, third, the perception of violence that is associated, not only with the symbolic and factual manifestations of violence, but also, and more broadly, historical and contemporary social conditions within which violence emerges. Examples of symbolic violence would be stereotypes related to race, gender and social geography – especially at the neighbourhood level – that predispose and justify the use of lethal force by the police (e.g. Butler 1993; James 1996).

'Ninguém é cidadão': Brazilian racialized regime of (non)citizenship

State violence in Brazil is an index of the precariousness of substantive citizenship, and the ways in which citizenship – or, rather, the lack of it – is inflected by and is reflected in the spatialization of race, gender and class. Disparities in employment, income, education, infant mortality and vulnerability to violent death are deeply influenced by the articulation of such categories as they influence the unequal distribution of privilege and social suffering (e.g. Hasenbalg 1979; Valle Silva 1980; Silva 1998; Mitchell and Wood 1999; Werneck 2000; Henriques 2001; Vargas 2005a, 2005b; PNAD 2005; Reis 2005). Such a system of inequalities shows how Afro-Brazilians experience state-sanctioned violence, not only by its most 'peculiar institution', the police, but also by the social and institutional mechanisms, embodied in schools and hospitals, for example, that perpetuate relative disadvantages for blacks while reproducing white privilege. From the perspective of Afro-Brazilians, citizenship has historically and socio-logically been tied to exclusions – social and spatial confinement, exclusion from education and work spheres – rather than to the guarantee of civil, political and cultural rights. It is within this Brazilian 'relational citizenship' (Da Matta 1991; Mitchell and Wood 1999), which we would rather call non-citizenship, that police assaults on black bodies need to be understood.

While the excessive use of force by police against impoverished communities in Brazil has been documented and is well understood, few scholars have denounced the racial underpinning of policing strategies, from racial profiling to deadly operations in their ordinary *favela* incursions (e.g. Silva 1998; Amar 2003; Batista 2003; Vargas 2005b.) In academic discourse, interpretations of police discretionary procedures against impoverished neighbourhoods, which are fre-quently majority black areas, reveal a hesitant, if not an overtly resistant approach to the significance of race. Such an approach against the relevance of race makes two contentions. First, the denial of the relevance of race appears in the claim of the impossibility of identifying who is black and who is white in Brazil. Here, the class-oriented approach takes primacy in the analysis of police killing and urban violence (e.g. Zaluar 2000). Second, such analyses tend to isolate the systemic practices of state violence in terms of the individual accountability of police officers, who are quickly identified as black (e.g. Sansone 2002).

In order to demystify this double bind, we argue for the inescapable centrality of race in producing both police strategies and the historical and contemporary social conditions within which violence emerges. The fact that the police have historically employed Afro-Brazilians does not undermine the well-known patterns of racialized violence that disproportionally affect non-white communities. Indeed, the presence of black bodies in the state apparatus obviously complicates, rather than contradicts, the racialized aspects of policing strategies. Patterns of police action that disproportionately negatively impact on

Afro-Brazilians is part of an institutional framework, itself immersed in and reproducing non-citizenship, that cannot be reduced by or separated from individual members of that framework. Instead of accepting the curious association that is frequently made between the presence of black police officers and the absence of racism in the police, we ask: how do military police practices reflect broader racial meanings in Brazilian society? How does Afro-Brazilian police officers' racialized experience inform their practice against other Afro-Brazilians? We propose, then, that, because blacks are victimized as a social group, individualized notions of accountability for their victimization undermine the historical, institutional and everyday meanings of policing predominantly black areas.

The denial of the relevance of race in policing practices is symptomatic of a larger social phenomenon. The 'hyperconsciousness/negation of race' (Vargas 2004) dialectic suggests that, while hegemonic constructions and practices of race relations in Brazil are based on the very negation of the relevance of race, such denial is often accompanied by thoughts and actions that unmistakably render race a key social fact, and thus the denial of race becomes itself a manifestation of the pervasiveness of race as an organizing principle of social relations. In other words, the systematic anxiety about taking race seriously is, in itself, an immanent expression of how Brazilians' understanding of the social world is deeply embedded in racial logic. It may be the case that the silence or evasiveness concerning racial dominance is part of the Brazilian etiquette of racial relations (e.g. Dzidzienyo 1971; Sheriff 2002), or, in the words of Florestan Fernandes (1972), the hyperconsciousness/negation of race dialectic is a manifestation and an underlying principle of the very Brazilian 'prejudice against having prejudice'.

The relevance of race, however, is not restricted to the realm of mythology/ideology and everyday talk of colour categories. Analyses of the political economy confirm and give a concrete and appalling dimension to the white/non-white binary informing Brazilian social structure: greater differences in life chances and outcomes (employment, education, infant mortality, susceptibility to police abuse, for example) persist between non-whites and whites than among non-whites (e.g. Valle Silva 1980; Mitchell and Wood 1999; Telles 1999; Henriques 2001; Khan 2002a).

The 1996 Pesquisa Nacional por Amostra de Domicílios (PNAD – National Household Sample Survey) observed that, whereas in the richest south-east region – comprising the states of São Paulo, Rio de Janeiro, Minas Gerais and Espírito Santo – infant mortality for whites stood at 25.1 per thousand infants born alive, for blacks the rate was 43.1. For black children under 5, mortality is 52.7 per thousand born alive; it is 30.9 per thousand white children born alive. In the country as a whole, whereas barely 50 per cent of black households are connected to a sewage system, the rate is 73.6 per cent for white households. When we apply the United Nation's Index of Human Development, utilized as a measure of life quality on a scale 0–1, we see that, whereas it stands at 0.796 for the Brazilian population as a whole, it is 0.573 for Afro-Brazilians.[2]

The 2007 PNAD data confirm the persistence of this pattern of racialized social exclusion. While 14.5 per cent of the white population is poor, poverty affects blacks at more than twice that rate, standing at 33.2 per cent. More specifically, blacks comprise 67.9 per cent of the population among the poorest 10 per cent. Nationally, blacks' monthly income averages R$502.02, about half of whites' income average, R$986.5. In São Paulo's metropolitan region, blacks earn on average R$3.98 per hour, whereas whites make R$7.33 per hour.[3]

Unemployment rates reproduce the same pattern: whereas 12.4 per cent of black women and 6.7 per cent of black men were unemployed, for white men the rate was 9.4 per cent and for white women 5.5 per cent. Also, children are disproportionately impacted upon due to their racialization: among working children between 5 and 6 years of age, 69.6 per cent are black; among working children 10–13 years of age, 65.1 per cent are black. The national household survey reveals an inconvenient truth to those who claim the irrelevance of race: the 8 million people living in *favelas* in Brazilian metropolitan areas are distributed in residences of whose total number 66 per cent are headed by blacks, twice the number of whites (33 per cent).[4]

All social-economic data available reveal that non-whites are subject to a 'process of cumulative disadvantages' (Valle Silva and Hasenbalg 1992) which blocks their social mobility. Whites, on the other hand, are markedly more successful in attaining upward social mobility. This process, by which blacks and whites have distinct life-trajectory paths, is similar to what happens in the US, as evidenced by Oliver and Shapiro (1995).

Police brutality, as it disproportionately affects blacks in Brazil, is another sad parallel that can be made with the US. The reality for Afro-Brazilians, however, is far worse than it is for African Americans: in Bahia, 2189 people were killed by agents of the state in 2008, almost twice the dreadful 1449 deaths registered in 2007.[5] In the state of São Paulo, the official lethality rate is 1.18 persons per day.[6] In the state of Rio de Janeiro, between January and August 2003, the police killed 900 people, almost 75 per cent of them in the *favelas* of Rio's metropolitan areas, in predominantly black communities.[7] Paul Amar reminds us that 'this trend, if continued, would have pushed the tally of police executions above 1,500 in 2003 in Rio state alone, approaching parity with Baghdad, beyond the realm of media metaphors, as the Iraqi capital suffered around 1,700 civilian fatalities during this year's war' (Amar 2003, p. 38). In a month, Rio police kills more than two and half times more people than the New York Police Department kills in a whole year (Cavallaro and Manuel 1997). The ubiquitous cases of police misconduct are part of an emblematic, persistent pattern of widespread anti-black racism that pervades Brazilian society, even though many scholars who study the police in Brazil, curiously but not surprisingly, refrain from making the argument about the centrality of race in such phenomena (e.g. Paixão 1995; Pinheiro 1995; Cano 1997; Cardia 2000).

Spatializations of police violence: an intersectional approach

The perception of violence merits further elaboration as it grounds our intersectional approach to police lethality. By differentiating the perception of violence from the symbolic and factual modalities of violence, we emphasize an intersectional method by which we approach lethal violence. The perception of violence is closely connected to – indeed derives from socially shared notions produced about – the social environment in which one finds oneself immersed. This social environment, as it produces and is reproduced by violence in factual and symbolic forms, is reflected in, as well as shaped by a particular social geography, or space. Henri Lefebvre's maxim, '[social] space is a [social] product' (Lefebvre 1991, p. 26) is here complexified to include social class, gender, age and race, among other variables, as they define and are marked by urban space. Since social relations are determined by, as well as shaping, power differentials, urban space is deeply implicated in and inflects the ways social hierarchies actualize themselves in a given historical moment. All urban spaces, all human geographies are the product of historical power struggles, and the social relations deriving from such struggles become spatialized according to the hegemonic political order: 'Every mode of production ... produces a space, its own space' (Lefebvre 1991, p. 53). While the resulting spatial relationships expressing degrees of subordination and privilege are normally maintained through consensus, there is often a need for explicit coercion. Police presence in general, but police lethality in particular, is a key element in the coercive apparatus as it enacts, to the limit, shared and normalized understandings about those it affects.

That police lethality, as we will show, is unevenly distributed in S. Paulo's urban geography reveals the contested nature of socially constructed, power-laden and deeply racialized and thus exclusionary social spaces. The unevenness of police lethality, while obviously determined by race, is also calibrated by social class, gender and age. Together – police lethality, race, social class, gender and their spatialized, combined expressions – produce the social climate in which violence is experienced. The perception of violence is a collective commentary about the ways in which social forces, including police lethality, intersect with, become energized by and define urban geographies. Such commentary guides members of distinct communities in their quotidian activities – drawing from shared historical memories as well as anticipated social outcomes – as it presents an analysis of the physical and symbolic threats associated with one's residential community.

We contend, and will develop this point as the essay unfolds, that the social environment's specificity not only provides the context within which police lethal violence occurs, but, more importantly, defines the very nature, frequency, perception and experience of police lethal violence. That is, while police lethality is certainly a core element in defining one's experience (pragmatic and symbolic) of a given locality, police lethality gains deeper meaning and explanations when juxtaposed to, and therefore contextualized in, the intersecting aspects of particular social environments. Even though police lethality appears difficult to analyse given the paucity of pertinent quantitative and qualitative data, it becomes rather graspable when contextualized and understood as part of – indeed animated by – a historical and contemporary web of multiple and intersecting social forces. In this essay, among such forces we will focus specifically on social class, gender, age and race, all understood in complex feed-back loops of mutual determination, in turn defining and affected by urban space.

This analysis builds from the following: police lethality and its unequal distribution on S. Paulo's social geography are results, as well as energizers, of historical and contemporary social inequalities. On this score, we want to complement case studies of the police *per se*, those that focus on law enforcement policies, employment of tactical technologies, self-understanding and their representation in the media (e.g. Benevides 1983; Kant de Lima 1994; Paixao 1995; Cano 1997; Silva 1998; Mitchell and Wood 1999). We present police lethality and its uneven distribution on S. Paulo's urban geography as a symptom, not a cause, of historical and contemporary inequalities; as an element of a social power constellation whose field of energy produces differentiated levels of violence and exposure to state-sanctioned death as markers of social inequalities: of privilege and citizenship to some and disadvantages and non-citizenship to many. To understand police lethality, then, we need to retrace its historical and contemporary roots. Police lethality, as part of actual, symbolic and perceived violence, acquires meaning as we analyse the various layers of social forces that determine it. What we describe as São Paulo's geography of death, in its social class, age, gender and race variants, explains key aspects of the historical and contemporary roots of police lethality. By emphasizing intersectionality, juxtaposition and multi-directional determinacy, following strands of critical race and black feminist theories (Collins 1990; Crenshaw 1994; James 1999), we argue that police lethality is a result of, at the same time as it is a manifestation of, São Paulo's multiply constituted geography of death.

The apparent progressive dilution of police lethality in our analysis – this slippage, if you will – is thus intentional: we start with basic data about police lethality; we then juxtapose such data to a series of other available social indicators, plotting the results in maps and charts, suggesting intersections as well as dissimilarities; the process of juxtaposition is repeated with different variables until, in the study's last section, we refocus on police lethality as a product, not a cause of historical, multiply constituted and spatially expressed social forces.

Cartographies of death in the urban setting

Figure 1, below, shows that, over the last decade, the city of São Paulo, *vis-à-vis* the city's metropolitan region and the interior of the state of São Paulo, staged, on average, over 50 per cent of all registered lethal police violence cases.

Figure 2 specifies and gives a spatial dimension to the above graph. Although there is a clear concentration of police violence in the city of São Paulo's districts *vis-à-vis* the greater metropolitan region, within the municipality of São Paulo there are some discernible patterns. Police violence is more intensely concentrated in the outer north-east, south and west areas of the city. While the city's inner districts register a much higher incidence of police violence than that measured in the greater metropolitan area, they are clearly not as impacted on as the outer eastern, western, northern and southern city districts.

Figure 1. *In absolute numbers, lethally shot by the military and the civil police in the state of São Paulo Sources: authors' cross-tabulation; Secretaria da Seguranca Publica Police Ombudsman (SSP-SP, 2008)*

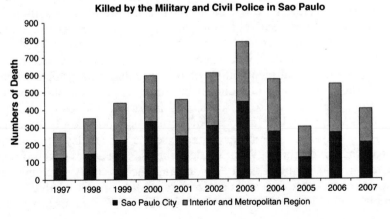

Killed by the Military and Civil Police in Sao Paulo

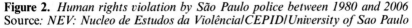

Figure 2. *Human rights violation by São Paulo police between 1980 and 2006*
Source*: NEV: Nucleo de Estudos da Violência/CEPID/University of Sao Paulo*

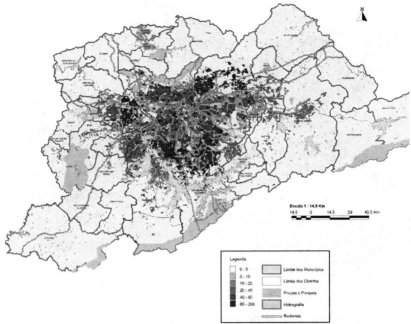

A first question that we may ask, then, is: who lives in those areas most affected by police violence? Answering the question would also allow us to reflect on the type of social profile of those least affected by police violence. To answer the question, let us start with data on income. Income, when considered with other quality-of-life factors (for example, vulnerability to violence, access to quality education and public transportation), serves as a proxy to social class. Figure 3 represents Sao Paulo's districts by income, in 2005 reais, the Brazilian currency.

Juxtaposing the two maps above, we detect meaningful intersections: areas with higher income, the centrally located city districts, correspond roughly to the city of S. Paulo's neighbourhoods less affected by police violence. Similarly, there are area overlaps between districts with the lowest incomes and those most affected by police violence. Of course the intersections pointed out are not sufficient to make a definite case. Rather, they suggest inverse correlations between economic power and likelihood of experiencing lethal police violence that must be further analysed. The urban space patterns that emerge, however, produce an added dimension to such correlations: they point to ways in which economic power and exposure to police violence

Figure 3. *Nominal income of the heads of household in the districts of the city of São Paulo* Source: *Indice de Vulnerabilidade Juvenil 2000, Fundação Seade*

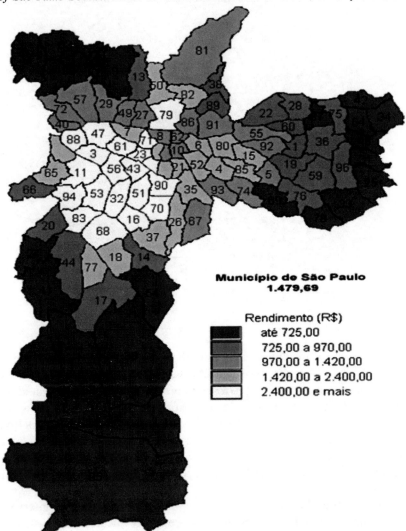

translate into, at the same time as they are influenced by, territorial boundaries.

To contextualize the previous findings, we now turn to a broader indicator of violence, that of distribution of homicide among the city's general population. By comparing and contrasting Figure 4 to our previous findings, we can reflect not only on correlations between police violence and incidence of homicide, but also on the ways in which exposure to police violence, homicide, income and urban space intersect. The juxtaposition of the spatial representations of police

Figure 4. *The map shows the spatial distribution of homicide rate among the districts of the city of São Paulo between 2000 and 2002* Source: *Sistema de Estatísticas Vitais, Fundação Seade*

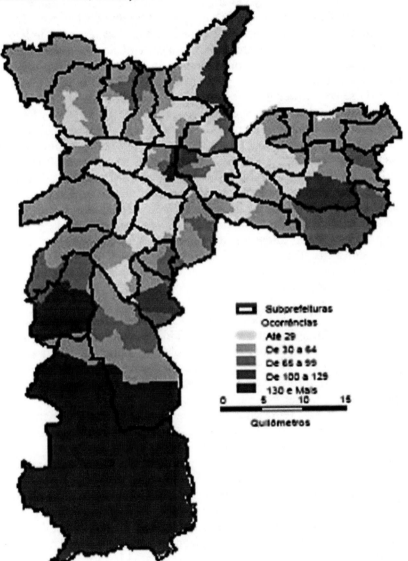

violence and homicide allows us to expand on each of these indicators of exposure to violence. Police violence and frequency of homicide, thus, can be analysed as important elements of a continuum that encompasses all experiences of violence in S. Paulo. Taken together, they produce a more complete spatial and temporal snapshot of violence than they would separately.

The combination of indices of police violence and homicide generates a more reliable approximation of the total of incidents of violence, including deadly violence, occurring in the city and how such deaths are distributed in the urban space. Moreover, when we add to this statement the findings in Figure 1, which locates the municipal boundaries as those where lethal police violence is concentrated relative to the greater metropolitan region and state, we are able to hypothesize that the areas of greater police violence, the ones that are also those with lower income, intersect in significant ways with those where lethal police violence occurs more frequently.

While the dissimilar exposure to civil and institutional lethal violence, the combination of which unfolds in a body count that is unevenly spread in zip code areas, should itself be a source of outrage, it does not prevent us from reflecting on the often silenced broader reality: the disproportionate violence and deaths in economically disadvantaged areas are part of a broader social and institutional context marked by the maintenance and reproduction of deep social inequalities. Maps allow us to examine these inequalities' spatial dimensions, as they occur concomitantly, and as such provide potentially sharp tools to denounce ongoing injustices and inequalities. Such maps suggest a geography of death that is constituted by, not only the actual police and civil society lethal violence, but also a social climate that can be accessed when we analyse various social indicators defining specific locations. This methodology allows us to gain entry into the perception of violence, including lethal police violence, graspable as socially shared and constructed knowledge that draws on the multiple, overlapping historical and contemporary forces affecting a particular geographical area.

Figure 5 below represents the variations in juvenile vulnerability indexes (JVI) in the city of São Paulo. Juvenile vulnerability, as defined by the Seade Foundation (Fundacao Seade 2000), varies on a 0–100 scale, in which 0 represents the district with the lowest vulnerability and 100 the highest. It comprises the following variables: annual rate of population growth between 1991 and 2000; proportion of youth in a district's total population; rates of mortality by aggression (in this case homicide) for male youths between the ages of 15 and 19 per 100,000 inhabitants; fertility rates for young women between the ages of 14 and 17; the proportion of youths between 15 and 17 who do not attend school per total number of people in this age group; and average monthly household income. All data are relative to the year 2000, except the rate of homicide, which was drawn from 1999, 2000 and 2001 indices, and the proportion of youths who do not attend school, which is relative to 1996.

The JVI are important as they provide an approximation of what we earlier defined as the perception of violence. The social commentaries

Figure 5. *Range of social vulnerability for youth among the districts of the city of São Paulo* Source*: Index of Juvenile Vulnerability/2000, Fundacao Seade*

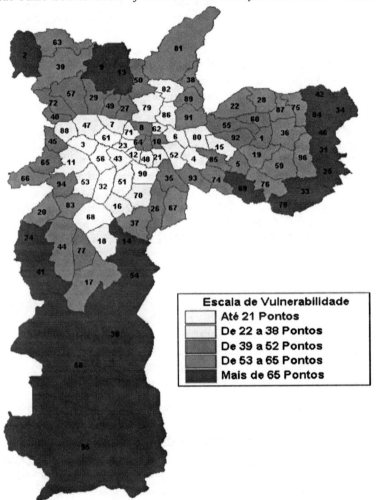

on violence and death that are shared about particular geographical areas – in this case neighbourhoods – take into account not only exposure to physical and symbolic threats, but also key social elements that define the climate within which one finds oneself.

The linear data combination, drawn from the analysis of a correlation matrix of the variables, produces a synthetic indicator that is able to explain 74.2 per cent of all data variability. This synthetic indicator, the vulnerability index, in turn produced five distinct groups of juvenile vulnerability, represented in Figure 5. These groups are the following:

- Group 1, up to 21 points: includes the nine less vulnerable city of S. Paulo districts: Jardim Paulista, Moema, Alto de Pinheiros, Itaim Bibi, Pinheiros, Consolação, Vila Mariana, Perdizes e Santo Amaro;
- Group 2, 22–38 points: Lapa, Campo Belo, Mooca, Tatuapé, Saúde, Santa Cecília, Santana, Butantã, Morumbi, Liberdade, Bela Vista, Cambuci, Belém, Água Rasa, Vila Leopoldina, Tucuruvi, Vila Guilherme, Campo Grande, Pari, Carrão and Barra Funda;
- Group 3, 39–52 points: República, Penha, Mandaqui, Cursino, Socorro, Ipiranga, Casa Verde, Vila Matilde, Vila Formosa, Jaguara, Brás, Vila Prudente, Vila Sônia, Freguesia do Ó, Bom Retiro, São Lucas, Limão, São Domingos, Jaguaré, Rio Pequeno, Pirituba, Aricanduva, Sé, Artur Alvim and Ponte Rasa;
- Group 4, 53–65 points: Sacomã, Jabaquara, Vila Medeiros, Cangaíba, Cidade Líder, Vila Andrade, Vila Maria, Tremembé, Ermelino Matarazzo, São Miguel Paulista, José Bonifácio, Jaçanã, Itaquera, Raposo Tavares, Campo Limpo, São Mateus, Parque do Carmo, Vila Jacuí, Perus, Cidade Dutra, Jardim São Luís and Jaraguá;
- and Group 5, 65 points and above: includes the 19 districts characterized by greater juvenile vulnerability: Cachoeirinha, Vila Curuçá, Guaianases, Sapopemba, Capão Redondo, Lajeado, Anhangüera, São Rafael, Jardim Helena, Cidade Ademar, Brasilândia, Itaim Paulista, Pedreira, Parelheiros, Jardim Ângela, Grajaú, Cidade Tiradentes, Iguatemi and Marsilac.

The relevance of the map in Figure 5 and these findings is that they provide information that, when intersected with our previous analyses, suggest a generational specificity to the geographically situated social groups regarding their likelihood of experiencing social marginalization, including violence and death by the police or otherwise. The spatial representation suggests the idea of a social environment that is geographically specific. As such, the environment is characterized by actual facts, i.e. average household income, and by patterns that are registered in a given time period, i.e. police violence. From the perspective of an individual, therefore, s/he does not have to experience direct acts of violence, including police lethality, to be in an excluded and excluding, violent, death-prone environment. The spatial quality of social facts, which emerges from the maps we are analysing, allows us to grasp both the facts and their collateral consequences – that is, the ways in which these facts produce a climate that is experiential and is probabilistically determined. Furthermore, such maps allow for the visualization of multiple, concomitant social events that both contextualize and shape the character and scope of each discrete social occurrence. Vulnerability indexes suggest a social configuration of factors – a structure – that influences the likelihood and the perception of violence, including lethal violence.

The areas in the Figure 5 map and those in the previous maps that intersect intimate that higher-income neighbourhoods are less susceptible to civil and institutionalized violence, which at its limit includes death; they also imply that such areas' youths are relatively shielded from exposure to challenging social environments marked by high incidence of school evasion, teenage pregnancy, acts of police misconduct and homicide. Youths in groups 1, 2 and 3, which roughly correspond to the affluent, middle-class and lower-middle-class areas, live in economically advantaged and geographically delimited environments that decrease their relative likelihood of experiencing, directly or indirectly, threats to their physical and psychological well-being. The young men and women in these areas also experience their peers dropping out of school with less frequency. Conversely, youths in groups 4 and 5, which mostly correspond to economically poorer areas of the city in the east, south and north west, live in environments that register the higher values of juvenile vulnerability. Connections between exposure to violence, social class and age suggest themselves in visual intersections. When juxtaposed, our previous maps propose that low-income youths residing in economically disadvantaged areas are the most likely to encounter and live in social geographies characterized by violence, the incidence of homicide being a case in point. Moreover, the areas with the highest indices of juvenile vulnerability correspond, in substantive measure, to those where police violence takes place with greater frequency (see Figure 2). Thus, a reasonable proposition would be that the higher the juvenile vulnerability index, the higher would be the likelihood of inhabiting a social and spatial environment marked by the violent presence of the state.

From the perspective of the youths placed in such conditions, their vulnerability to death by state (the police) and civil means (homicide) stresses accumulated social disadvantages that, themselves, become predictors of further disadvantages. To stress again a point made in the introduction: police violence, including police lethality, would thus be the product of such historically accumulated and socially reproduced disadvantages. Accordingly, in areas defined by low levels of juvenile vulnerability, the accumulated privileges, themselves the result of a constellation of access to financial, educational, political and cultural resources, just to name a few, are such that the likelihood of experiencing violence in general, and police lethal violence in particular, is, relative to the more stigmatized geographies, minimized. Police lethality, then, becomes one of many indicators that reveal – and is arguably produced by – a web of multiply determined social forces.

Figure 6, charting the rates of homicide of young men (between 15 and 19 years of age) in S. Paulo, when added into our previous analyses, allows us to further visualize spatial patterns of social belonging. In accordance with our findings relative to police abuse, income, homicide and juvenile vulnerability, the rates of homicide for young men, and their spatial distribution, give further credence to the idea of a geography of death – the highest rates of homicide of young men, like the lowest incomes, the highest homicide in general and the highest indices of juvenile vulnerability, occur in the most eastern, southern and parts of the most northern city areas. At the same time, and obviously connected, the geography relative to lower rates of young male homicide often intersects with the areas marked by the highest incomes, the lowest rates of homicide in general and the lowest indices of juvenile vulnerability.

The intermediate areas, those that were categorized as groups 2, 3 and 4 relative to their indices of juvenile vulnerability, constitute a buffer zone – admittedly not as well defined as the centre, wealthier areas and the outlying, poorer neighbourhoods in the far east, south and north. Yet, such intermediate areas, whose roughly concentric layout mirrors the spatial patterns encountered in our previous maps charting income, homicide, juvenile vulnerability and male homicide, suggest at least three social geography configurations.

One is the peripheral, especially eastern, southern and northern areas, in which indicators of social exclusion by social class (here approximated by income, which provides an incomplete measure), age and gender indicate that socially disadvantaged young men find themselves in urban communities whose layers of accumulated disadvantages produce and reproduce the very dynamics of their exclusion. Homicide rates and levels of police abuse, including lethal police force, at the limit, point to patterns of imposed social marginalization that find, in spatial arrangements, their expression and reproductive engine. The second geographical configuration points to the highest incomes, lower juvenile vulnerability indices, lower homicides and lower homicides of young men (the Shantytown of Paraisopolis, in the middle of the elite neighbourhood of Morumbi is an exception that merits deeper analysis). If these stark differences are manifest in obvious accumulated, overlapping and multiple social advantages, they become even more obvious and, we would say, effectively maintained by the geographical separation that exist between the relatively homogenous central districts and the relatively homogeneous outer, poorer, more vulnerable and violent outer areas. The relative lower indices of homicide in general, young male homicide, police violence and police lethality in such affluent geographies, at the limit, suggest that accumulated social advantages and privileges – i.e. the privilege of not being subjected to early violent

Figure 6. *The distribution of homicide among young males per 100,000 population in the districts of the city of São Paulo* Source: *Sistema de Estatísticas Vitais, Fundação Seade*

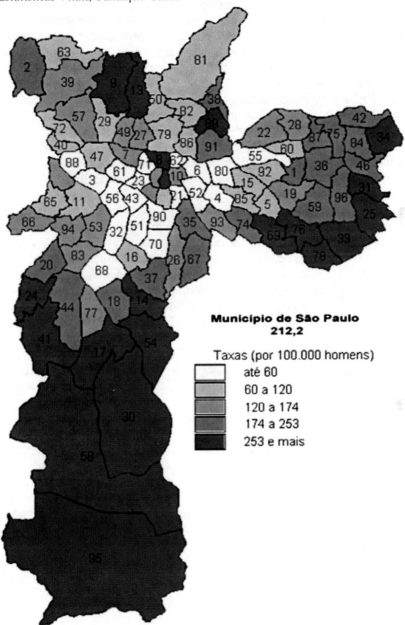

Município de São Paulo
212,2

Taxas (por 100.000 homens)
até 60
60 a 120
120 a 174
174 a 253
253 e mais

death, by the police or otherwise – find expression and indeed their energizer in spatial configurations.

The third geographical pattern is perhaps the most complex. Compressed between accumulated affluence and persistent disadvantage, in physical contact with (because bordering) both extremes (Caldeira 1985, 2001; Vargas 1993), such intermediate, buffer-zone areas are marked by their populations' sense of instability and need for resolution. As the specialized literature on electoral politics has shown (e.g. Pierucci 1989), anxieties produced by a sense of cultural deficit *vis-à-vis* the more affluent areas, as well as perceived threats emanating from the proximity of '*nordestinos*' and '*bahianos*' in their own neighbhourhoods (Vargas 1993), are often expressed in allegiance to conservative, law-and-order political platforms and candidates. This intermediate zone is where the right, historically, finds its electoral home. Middling levels of income, homicide in general, homicide of young men and juvenile vulnerability become expressed in and are reproduced by these transitional, in-between geographies. Within their borders, dominant social groups strive to resolve their transitional, intermediary location by distancing themselves from the more disadvantaged areas and by suggesting proximity to the historically privileged neighbourhoods. Such desired proximity is expressed through political choices, cultural understandings of their perceived instability (that becomes linked to the presence of non-whites in or close to their neighbourhoods) and everyday talk and actions relative to crime and violence (Caldeira 2001).

There is perhaps no more meaningful expression of this sensed instability than the ubiquitous presence of high metal and iron gates over doors and windows, isolating residences, as well as a plethora of accompanying security devices – they translate, pragmatically and symbolically, the desires to resolve the social and geographical nature of the experienced instability. While the more obvious aspect of privilege and exclusion is exposure to death (homicide and police lethality) – or, to put it another way, exposure to death frames and gives added meaning to social class, place of residence, access to quality education and health care – in the intermediate zones the threat of death is acknowledged via the ubiquity of security mechanisms. Insofar as such security mechanisms are meant to protect both property and body, they symbolize the need to preserve one's space as an expression of social belonging and therefore an as an index of social and geographical distance from areas and peoples associated with instability and death.

Racialized spaces/multifaceted violence

The social geography patterns of accumulated privilege and exclusion analysed through our various maps provide grounds for insight, not only about accumulated disadvantages and privileges, but also into the meanings of police lethality. If the intersectional and cumulative patterns of social exclusion find expression in corresponding geographical arrangements; if such patterns intersect with, and thus correspond in considerable measure to, those relative to police abuse; and if patterns of police abuse can be taken as indicators of the probability of police lethality; then we can ascertain, at least as a working proposition, that police lethality follows and indeed is produced by these same multiply constituted and cumulative patterns. These patterns, expressing the mutual determinacy of social class, gender and age as they relate to and are inflected by urban space, become further defined when we take into account race. Thus far, we have indicated that young men residing in less affluent areas are the most likely to continually experience the effects of accumulated social disadvantages. At the limit, such disadvantages lead to exposure to death by the state or via homicide. If we rank S. Paulo's districts by juvenile vulnerability and are able to trace correlations between this rank and race, then we may be able to draw analytical propositions regarding the role of race in the geographical patterns we have discussed so far.

Table 1 ranks ten districts by juvenile vulnerability. It also provides the racial breakdown of such districts by white and black population, as defined by the official Brazilian census. Two obvious correlations between race and juvenile vulnerability can be drawn: first, the higher the proportion of whites *vis-à-vis* blacks inhabiting a district, the lower that district's index of juvenile vulnerability; and, second, conversely, the lower the proportion of whites *vis-à-vis* blacks, the higher juvenile vulnerability becomes. Of course, we could present these same correlations emphasizing the proportions of blacks in given districts. We would thus arrive at the following, second set of correlations: the higher the proportion of blacks *vis-à-vis* whites in a particular district, the higher the indices of juvenile vulnerability; conversely, the lower the proportion of blacks relative to whites, the lower the juvenile vulnerability index. These two sets of correlations seem interchangeable. To emphasize blacks or whites, as we did above, does not seem to alter the results regarding juvenile vulnerability indexes – that is, the *proportion* of whites *vis-à-vis* blacks and vice versa seems to be the obvious determinant of social outcomes, in this case regarding juvenile vulnerability.

Another way of making this case would be to take into account that the city of S. Paulo registers 30.1 per cent of blacks and 68 per cent whites (*pretos* and *pardos*) in its population (IBGE/PNAD 2005). Rankings in social vulnerability for youth, thus, would be correlated with the distribution of black and white populations in specific districts. To wit, where blacks are overrepresented and whites are

Table 1. *Spatial distribution by race in the ten most and the ten least vulnerable districts of the city of São Paulo*

	Most socially vulnerable neighborhoods				Least socially vulnerable neighborhoods			
Rank	District	Total population	Whites (%)	Blacks (%)	District	Total population	Whites (%)	Blacks (%)
1	Marsilac	8,398	58.6	40.2	Jd. Paulista	83,663	90.9	5.2
2	Iguatemi	101,772	63.3	36.1	Moema	71,269	91.9	4.7
3	C. Tiradentes	190,652	49.4	49.8	Pinheiros	62,991	88.4	7.2
4	Grajaú	334,283	49.6	48.8	Consolacao	54,518	87.9	8.3
5	Jd. Ângela	245,799	47.2	51.4	Itaim Bibi	81,450	90.1	6.5
6	Parelheiros	102,830	49.7	48.5	Perdizes	102,440	90.1	7.0
7	I. Paulista	212,727	50.2	48.5	V. Mariana	123,677	83.5	7.2
8	Brasilandia	247,322	58.4	39.7	S. Amaro	60,533	89.3	6.9
9	Cid. Ademar	243,367	56.1	41.5	Mooca	63,274	89.9	7.1
10	Guaianazes	98,539	51.8	47.3	Morumbi	34,581	81.6	14.7

Sources: IBGE Population Census 2000, Coordenadoria de Assuntos da População Negra (Cone) and Fundação Sistema Estadual de Análise de Dados – SEADE

underrepresented *vis-à-vis* the city's general population, the indices of juvenile vulnerability are the highest, and these areas are the most likely to stage multiple types of social exclusion as well as, at the extreme, death by homicide or the police. In these areas, then, the negative effects of social exclusion, obviously strongly correlated with race, are disproportionately evident. Accordingly, where blacks are underrepresented and whites are overrepresented, the indices of juvenile vulnerability are the lowest.

The privileges associated with whiteness, necessarily linked to the disadvantages emanating from blackness, gain in this multidimensional, intersectional analysis an apparent geographical expression. Is it not the case that the geographical inscription of gendered, sexed and classed dimensions of violence upon black bodies conjures up *Brazilian apartheid* (Vargas 2005a)? We suggest that the geography of death in São Paulo is a product of systematic and multi-layered dimensions of violence in the urban setting. Read in conjunct with the previous illustrations, Figure 7 also allows us further to visualize spatial patterns of social and racial belonging and their correlation with urban violence.

While the persistence of class differences and their impact on the lives of differently situated community members are generally supported by scholarly contributions (e.g. Holston and Caldeira 1999; Zaluar 2000; Caldeira 2001), the same does not hold when it comes to recognizing and analysing the full impact of racial differences. It can be safely argued that debates regarding the relevance

Figure 7. *Spatial distribution of black population in the city of São Paulo Source: IBGE Census 2000/Fundação Seade*

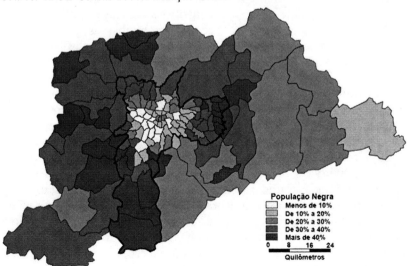

População Negra
Menos de 10%
De 10% a 20%
De 20% a 30%
De 30% a 40%
Mais de 40%
0   8   16   24
Quilômetros

of race in Brazilian social relations and institutions, mass news media support of the dominant views defending the *irrelevance* of race notwithstanding, remain unresolved (e.g. Hanchard 1994; Bourdieu and Wacquant 1999). Our findings engage the debates and propose an argument for the centrality of race in geographically situated, multiply constituted, yet deeply unequal social outcomes

Conclusion

In this essay we approached police lethality as emanating from a constellation of multiply and inter-determined sets of social events that result in concrete, geographically located privileges and disadvantages. Such social results need to be understood as deriving from the effects of social class (which we approached via the plausible but evidently insufficient indicators of income) and as being multiply determined by a range of vectors, among which social class features prominently but is not, by any means, unaccompanied or unaffected by multiple social forces such as homicide in general, male homicide, teen pregnancy, school evasion, etcetera. As well, while we recognize the incisive yet still relatively marginalized scholarship that seeks connections between police action and race, we explored the gender and age implications of such connections as they are expressed in and shaped by urban space.

We proposed an explanation of the deaths perpetrated by the police by contextualizing them within broader social patterns that character-ize the city's urban social geography. The explanation derives from an examination of the ways in which a) the variables of vulnerability to violence, social class, age, gender and race both inflect and are inflected by each other and b) in turn are manifested in spatial patterns. Urban space, therefore, constitutes the stage on which police violence and police lethality become intelligible as part of, and energized by, a constellation of social variables. Through the analyses of multiple social variables and their unequal manifestation in urban spaces, we showed how historical inequalities become expressed by and reproduced in differentiated social geographies. More specifically, we suggested that, to understand police lethality, it is necessary to place it in the web of social forces that define and become reproduced by urban space. In other words, as an expression of deeply ingrained social inequalities that are marked by spatial boundaries of belonging, police lethality is a manifestation of the state's complicity in reproducing such boundaries. At the extreme, the deaths caused by the police work culturally and pragmatically by constantly redrawing the racial lines of privilege and exclusion. As the result of multiply intersecting social vectors that become actualized in urban space, the lines of privilege and exclusion thus become reliable predictors – and, we claim, energizers – of violent death.

Notes

1.   São Paulo's Secretary of Public Safety releases an annual report on police abuse but it is not categorized by race, class or age. See São Paulo Police Ombudsman in http://www.ouvidoria-policia.sp.gov.br/pages/Relatorios.htm
2.   Pesquias Nacional por Amostra de Domicílios (PNAD), Brazil: Instituto Brasileiro de Geografia e Estatística IBGE, 1996.
3.   DIEESE (Intersindical Department of Statistics and Socioeconomic Studies) 2006. 'O negro no mercado de trabalho'. *Estudos e Pesquisas*, 26, November, p. 6.
4.   See Retrato das Desigualdades Raciais e de Genero, and PNAD 2007. IPEA/Brasília 2007.
5.   Comissão Justiça e Paz da Arquidiocese de Salvador. See also Revista Carta Capital, 8 February 2008. Available at www.cartacapital.com.br/app/materia.jsp?a=2&a2=6&i=48
6.   Ouvidoria da Polícia do Estado de São Paulo – Relatórios trimestrais e anuais. Available at http://www.ouvidoria-policia.sp.gov.br/pages/Relatorios.htm
7.   Jon Jeter, 'Death squads feed terror in Rio slums', *Seattle Times* 27 October 2003.

References

AMAR, PAUL 2003 'Reform in Rio: reconsidering the myths of crime and violence', *NACLA Report on the Americas*, vol. 37, no. 2, pp. 37–42

BATISTA, VERA MALAGUTTI 2003 *Medo na Cidade do Rio de Janeiro: Dois Tempos de uma História*, Rio de Janeiro: Editora Revan

BENEVIDES, M. VICTORIA 1983 *Violência, Povo e Polícia: Violência Urbana no Noticiário de Imprensa*, São Paulo: Brasiliense

BOURDIEU, PIERRE 1977 *Outline of a Theory of Practice*, Cambridge: Cambridge University Press

BORDIEU, PIERRE and WACQUANT, LOIC 1999 'On the cunning of imperialist reason', *Theory, Culture & Society*, vol. 16, no. 1, pp. 41–58

BUTLER, JUDITH 1993 'Endangered/*endangering*: schematic racism and white paranoia', in Robert Gooding-Williams (ed.), *Reading Rodney King/Reading Urban Uprising*, London: Routledge

CANO, IGNACIO 1997 *Letalidade da Ação Policial no Rio de Janeiro*, Rio de Janeiro: ISER

CALDEIRA, TEREZA P. 1985 *A Política dos Outros*, São Paulo: Brasiliense

——— 2001 *City of Walls: Crime, Segregation, and Citizenship in São Paulo*, Berkeley: University of California Press

CARDIA, NANCY 2000 *Urban Violence in São Paulo*, Comparative Studies Occasional Papers, 33, Washington, DC: Woodrow Wilson International Center for Scholars

CAVALLARO, JAMES and MANUEL, ANNE 1997 *Police Brutality in Urban Brazil*, New York: Human Rights Watch/Americas

COLLINS, PATRICIA HILL 1990 *Black Feminist Thought: Knowledge, Consciousness, and the Politics of Empowerment*, Boston, MA: Unwin Hyman

CRENSHAW, KIMBERLE 1994 'Mapping the margins: intersectionality, identity politics, and violence against women of color', *Stanford Law Review*, vol. 43, no. 6, pp. 1241–99

DA MATTA, ROBERTO 1991 *A Casa e a Rua*, Rio de Janeiro: Guanabara Koogan

DZIDZIENYO, A. 1971 *The Position of Blacks in Brazilian Society*, London: Minority Rights Group

FERNANDES, FLORESTAN 1972 *O Negro no Mundo dos Broncos*, São Paulo: Difel

FUNDACAO SEADE 2000 *Indice de Vulnerabilidade Juvenil/IVJ2000*, São Paulo: Fundação Seade. Available at http://www.seade.gov.br/produtos/ivj

HANCHARD, MICHAEL 1994 *Orpheus and Power: The Movimento Negro of Rio de Janeiro and São Paulo, Brazil 1945–1988*, Princeton, NJ: Princeton University Press

HASENBALG, C. 1979 *Discriminação e Desigualdades Raciais no Brasil*, Rio de Janeiro: Graal

HENRIQUES, RICARDO 2001 *Desigualdade Racial no Brasil: Evolução das Condicoes de Vida na Década de 90*, Rio de Janeiro: IPEA

HOLSTON, JAMES and CALDEIRA, T. P. R. 1999 'Democracy and violence in Brazil', *Comparative Studies in Society and History*, vol. 41, no. 4, pp. 691–729

IBGE (BRAZILIAN INSTITUTE OF GEOGRAPHY AND STATISTICS) 1996, 2005, 2007 Pesquisa Nacional por Amostra de Domicílios (PNAD)

JAMES, JOY 1996 *Resisting State Violence*, Minneapolis: University of Minnesota Press

——— 1999 *Shadowboxing:* Representations of Black Feminist Politics, New York: St. Martin's Press

KANT DE LIMA, R. 1994 *A Policia da Cidade do Rio de Janeiro: Seus Dilemas e Paradoxos*, Rio de Janeiro: Policia Militar do Rio de Janeiro

KHAN, TULIO 1998 'Os negros e a polícia: recuperando a confiança mútua', *Boletim Conjuntura Criminal*, no. 7. Available at www.conjunturacriminal.com.br

——— 2002 *Velha e Nova Polícia: Polícia e Políticas de Segurança Pública no Brasil Atual*, São Paulo: Editora Sicurezza

LEFEBVRE, H. 1991 *The Production of Space*, Oxford: Blackwell

MITCHELL, MICHAEL and WOOD, CHARLES 1999 'Ironies of citizenship: skin color, police brutality, and the challenge to democracy in Brazil', *Social Forces*, vol. 77, no. 3, pp. 1001–20

NEV NUCLEO DE ESTUDOS DA VIOLENCIA/USP http://www.nevusp.org/portugues/index.php?option=com_content&task=category&sectionid=3&id=7&Itemid=55

OLIVER, MELVIN and SHAPIRO, THOMAS 1995 *Black Wealth/White Wealth: a New Perspective on Racial Inequality*, New York: Routledge

PAIXAO, LUIZ ANTONIO 1995 'O problema da polícia', in *Violência e Participação Política no Rio de Janeiro*, Série Estudos no. 91, Rio de Janeiro: IUPERJ

PIERUCCI, ANTONI FLAVIO 1989 'A direita mora do outro lado da cidade', *Revista Brasileira de Ciências Sociais*, vol. 4, no. 10, pp. 46–64

PINHEIRO, PAULO SERGIO 1995 'Autoritarismo e transição', *Revista da USP*, vol. 108, no. 5, pp. 937–75

REIS, VILMA 2005 'Atucaiados pelo estado: as políticas de segurança pública implementadas nos bairros populares de Salvador e suas representações, 1991–2001', dissertação de Mestrado, Universidade Federal da Bahia, Salvador

PNAD/National Household Sample Survey 2005 Brazilian Institute of Geography and Statistics/IBGE, Brazilia

SANSONE, LIVIO 2002 'Fugindo para a força: cultura corporativista e "cor" na polícia militar do estado do Rio de Janeiro', *Estu dos Afro-Asiáticos*, vol. 24, no. 3, pp. 513–32

SHERIFF, ROBIN E. 2001 *Dreaming Equality: Color, Race, and Racism in Urban Brazil*, New Brunswick, NJ: Rutgers University Press

SILVA, JORGE 1998 *Violência e Racismo no Rio de Janeiro*, Niterói: EDUFF

TELLES, EDWARD 1999 'Ethnic boundaries and political mobilization among African Brazilians: comparisons with the U.S. case', in M. Hanchard (ed.), *Racial Politics in Contemporary Brazil*, Durham, NC: Duke University Press

VALLE SILVA, NELSON 1980 *O Preço da cor: diferenciais raciais na distribuição da renda no Brasil*, ipea: Rio de Janeiro

VALLE SILVA, NELSON and HASENBALG, C. 1980 'O preço da cor: diferenças raciais na distribuição de renda no Brasil', *Rio de Janeiro: Pesquisa e Planejamento Econômico*, vol. 10, no. 1, pp. 21–44

——— 1992 *Relacoes Raciais no Brasil Contemporâneo*, Rio de Janeiro: Iuperj

VARGAS, JOAO COSTA 1993 'As transformações recentes de São Paulo vistas de seu epicentro', Master's thesis, Universidade Estadual de Campinas

——— 2004 'Hyperconsciousness of race and its negation: the dialectic of white supremacy in Brazil', *Identities: Global Studies in Culture and Power*, vol. 11, pp. 443–70

——— 2005a 'Apartheid Brasileiro: raça e segregação residencial no Rio de Janeiro', *Revista de Antropologia*, vol. 48, no. 1
——— 2005b 'Genocide in the African diaspora', *Cultural Dynamics*, vol. 17, no. 3, pp. 267–90
WERNECK, JUREMA, *et al.* 2000 *O Livro da Saúde das Mulheres Negras: Nossos Passos Vêm de Longe*, Rio de Janeiro: Pallas
ZALUAR, ALBA 2000 'Perverse integration: drug trafficking and youth in the favelas of Rio de Janeiro', *Journal of International Affairs*, vol. 53, no. 2, pp. 654–71

Appendix

Municipality of São Paulo by districts

#	District	#	District	#	District	#	District
1	Artur Alvim	25	Cidade Tiradentes	49	Limão	73	Sé
2	Anhanguera	26	Cursino	50	Mandaqui	74	São Lucas
3	Alto de Pinheiros	27	Casa Verde	51	Moema	75	São Miguel
4	Agua Rasa	28	Ermelino Matarazzo	52	Mooca	76	São Mateus
5	Aricanduva	29	Freguesia do Ó	53	Morumbi	77	Socorro
6	Belem	30	Grajaú	54	Pedreira	78	São Rafael
7	Barra Funda	31	Guaianases	55	Penha	79	Santana
8	Bom Retiro	32	Itaim Bibi	56	Pinheiros	80	Tatuapé
9	Brasilândia	33	Guatemi	57	Pirituba	81	Tremembé
10	Brás	34	Itaim Paulista	58	Parelheiros	82	Tucuruvi
11	Butantã	35	Ipiranga	59	Parque do Carmo	83	Vila Andrade
12	Bela Vista	36	Itaquera	60	Ponte Rasa	84	Vila Curuçá
13	Cachoeirinha	37	Jabaquara	61	Perdizes	85	Vila Formosa
14	Cidade Ademar	38	Jaçanã	62	Pari	86	Vila Guilherme
15	Carrão	39	Jaraguá	63	Perus	87	Vila Jacui
16	Campo Belo	40	Jaguara	64	República	88	Vila Leopoldina
17	Cidade Dutra	41	Jardim Ângela	65	Rio Pequeno	89	Vila Medeiros
18	Campo Grande	42	Jardim Helena	66	Raposo Tavares	90	Vila Mariana
19	Cidade Lider	43	Jardim Paulista	67	Sacomã	91	Vila Maria
20	Campo Limpo	44	Jardim São Luís	68	Santo Amaro	92	Vila Matilde
21	Cambuci	45	Jaguaré	69	Sapopemba	93	Vila Prudente
22	Cangaiba	46	Lajeado	70	Saúde	94	Vila Sônia
23	Consolação	47	Lapa	71	Santa Cecília	95	Marsilac
24	Capão Redondo	48	Liberdade	72	São Domingos	96	Jose Bonifacio

SEMPLA: Municipal Secretary of Urban Planning/São Paulo Municipality, 2009. Available at: http://sempla.prefeitura.sp.gov.br/infocidade/index.php?sub= mapas&cat=7&titulo=Demografia&subtit=%20-%20Mapas&mpgraf=1

Order and security in the city: producing race and policing neoliberal spaces in South Africa

Tony Roshan Samara

Abstract

This paper examines the reproduction of racialized urban spaces in post-apartheid South Africa through a case study of the Central City Improvement District in Cape Town. Urban neoliberalism provides mechanisms of governance that reproduce spaces generated by apartheid under conditions of democracy. My focus is on private policing and the regulation of the central city through the socio-spatial ordering of downtown in ways that secure the interests of property owners and more affluent consumers. Private policing in this context produces a form of social ordering based on emerging conceptions of racialized citizenship linked to market access. It works to exclude or tightly regulate the black urban poor, who are unable to participate freely in this quasi-public neoliberal space, and to remove these 'undesirable' elements back into the townships. In doing so, it contributes to reproducing the spatial segregation and the racial identities of the apartheid period.

Introduction

Racialized policing practices are central to the ordering of public and quasi-public urban spaces; often, they are intimately linked to the ordering functions of urban revitalization policies themselves. Urban redevelopment programmes, as increasingly ubiquitous expressions of neoliberalism in cities, are powerful examples of 'colour-blind' discourse and public policy that are deeply implicated in the reproduction of racial inequalities (Omi and Winant 1994; Bonilla-Silva 2006). Some scholars have even suggested that urban neoliberalism constitutes a new racial project under conditions of democracy (Hetzler, Medina and Overfelt 2006), one in which the regulatory functions of the state are transferred to the market, or to the heralded 'public-private partnership'. This research pushes us to interrogate the kinds of urban spaces being produced under conditions of formal democracy and the relationship between spatial production, governance and social exclusion. Market-driven urban revitalization has simultaneously driven up the value of urban real estate, producing sharper socio-spatial inequalities, and contributed to intensified struggles over land in many cities around the world. These struggles and the management of conflict have thus become central issues in urban governance debates and practices. As the world continues to urbanize, undergoing competing pressures of connection and fragmentation, the city is proving to be a vibrant and often violent crucible for the creation of new forms and practices of citizenship, rights and exclusion (Sassen 2002; Purcell 2003; Kurtz and Hankins 2005).

This paper is organized around a case study of urban governance mechanisms in Cape Town, South Africa. South Africa is of particular interest because racialized spatial governance of urban areas was state policy for decades. This has given way to a vision of racial and spatial reintegration that, while not realized, continues to animate discussions of post-apartheid society and urban social policy more specifically. The expected, or hoped-for, transformation has yet to occur; indeed the nation's urban spaces remain very much racially segregated. My goal here is to identify important links between how segregation is reproduced and how contested space is governed. To do so I focus on the central city, or downtown, arguably the most valuable piece of real estate in the entire metropolitan region, and an urban space which apartheid designated as racially white and culturally European (Nahnsen 2003). I pay particular attention to the Central City Improvement District [CCID] and the private security firm G4S Security Services-South Africa (Securicor), which was primarily responsible for securing this space between 2001 and 2008. The improvement district is a quasi-public space structured, in large part, by a neoliberal logic organized around the protection of property, consumption and the securing of market-oriented accumulation processes more generally. This neoliberal urban space is governed by a transnational network of actors and agencies in which private security forces play a central role.

The significance of examining neoliberal urban governance lies in the growing prevalence of such spaces and the potential light such an examination sheds on a key question in studies of race and ethnicity: how are racial and ethnic inequalities reproduced under conditions of democracy and in societies that explicitly reject discrimination (Gold 2004)? It is important to keep in mind throughout that the relationship of neoliberalism to racial inequality is contingent and historical. South Africa's own past is reminder enough that neither neoliberalism nor private police are required for the production or reproduction of racialized urban spaces. Nevertheless, we are today confronted with the reality of neoliberal urban spaces marked by growing inequality, and which are in many cases managed by private interests and secured by private police in their employ. Understanding the processes of governing and reproducing racialized spaces as they operate today requires that we engage with neoliberalism while avoiding the tendency to dehistoricize it.

The research for this study was conducted between 2003 and 2008, over the course of four visits to the city. The primary source of data is interviews with social development workers in the city centre, whose experience and insights provide a perspective absent from city documents, interviews with powerful local officials and police. Most of the people I interviewed work with street children specifically, although I also visited one organization that works with adults, and spoke with two former social development coordinators employed by the CCID. I also rely on documents published by the relevant governing bodies, media reports and field observation from eight years of travel to and research in the city. The paper is divided into three sections: the first addresses the relationship between neoliberal governance, race and policing; the second introduces the private security firm, G4S, and provides background on the parameters of security governance within the quasi-privatized space of the city improvement district; the third section presents data on the policing of this everyday space by Securicor from the perspective of those who work with vulnerable populations that inhabit it.

Private policing and the neoliberalization of racial governance

The empirical concern of the paper is with exclusionary policing, the more active and often more repressive arm of disciplinary neoliberal governance, private security and the city. In South African cities exclusion has historically been explicitly racial at its foundations and downtown Cape Town in particular was seen by apartheid leaders as an important cultural/racial site for Afrikaaners (Western 1996). Since the mid-1990s there has been at least a rhetorical commitment to transformation but, as we will see, in carrying out their mandate of keeping the central city improvement district 'clean and safe', private police, in the employ of coalitions of property owners, are strengthening these foundations. Although nominally a democratic, public and open space, the geographic area now bound by the CCID continues to be defined by practices and structures of racial governance.

Building on Glover (2008) I take racial governance to refer to forms and processes of governance in which the production or reproduction of racial boundaries and of racially exclusionary spaces is the effect. Of special concern here are neoliberal forms and processes, which represent important advances in racial governance and provide a window into how apartheid inequalities are reproduced under conditions of liberal democracy. In creating exclusionary spaces, racial governance relies upon and reproduces 'common' sensibilities about belonging in which race plays a central role, sensibilities which suffuse the consciousness of those who govern and those who are governed (Jensen 2008). We have seen this in studies of how urban spaces in liberal democracies are coded according to perceived levels of disintegration and racial composition (McCann 1999; Meehan and Ponder 2002), how these perceptions can shape the actions of police (Sampson and Raudenbush 2004; Clement 2007) and penalize people of colour (McArdle and Erzen, 2001; Wacquant 2005). What these studies suggest, and what I would like to explore further here, is the idea that the governance of security can function as a form of racial governance under conditions of democracy.

A vast literature in urban studies has documented the rise of the neoliberal city and a parallel increase in repressive and exclusionary governance, including but not limited to policing (Davis 1990; Smith 1996; Aguirre and Brooks 2001; McArdle and Erzen 2001; Coleman 2003; Herbert and Brown 2006; Kohn 2004; Wacquant 2006; Atkinson and Helms 2007; Clement 2007). There is a related of body of research documenting the aesthetic and cultural dimensions of the new city, much of it focused on the politics of consumption and the production of urban landscapes that are both disconnected from their immediate surroundings yet linked to similar urban spaces across the globe (Sorkin 1992; Hannigan 1998; Eisenger 2000; Urry 2002). We can term these twin developments the rise of the fantasy city alongside the rise of the carceral and panoptic city.

As much of the aforementioned research has shown, there is an important connection between these developments. The dynamic economic growth of many cities over the past twenty years is implicated in a deepening of inequality and the socio-spatial fragmentation of the urban environment, as growth is often predicated on reclaiming, rehabilitating and rebranding newly valuable central city real estate. A focus on policing is appropriate because of the central role of security in contemporary urban politics and the part played by policing agents in the day-to-day governance of divided cities. Although police, whether private or public, are not the only agents of security in affluent entertainment and commercial spaces (Shearing and Stenning 1987) they are often a key agent in the governance process. In many cities, discourses of crime and disorder have become central to public debates and figure prominently in the production of certain kinds of urban spaces. Two related trends in policing have received a great deal of attention in this context, both connected to deeper shifts in neoliberal governance: one is the shift to the policing of space (Merry 2001; Coleman 2003; Johnston and Shearing 2003); the other is the rise of non-state agents of policing, particularly private police and security forces (Shearing and Stenning 1987; Sklansky 2006).

Of concern here is the ways these trends combine to produce not only new forms of exclusion from certain urban spaces, but also new forms of urban space that are themselves exclusionary. The policing of space is closely linked to the interests of private property and commodity regimes in cities and the types of security and order – the types of spaces – such regimes require or demand. Policing here should be understood in its more literal and traditional meaning, but also as a broader process of structuring or ordering common space (Dikeç 2002; Kempa, Stenning and Wood 2004). Indeed, 'public order' has become one of the primary discursive formations through which neoliberal spaces are policed and non-criminal behaviours brought into the regulatory regime of modern cities and the criminal justice system (Hörnqvist 2004). Policing produces (or reproduces) space as much as it regulates behaviour within it. That is, police can and do contribute significantly to maintaining the architecture of exclusionary spaces, or spaces that suggest, expect and demand certain kinds of behaviour and a particular order (Merry 2001).

Private police or security agents have come to play an important role in governance regimes that separate questions of security and public order from deeper political questions of social and economic justice (Kempa and Singh 2008). Private refers here not only to policing as a business, but also, in the context of governance, as outside the public realm and, in many cases, effectively outside public control and scrutiny. Although nominally under the control of the state (Berg 2007), private policing and security firms, as profit-oriented entities, are primarily accountable to their clients but can exercise significant power over members of the public and over public space more generally. In their role as agents of governance within these spaces, private police have become, in a sense, both enforcers and producers of a new understanding of privatized citizenship linked to new neoliberal urban spaces and, in cities like Cape Town, to racial governance. Private police in Cape Town's central city operate within a governance regime marked very explicitly by an emphasis on the protection of private property, the culture and economy of commodity consumption and leisure, and the disruptive effects of visible poverty. Their engagement with marginalized inhabitants of downtown, though organized and articulated through a very different discursive logic, is in many respects strikingly similar to that of their public counterparts during the pre-democratic period. Their role in a highly political form of policing is, however, rendered less visible by virtue of the multiple layers of privacy within and through which they operate.

Policing space and governing race in the post-apartheid city

Until 2008 the primary private security provider in Cape Town was G4S Security Services-South Africa (Securicor), a division of Group4-Securicor [G4S], the second largest private security company in the world after the Swedish-based Securitas and the current incarnation of a massive, transnational security services corporation that has grown remarkably in just the last decade. In 2000 the Danish company Falck merged with the UK's Group4, forming Group4Falck. In 2002 Group4Falck took over Wakenhut, the second largest private security company in the United States at the time, creating a company of 230,000 employees operating in 85 countries. In 2004 the company merged with UK-based Securicor, which had purchased the South African private security firm Gray Security in 2000, and was again renamed as Group4Securicor (Abrahamsen and Williams 2007). The company currently has 530,000 employees and operates in over 110 countries. In 2007 its annual revenue reached $8.8 billion and it earned pre-tax profits of $375 million (*Economic Times* 2008; Weisbecker 2008).

The company is performing well across the globe, but particularly in the developing world, where it grew by 17 per cent in 2007, compared to 7 per cent in Europe and the United States. Much of this growth is attributed to expansion in the Middle East, Saudi Arabia and India. In India growth reached an impressive 28 per cent as the company recently won contracts in that country to provide security for airports in Delhi, Mumbai, Hyderabad and Cochin. G4S also expanded operations across Mauritius, Mauritania, Cambodia and Sri Lanka (*Economic Times* 2008). In South Africa Securicor employs over 15,000 people and works across a range of sectors. According to the corporate website, clients include public authorities, small, medium and large businesses, residential customers, embassies and NGOs. In addition to 'manned security' (e.g. mobile patrols, VIP guards, stationary guards, event security, alarm response services) Securicor also conducts corporate investigations and provides security training and consultancy services (Group4Securicor n.d.).

G4S's growth has been accompanied by controversies which suggest how deeply privatization can be linked with processes of racialization and neoliberal governance. The company has become the target of an international labour campaign alleging it abuses workers, violates or prevents collective bargaining arrangements and engages in racist practices. The allegations, which include cases in South Africa, led to a call by labour unions to exclude the company from bidding on security contracts for the 2010 World Cup and 2012 Olympics (PRNewswire 2006; UNI Global 2006; Hawker 2007). The company has also become enmeshed in conflicts linked directly to the rise of private governance and neoliberal urban policies, in particular the privatization of city services and the enforcement of neoliberal cost-recovery policies implemented across urban South Africa; on numerous occasions these conflicts have turned violent (Abahlali baseMjondolo 2008, 2009).

These conflicts between G4S, labour and social movements are important aspects of neoliberal governance that contribute to the reproduction of racial inequalities and racialized urban spaces. Through explicit market mechanisms (labour relations and municipal cost recovery programmes) a private corporation plays a pivotal role in reproducing both the underdeveloped black working class and the underdeveloped black township.[1] Crucial as these processes are to understanding the neoliberalization of racial governance, however, they only indirectly illuminate the simultaneous process of reproducing the racial hierarchy and culture of downtown Cape Town. Furthermore, they constitute relatively well-known aspects of racial governance and the struggles over urban space and resources in the neoliberal city. Less visible are the everyday conflicts in which the black urban poor and private security firms engage on a daily basis across the central city and through which the racialized order of the CCID is reproduced. It is within the confines of this well-defined and tightly regulated social space that we can observe this central dynamic of the governance of inequality that exists, in a variety of forms, across the gentrified, divided and fragmented spaces of urban world.

The Cape Town Central City Improvement District [CCID], the metropolitan region's economic engine, is based on a model emulated in many aspiring world-class cities. Central improvement districts, sometimes referred to as business improvement districts, originated in Canada and the United States in the 1970s as institutions of local government and mechanisms of public governance despite their highly exclusive and private character (Zukin 1995; Berg and Shearing 2008). They are clearly and legally defined neoliberal spaces, generally non-profit corporations, created by property owners and local government in often contested urban environments for purposes of urban redevelopment or revitalization. As discussed above, private police often play a central role in the day-to-day governance of security in central improvement districts. During its contract with the CCID, for example, Securicor had a representative on the Cape Business Forum, which links the business community to the Cape Town Partnership, the non-profit corporation which manages the CCID (Cape Town Partnership, Business Forum n.d.). The fear of inner-city decline and the need to 'save' the area, which began in the mid-1990s, led to the formation of the Cape Town Partnership in 1999. The partnership, it could be argued, took up the 'civilizing mission' that underpinned mostly successful efforts to drive out the coloured and small black African population from the city centre during the Group Areas period (Zukin 1995; Western 1996; Nahnsen 2003; Miraftab 2007). From the mid-1990s eviction of hundreds of squatters during the construction of the upscale V & A Waterfront, located adjacent to the CCID, to the more recent controversy over the siting of the 2010 World Cup stadium, the poor and black mar the fantasy of the perfect city (Bingham 2004, p. 3; Ryan 2005). The result is 'a continuous turf war ... between those entrusted with maintaining the illusion and encroaching representatives of urban poverty' (Ryan 2005, p. 36).

Although not a large area – one could easily walk its perimeter in under an hour – the CCID contains major corporate offices, government buildings, a high concentration of restaurants, bars, clubs and cafes, and the majority of the city's built skyline. Beginning in the mid-1990s and continuing into the present, a security network has emerged in and around the CCID in response to fears of the early post-apartheid period. Today the network of governance in the CCID includes the South African Police Service [SAPS], specialized units of the municipal police and private security companies. Additional layers of governance and security are provided for informally by property and business owners, representatives for foreign real estate investors – who are in regular contact with security forces and the CCID management – social development workers employed by the CCID and an array of street cleaners and other semi-employed low-wage workers who police the homeless and informal traders living and working on the streets.

The organizing principle of this network is a proactive and exclusionary form of policing underpinned by a vision of downtown space originally framed by apartheid in a national-racial context and now reframed by neoliberalism in a transnational-economic context. Implicit and explicit in the city improvement district as a well-defined (and well-defended) economic and cultural space is a politics of belonging organized around consumption, leisure and recreation. Here, in this new polity, the citizen is the consumer and the consumer the citizen. Belonging is rooted in access to the market (Ryan 2005) and participation in the culture of consumption, neither of which is indicated by the visible signs of poverty borne by black street children, 'vagrants' and homeless adults. While exclusion is rightly understood in class terms, in Cape Town and countless other cities it also involves a powerful racial dimension that continues to be intrinsic to the CCID.

Although public policing has played a role, and continues to do so, in securing the central city, the clear drift has been towards the an increased role for private security and a hybridization of security governance, concurrent with the 'revitalization' and *de facto* privatization of public downtown spaces. Melanie Dugmore (2003) documents this shift in policing, beginning with the creation in 1995 of the Community Patrol Office Scheme [CPOs] as a non-profit company in an agreement between the city, the provincial government and the National Department of Safety and Security. Limited to 770 officers, trained and equipped by the SAPS, the CPOs were the equivalent of police reservists. Deployed primarily in the city centre, they represented an attempt by the city to introduce visible policing as the fight against crime in the inner-city intensified. The CPOs were phased out in 2004 and replaced by the Municipal Police (Muni), created three years earlier (Berg 2004). The Muni police are responsible for general traffic and law enforcement. Although they are a city-wide force, it is worth noting that their six strategic areas of emphasis include securing and promoting investment in the city centre (Dugmore 2003).

Until the end of their contract in 2008, however, most of the day-to-day security work in the CCID was carried out by Securicor, and a former social development coordinator for the CCID referred to them as the improvement district's 'personal little army' (interview, December 2008). The company provided the core of the CCID security network, consisting of 80 foot officers per day shift and 60 at night. There were also six 24-hour mobile units and eight horse units seven days a week, overseen by a team of four managers. The foot officers were in addition to any regular SAPS officers and Muni police (Cape Town Partnership n.d.). Although Securicor's private guards were the primary policing force in the CCID, they cooperated closely with the Muni police and SAPS (Berg 2004). Abrahamsen and Williams (2007) point out that Muni police officers rode along in Securicor patrol cars, and that Securicor shared intelligence with SAPS and Muni police, and supported police operations; the result was a 'network of public and private, global and local security actors' operating within the CCID (ibid., p. 247). Securicor was also deeply embedded in the next layer of protection for the CCID as well, the closed circuit television (CCTV) system. Securicor was responsible for the control room operating the city's CCTV system, providing 50 officers in addition to eight Muni police, and was connected directly to the SAPS and Muni police for rapid response (ibid.).

The targets of these mechanisms are generally street children, the unemployed/homeless, street vendors and informal workers, and unlicensed performers. These marginalized inhabitants of downtown are virtually all coloured and black African men, women and youth from the townships or migrants and refugees from neighbouring states. As I document elsewhere (Samara 2009) during the early days of the Partnership and the CCID, a moral panic primarily around street children and crime in the city centre emerged that evoked well-known racial codes linking black youth with urban disorder, translated from the language of apartheid into a more acceptable democratic language of crime, safety and security. Although the panic was of a relatively short duration it functioned to crystallize anxieties around race, the security of the city centre, social order and neoliberal economic growth into a law enforcement-driven governance plan under the CCID rubric. Clearly driven by CCID and partnership officials, who regularly referred to street children as the primary threat to public safety and revitalization, the panic provided a discursive context through which public policies built around the exclusion of poor black youth from the city centre could successfully be implemented with minimal protest.

Race, crime and the violence of neoliberalism

Central to contemporary law enforcement in the city centre is attention to 'quality of life', recently discussed in the city around a heavily contested municipal by-law regarding 'nuisances' (City of Cape Town 2007). As its defenders in the city often point out, the poor and the non-white are not singled out in the by-law regulations. However, in practice, this is precisely who is targeted, particularly when behaviours such as begging and sleeping in public are specified. This by-law in particular gives private security guards unchecked power to move along people living on the street with no need for justification beyond the authority vested in them by the property owners of the CCID, a power that in a sense far exceeds the power of the public police (Shearing and Stenning 1983). While the CCID claims a commitment to social development, pointing to the creation of a social development coordinator's position soon after its formation, Clinton Osbourne, a former coordinator I spoke with, challenged the substance of this commitment. Although approximately 50 per cent of the CCID budget goes to security, he felt their attention to it was even higher, and that the concern for social development was mostly a marketing ploy.

> Security? Sixty per cent to 70 per cent [of the CCID's attention], maybe even 75 per cent. And then clean, the other ... the rest. [laughs]. And then social development maybe 5 per cent. They would always talk about raising the profile of social development. It was definitely seen as something they could milk for all its PR [public relations] worth. They were very keen on me sending things to the media, and "oh you've done this, wonderful!" (interview, December 2008)

He added that during his time with the CCID, the security budget for one month exceeded the social development budget for the entire year.

A focus on quality of life generally, and crime more specifically, provides a clear and powerful governing rationale for this neoliberal space and a moral authority to private security personnel. As Kempa and Singh (2008) point out, speaking of private policing in South Africa more generally, this approach to public order replaces violations of apartheid's racial order with violations of private property as the trigger for repressive police action. At the same time, it mobilizes the same disproportionately white 'public' against the threat to order posed by the now superficially 'deracialized' urban poor who find themselves in the CCID. In the process of the interactions between private police and the black urban poor generated by this mobilization, the very images of the black urban poor that mobilized this public in the first place are reinforced and reproduced.

The intensity of policing in this constructed space is not static, but appears to move in cycles, and has both repressive and exclusionary aspects. The creation of the CCID in 2000 contributed to a new cycle of violence against poor black youth in the city, according to Pam Jackson, director of Ons Plek, a social service organization for young girls on the street, and supported by reports in local media (interview, July 2006). The deployment of its 'private army' appears to have been instrumental in this, as the police have often shown themselves to be at best ambivalent about the by-law and 'quality of life' policing more generally, but feel pressured by business interests and the CCID (Dugmore 2003; Miraftab 2007).

Speaking of this in relation to street children, Pam Jackson said of the SAPS in the city centre:

> They understand some of the deeper dynamics and so they are trying to work together with the NGOs and with children. ... I think the Cape Town police are doing their best given that they have a lot of pressure on them to clear the children off the streets and that their brief is not to care for children but to keep the streets clear of crime. (interview, July 2006)

Although she acknowledges that there is brutality by police, she adds:

> There have been more reports of abusive behaviour towards the children by private security companies employed by the CCIDs and the Partnership than there are reports of children being treated badly by the police. (email communication, January 2004)

When I asked in 2003, prior to the municipal by-law, whether the formation of the CCID had led to an increase in harassment and beatings, she replied:

> Yes it has ... it's not the police as much as the private security firms in particular Gray Security [Securicor]. Gray Security have chased a number of the children out of town onto the periphery. ... We've had reports of children being picked up by security firms in Cape Town and dumped in Camps Bay and then being picked up in Camps Bay by police there and then being dumped back in town. And so it goes. (email communication, January 2004)

Her last comment points to an exclusionary aspect of policing the CCID as well. Clinton Osboure, who resigned from the CCID over objections to the treatment of poor and homeless people in the city centre, told me in 2008 that, although the CCID purports to be 'caring' as well as concerned with making the area clean and safe,

> [T]he reality is that what these people are actually doing is not that kind or caring and their primary concern is moving these people on, their primary concern is not the best interest of these people. ... And they [the CCID] feel like, anything, just do whatever needs to be done to get them off there. I don't think any of them have really malicious intent, but at the same time they also have no real concern for the people. (interview, December 2008)

Linda Ambor, of One Love, a service provider for adults living on the street, draws a direct link between the CCID and the decrease in street people in the city centre after 2004, and highlights the exclusionary effect of repressive policing.

> I think without the heavy handed tactics of the CCID the numbers would probably have increased. ... I think we would have had much larger numbers if it wasn't for the security ... ja, I'm sure there would have been much greater figures. (interview, June 2006)

When I inquired about the reasoning behind the behaviour of security personnel, she replied:

> Their brief is by big business, by the city. "Keep the children away from our doorways, keep them away from our shops." So that's their immediate brief, is keep the city clean. And I hate that phrase, it's sort of like ethnic cleansing, they're dirty, they're vermin. ... And the city belongs to everybody, not just wealthy tourists. It smacks a little bit of Group Areas act to me, and the pass laws. (interview, June 2006)

Explaining how this brief at times plays out, Osbourne refers to calls he would received from Derek Bock, formerly the head of security for the CCID, now chief of operations for Eurocape Holdings, the South African subsidiary of a foreign company and one of the largest owners of property in the CBD, and Theodore Yach, chair of the CCID board and a major local property owner.

> They would phone and they would send messages like "there's two children on Long Street. There's a man pushing a dustbin down Bree Street. There's this man begging on this corner." All the time, sending me these things like "just go and take them away". And that's the attitude, just go and take them away. (interview, December 2008)

The drive to remove the black urban poor from the city centre came up often in discussions with social development workers. Pam Jackson and Renée Roussouw, a co-worker, relate one story of removal.

> Pam: We also got a report, which we couldn't verify, from a fairly reliable source, one of Ons Plek's committee members who worked with a church in Langa [a nearby black African township], saying that the church is very upset – this is last year [2005] – because somebody keeps arriving on a daily basis with street children from the city to dump them in Langa and to ask the church and other community members to take these kids in.
> [TRS: Who was dropping kids in Langa?]
> Renée: We're not clear.
> Pam: It was a small *bakkie* [truck] of the kind that the CCID drive. (interview, July 2006)

Efforts to make downtown inhospitable include confiscating the belongings of the homeless and demolishing their temporary structures. According to the Osbourne:

> [W]ithout a doubt, they [Securicor] take [street] people's blankets, not only their blankets, take everything. Usually when they're not there. So they would know where the people keep everything, then they would go and take them. ... When the CCID used to go on their night operations, they used to make sure they had one of the cleaning contractors with the big lorry so that they could load all this stuff, the belongings, blankets, pots and pans, all of the stuff into the thing. (interview, December 2008)

This confiscation was also at times carried out by other homeless people contracted by the CCID from Straatwerk (Street Work), an evangelical Christian NGO. The CCID credited Straatwerk with clearing 24 tons of debris from city storm drains in 2007 (CCID

2007); the drains, as Osbourne notes, are where many street people hide their belongings.

Osbourne confirmed the suspicions of the other social development workers that the CCID was actively excluding street people from the city centre. In doing so he also revealed the difficult position the street level security guards are put in.

> I mean, they [Securicor guards] used to phone me all the time, desperate. Because they would be told "there's these two children, go pick them up". And then they'd go pick them up and they didn't know what to do with them. And then they'd phone me desperately "don't you know what we can do with these children?" And I'd be like "don't give me any children, I don't want any children from you." I mean, obviously I'd speak nice to them because I also understood that they're just doing what they get told to do, and they get put in a position where there's no options available to them. They've been told to do something but there isn't really any real options. (interview, December 2008)

The creation of a policing force directly tied to the interests of property owners thus not only appears to have contributed to an increase in harassment of poor black people in the downtown, but also contributes to the power of property owners and other elite parties to regulate who can and cannot pass through or occupy CCID space unmolested. The race and class markers here are clear. Private security is hired by, and accountable to, property owners, and they lack a broader crime reduction or social development mandate. What they do have is a mandate to keep the CCID free of nuisances and undesirable elements as defined by the affluent, disproportionately white clientele and the downtown businesses and property owners who profit from them. Private security companies should therefore be understood here in terms of the central role they play as a transnational actor, employing the local working poor and reproducing racialized, local public spaces through their service to a network of local, national and transnational elites.

Conclusion

The Cape Town CCID has shown itself in a short eight years to be remarkably efficient as a mechanism through which private actors can pursue a 'public' agenda. In doing so, the CCID plays a crucial role in working against the stated desires of most city officials: to transform the divided city inherited from apartheid into a diverse yet unified whole emblematic of the new South Africa. A city centre whose white, European character was created and protected by laws designed explicitly for that purpose has become a city centre governed by the logic of the market, shaped by the interests of property owners and investment capital, and patrolled by a transnational private security network. The net effect has been to preserve the hegemony of the very same social groups that held sway under apartheid and to exclude the very same groups cast out by the logic of white supremacy. At the end of the day central Cape Town at the dawn of the twenty-first century is as remote from the majority of city residents as it was for most of the previous century: physically, socially and culturally.

Securicor played a central role in this new form of market-driven racial governance. As the observations of the youth workers cited above show, the general pattern of policing in the CCID is to remove certain black people from the city centre and back to the townships where 'they belong'. As I mentioned at the outset, private policing has to be understood within the context of shifting understandings of citizenship, rights and belonging that are occurring below (as well as above) the national scale. In a city like Cape Town, belonging and rights are not, on a day-to-day basis, grounded in citizenship as it is commonly understood, but in other, often more salient, identities such as race, class and gender. In enforcing quality of life and nuisance by-laws, Securicor works at the front lines of this new racial project of exclusion under conditions of democracy. Working under the authority of the city, but in the interests of property owners, private police have both the legitimacy granted by existing in a formal democracy and the freedom guaranteed to the private sector. The result is a powerful force that, ironically, is itself built upon the exploited labour of black workers; this, too, however, echoes the apartheid past.

The example of Cape Town's CCID pushes us to take seriously the argument that the central improvement district can function as an apparatus of legitimate racial exclusion in a neoliberal democracy, as an undemocratic urban space protected by property law in a demo-cratic nation. Here, the language of economic growth and investment is at the same time a language of security, narrowly tailored to refer to securing certain processes and populations in certain places and excluding others from these same places. These are languages of concealment, which submerge race under class, and class under 'order'. In the post-apartheid city, this concealment facilitates an exclusion that has grown vibrant transnational roots, in terms of both the private company that does the securing and the tourists, business travellers and investments to be secured. In this, neoliberalism has proved itself invaluable as more than an economic development strategy; it is a much further reaching strategy for governing, one that builds upon and extends the social exclusions and divisions many hoped would wither away with the demise of apartheid, but whose reality is obvious to even the most casual observer of cities around the globe.

Discussing and documenting the many connections between race and poverty or race and class is so common that we risk taking for granted the socio-political power and centrality of race to social life, reducing it, as has happened in the past, to a question of class. The constructed link between race, poverty and criminality, however, is essential, and perhaps the most important aspect of racism under liberal democracy and in the neoliberal city. In policing quality of life and producing order, Securicor guards and the public police that partnered with them reproduced the city centre as white space and, just as importantly, the townships as black space. Exclusion in Cape Town may, on the surface, be based on class and not race, but class is of course another way of talking about race in South African and many other contexts. What we must not forget is that, as much as some of us may take this relationship for granted, general public and formal political discourses in many cities and many societies continue to ignore, deny or reformulate the relationship in ways that serve to hide it. To pay attention to the targets of public order and private policing and the spaces they violate, however, is to see that race continues to serve as a rationale for social ordering.

Note

1.   Throughout the paper, I will use the basic racial categories employed by the census (Statistics South Africa 2001) – black African, coloured and white. However, in contrast to the census terminology, I use the term 'black', as distinct from African, to refer to all 'non-whites'.

References

ABAHLALI BASEMJONDOLO 2008 'Arnett Drive resident shot with live ammunition, by Securicor guard', 2 December, http://antieviction.org.za/2008/12/03/abm-arnett-drive-resident-shot-with-live-ammunition-by-securicor-guard/ (accessed 25 May 2009)
——— 2009 'Electricity disconnected and three women arrested in Arnett Drive', http://antieviction.org.za/2009/02/19/abm-electricity-disconnected-and-three-women-arrested-in-arnett-drive/#more-1840 (accessed 25 May 2009)
ABRAHAMSEN, RITA and WILLIAMS, MICHAEL C. 2007 'Securing the city: private security companies and non-state authority in global governance', *International Relations*, vol. 21, no. 2, pp. 237–53
AGUIRRE JR., ADALBERTO and BROOKS, JONATHAN 2001 'City redevelopment policies and the criminalization of homelessness: a narrative case study', in Kevin Fox Gotham (ed.), *Critical Perspectives on Urban Development*, Oxford: Elsevier Science, pp. 75–105
ATKINSON, ROWLAND and HELMS, GESA (eds) 2007 *Securing an Urban Renaissance: Crime, Community and British Urban Policy*, Bristol: Policy Press
BERG, JULIE 2004 'Private policing in Cape Town: the Cape Town city improvement district – pluralism in practice', *Society in Transition*, vol. 35, no. 2, pp. 224–50

────── 2007 *The Accountability of South Africa's Private Security Industry: Mechanisms of Control and Challenges to Effective Oversight*, Newlands, South Africa: Criminal Justice Initiative of the Open Society Foundation for South Africa

BERG, JULIE and SHEARING, CLIFFORD 2008 'Integrated security: assembling knowledges and capacities', In: Tom Williamson (ed.), *The Handbook of Knowledge Based Policing: Current Conceptions and Future Directions*, Malden, MA: Wiley Blackwell, pp. 389–404

BINGHAM, ANNE 2004 *Twilight Children: Helping the Street Children of Cape Town*, Occasional Paper 16, Cape Town: Southern African Bishops' Conference, Parliamentary Liaison Office

BONILLA-SILVA, EDUARDO 2006 *Racism without Racists: Color-Blind Racism and the Persistence of Racial Inequality in the United States*, Lanham, MD: Rowman & Littlefield

CAPE TOWN CENTRAL CITY IMPROVEMENT DISTRICT (CCID) 2007 *Annual Report*, Cape Town, http://www.capetownpartnership.co.za/files/CCIDannual.pdf (accessed June 2008)

CAPE TOWN PARTNERSHIP n.d. www.capetownpartnership.co.za (accessed May 2008)

CAPE TOWN PARTNERSHIP, BUSINESS FORUM n.d. http://www.capetownpartnership.co.za/default.aspx?pageid=26a233ab-814f-4c37-af1b-44028b375a49 (accessed July 2008)

CITY OF CAPE TOWN 2007 *By-law Relating to Streets, Public Places and the Prevention of Nuisances*, approved by City Council on 24 May

CLEMENT, M. 2007 'Bristol: "civilising" the inner city', *Race and Class*, vol. 48, no. 4, pp. 97–114

COLEMAN, ROY 2003 'Images from a neoliberal city: the state, surveillance and social control', *Critical Criminology*, vol. 12, pp. 21–42

DAVIS, MIKE 1990 *City of Quartz*, New York: Vintage

DIKEÇ, MUSTAFA 2002 'Police, politics, and the right to the city', *Geojournal*, vol. 58, pp. 91–8

DUGMORE, MELANIE LUE 2003 *A Review of New Developments in Policing in the Cape Town Metropolitan Area*, Occasional Paper Series, University of Cape Town: Institute of Criminology

ECONOMIC TIMES 2008 'Global expansion boosts GRS profits', 13 March, http://economictimes.indiatimes.com/Latest_News/Global_expansion_boosts_G4S_profits/articleshow/2860316.cms (accessed July 2008)

EISENGER, PETER 2000 'The politics of bread and circuses: building the city for the visitor class', *Urban Affairs Review*, vol. 35, no. 3, pp. 316–33

GLOVER, KAREN S. 2008. 'Citizenship hyper-surveillance, and double-consciousness: racial profiling as panoptic governance', *Sociology of Crime, Law and Deviance*, vol. 10, pp. 241–256

GOLD, STEVEN J. 2004 From Jim Crow to racial hegemony: evolving explanations of racial hierarchy', *Ethnic and Racial Studies*, vol. 27, no. 6, pp. 951–68

GROUP 4 SECURICOR n.d. http://www.g4s.com/home/g4s_worldwide/south_africa.htm (accessed August 2008)

HANNIGAN, JOHN 1998 *Fantasy City: Pleasure and Profit in the Postmodern Metropolis*, New York: Routledge

HAWKER, DIANNE 2007 'Bid to bar Securicor from 2010 contracts', *Cape Argus*, 31 May

HERBERT, STEVE and BROWN, ELIZABETH 2006 'Conceptions of space and crime in the punitive neoliberal city', *Antipode*, vol. 39, no. 4, pp. 755–77

HETZLER, OLIVIA, MEDINA, VERONICA E. and OVERFELT, DAVID 2006 'Gentrification, displacement and new urbanism: the next racial project', *Sociation Today*, vol. 4, no. 2

HÖRNQVIST, MAGNUS 2004 'The birth of public order policy', *Race and Class*, vol. 46, no. 1, pp. 30–52

JENSEN, STEFFEN 2008 *Gangs, Politics and Dignity in Cape Town*, Oxford: James Currey; Chicago: University of Chicago; Johannesburg: Wits University Press

JOHNSTON, LES and SHEARING, CLIFFORD 2003 *Governing Security; Explorations in Policing and Justice*, London: Routledge

KEMPA, MICHAEL and SINGH, ANITA MARIE 2008 'Private security, political economy and the policing of race: probing global hypotheses through the case of South Africa', *Theoretical Criminology*, vol. 12, no. 3, pp. 333–54

KEMPA, MICHAEL, STENNING, PHILIP and WOOD, JENNIFER 2004 'Policing communal spaces: a reconfiguration of the "mass private property" hypothesis', *British Journal of Criminology*, vol. 44, no. 4, pp. 562–81

KOHN, MARGARET 2004 *Brave New Neighborhoods: The Privatization of Public Space*, New York: Routledge

KURTZ, H. and HANKINS, K. 2005 'Geographies of citizenship', *Space and Polity*, vol. 9, no. 1, pp. 1–8

MCARDLE, A. and ERZEN, T (eds) 2001 *Zero Tolerance Policing and the New Police Brutality in New York City*, New York: New York University Press

MCCANN, EUGENE J. 1999 'Race, protest, and public space: contextualizing Lefebvre in the US city', *Antipode*, vol. 31, no. 2, pp. 163–184

MEEHAN, ALBERT J. and PONDER, MICHAEL C. 2002 'Race and place: the ecology of racial profiling African American motorists', *Justice Quarterly*, vol. 19, no. 3, pp. 399–430

MERRY, SALLY ENGLE 2001 'Spatial governmentality and the new urban social order: controlling gender violence through law', *American Anthropologist*, vol. 13, no. 1, pp. 16–29

MIRAFTAB, FARANAK 2007 'Governing post apartheid spatiality: implementing city improvement districts in Cape Town', *Antipode*, vol. 39, no. 40, pp. 602–26

NAHNSEN, ANTJE 2003 Discourses and procedures of desire and fear in the re-making of Cape Town's central city: the need for a spatial politics of reconciliation, in Christoph Haferburg and Jurgen Oßenbrügge (eds), *Ambiguous Restructuring of Post-Apartheid Cape Town: The Spatial Forms of Socio-Political Change*, London: LitVerlag, pp. 137–56

OMI, MICHAEL and WINANT, HOWARD 1994 *Racial Formation in the United States: From the 1960s to the 1990s*, New York: Routledge

PRNEWSWIRE 2006 'Trade unionists encourage South Africa Football Association to rule out Group 4 Securicor as a security provider for World Cup games', 22 December, http://www.prnewswire.co.uk/cgi/news/release?id=187206 (accessed September 2008)

PURCELL, M. 2003 'Citizenship and the right to the global city: reimagining the capitalist world order', *International Journal of Urban and Regional Research*, vol. 27, no. 3, pp. 564–90

RYAN, LINDSAY 2005 'Identity, conflict, and memory in Cape Town's public spaces: unearthing the waterfront', *postabmle*, vol. 1, no. 2, pp. 34–43

SAMARA, TONY ROSHAN 2008 'Marginalized youth and urban revitalization: street kids and moral panics in Cape Town', in Charles Krinsky (ed) *Moral Panics over Contemporary Children & Youth*, Surrey, UK: Ashgate Publishing, pp. 187–202

SAMPSON, ROBERT J. and RAUDENBUSH, STEPHEN, W. 2004 'Seeing disorder: Neighborhood stigma and the social construction of "Broken Windows"', *Social Psychology Quarterly*, vol. 67, no. 4, pp. 319–342

SASSEN, SASKIA 2002 'The repositioning of citizenship: emergent subjects and spaces for politics', *Berkeley Journal of Sociology*, vol. 46, pp. 4–25

SHEARING, CLIFFORD D. and STENNING, PHILIP C. 1983 'Private security: implications for social control', *Social Problems*, vol. 30, no. 5, pp. 493–506

——— (ed.) 1987 *Private Policing*, Thousand Oaks, CA: Sage

SKLANSKY, DAVID ALAN 2006 'Private police and democracy', *American Criminal Law Review*, vol. 43, no. 89, pp. 89–105

SMITH, NEIL 1996 *The New Urban Frontier: Gentrification and the Revanchist City*, New York: Routledge

SORKIN, MICHAEL (ed.) 1992 *Variations on a Theme Park: The New American City*, New York: Hill Wang

STATISTICS SOUTH AFRICA 2001 *Census 2001*, Pretoria

UNI GLOBAL 2006 12 December http://www.unionnetwork.org/UNIPropertyN.nsf/0/
30B1C661E09B72B1C1257242003B0DEA?OpenDocument
URRY, JOHN 2002 *The Tourist Gaze*, London: Sage
WACQUANT, LOIC 2005 'Race as civic felony', *International Social Science Journal*, vol.
57, no. 183, pp. 127–42
―――― 2006 *Urban Outcasts: A Comparative Sociology of Advanced Marginality*, New York:
Polity Press
WEISBECKER, LEE 2008 'Security giant G4S buys MJM Investigations', *Triangle Business
Journal*, 23 May http://www.bizjournals.com/triangle/stories/2008/05/26/story1.html (accessed
July 2008)
WESTERN, JOHN 1996 *Outcast Cape Town*, Berkeley: University of California Press
ZUKIN, SHARON 1995 *The Cultures of Cities*, Malden, MA: Blackwell

Police marginality, racial logics and discrimination in the *banlieues* of France

Sophie Body-Gendrot

Abstract

Youth in 'high-risk' urban zones in France see police discrimination and brutality as a fundamental problem in their relationship to the state, but the state insists on marginalizing or silencing issues of racism and police impunity. At first glance, it seems that mainstream society and its political representatives are indifferent to the racial and ethnic dimension of violence that takes place in marginalized minority neighbourhoods. This paper takes a closer look at how the strength of entrenched French institutions and of police unions play a large role in institutionalized racism. This paper argues that a lack of institutional accountability within the French culture of governance also helps us to understand why the French national police are so reluctant to embrace the community policing model or to register the persistent histories and geographies of intersecting racial, post-colonial and class hierarchies.

Introduction

Are 'visible minorities'[1] in France experiencing racial discrimination? How many young people are stopped and searched by the police because they look North African or African, rather than British or Alsatian? Countries such as the United States and the United Kingdom recognize *institutional racism*, which exposes ideological and political racism buried in the practices and institutional cultures of housing, employment, education, healthcare and police work, and they attempt to address the problem. By contrast, France is silent on questions of potential institutional racism. Unions protect public employees and strongly resist debates on racism in general. As Poli argues, in France 'the first reaction to questions related to racism is silence' (2001, p. 198).[2] Currently, however, there is an emerging consensus around the idea of race as a 'political object referring to boundaries between social inclusion and exclusion' (Balibar 2005, pp. 14–15) and to rights and legitimate grievances.

However, tools like ethnic statistics, which other countries use to fight racial discrimination, have not been gathered by the state, as this practice, itself, is still taboo. For example, after the GIA, a radical Algerian Islamist group, carried out terrorist attacks in 1995 and 1996 on French soil, the commission monitoring the processing of personal data [CNIL] agreed that 'objective, unalterable distinguishing physical marks' could be included in the police database. This was done despite loud protests by both civil rights advocates and right-wing conservatives. However, later, when the police tried to mention the skin colour of those arrested for suspected participation in collective urban violence, the Socialist Minister of the Interior stated that it was against 'the values of the Republic' to do so, and the practice was discontinued (*Le Monde* 8, 11 July 1997; Zauberman and Levy 2003). As of 2009, the debate on the use of ethnic statistics to address discrimination still divides social scientists and public authorities.

Heavily centralized French institutions such as the police are characterized by a culture of denial, particularly when populations of unorganized, poor, immigrant young denounce abusive practices. Increasing denials of different treatment clash with the intensification of identity checks in the *banlieues*. Social relations have been increasingly ethnicized in the last twenty-five years in multicultural neighbourhoods where people mark their difference, through clothing, behaviour or patterns of association, whether with a xenophobic bias or with a sense of pride or of cultural assertion. Policemen are not immune to that culture. Reactive forms of 'functional racism' are part of police culture in numerous countries,[3] but what is specifically French is the fact that policemen and gendarmes are not accountable to anyone but the Interior Ministry.

This study, based on fieldwork and on my experience at the National Commission of Civilian Police Review [CNDS], examines key features of police, race and ethnic relations in France during the last two decades. I examine policing in what the French administration has labelled 'urban sensitive zones' (ZUS): high-risk zones characterized by the isolation and concentration of numerous first- and second-generation immigrants living in massive public housing projects or in dilapidated private homes devoid of adequate public services. I argue that both police who are themselves guilty of crimes and juveniles suffer the indifference of mainstream society and its political representatives to what takes place at the margins, except during outbreaks of violence. As this paper will show, in general, neither policy-makers nor the police force (which is not decentralized in France) seem committed to these neighbourhoods. The institution of policing in France lacks accountability, operating under internal forms of supervision rather than external monitoring, and theoretically observes a strict code of ethics and loyalty. French institutional traditions and practices make it difficult for young residents of immigrant origin to challenge police harassment and institutional neglect. The stigmatization of such youth and of the areas where they live may explain the lack of public debate regarding their rights as citizens and the need for reforms.

As the journal *Ethnic and Racial Studies* has demonstrated forcefully before, while there has been an explosion of theoretical debates related to race and racism, French scholars have been slow to come forward and join these debates, with certain significant exceptions.[4] In general, French intellectuals have been reluctant to discuss racism, an issue they see through the lens of the history of anti-Semitism. In a conference organized on 27–8 March 1992 at the Senate by a French university, social scientists questioned whether the term *race* should be removed from the French Constitution, since some argued it was devoid of substance (Bonnafous, Herszberg and Israel 1992). Others argued that, even if racism was real, the concept of race was unscientific.[5] Nevertheless, the term was not banned, and studies of race continued to emerge in France.[6] While French scholars have indeed recognized that complex identities, including racial ones, are constructed through time and place individually and collectively (Hall 1997), this acknowledgment occupies a minor position compared with debates on inequality, poverty and social justice. Racism in France is understood so broadly that it includes 'any form of violence exerted against another human group, from prejudice and/or contempt to discrimination; from segregation to random or organized murder' (Guillaumin 1994, pp. 67–8).

However, because of France's history of ethnicized religious strife, the racial quotas imposed on Jews during the Second World War (access to many public goods were denied to them as Jews)[7] and the explicitly racist legislation in Algeria and the other French colonies, there is a historic wariness on the part of public officials about deploying racial categories, especially when fighting ethnic and racial discrimination. A popular French mode of thinking was expressed by former President Pompidou, who asserted that 'merely mentioning a term like race calls for the idea of racism and then makes it reality.'[8] I will examine this official attitude in regard to conflicts between youth and police forces in the 'urban sensitive zones' and the functional racism that complicates this relationship.

Racism and resistance in the urban sensitive zones

The term *banlieue* itself is deceptive. On the one hand, it merely designates an urbanized area on the outskirts of a large city. As it is now used by the media and in popular discourse, the term refers to urban deprivation, illiteracy, segregation, poverty, drugs and crime, the subtext being that large immigrant families concentrated in public housing estates are, themselves, the source of the problems. Thus to avoid the culturalist or racializing subtexts now embodied by the term *banlieue* I prefer the administrative label *urban sensitive zones* (ZUS) or 'high-risk zones', coined when a territorial form of affirmative action was launched at the beginning of the 1980s. Many of the 751 ZUS area are currently located in the Parisian region. In some of these localities, 70 to 80 per cent of the housing is public. The rate of unemployment is on average 18 per cent in 2008; however, in some zones it can reach as high as 40 per cent, and then climb to 14 per cent higher than that for juveniles and immigrants. Meanwhile, the average unemployment rate in France in 2008 was around 9 per cent (Le Monde, 23 October 2009, p. 19). Overall, 27 per cent of the ZUS population (4.5 million) is poor – a rate three times higher than elsewhere.

Segregational modes in the distribution of public housing help explain the rise in collective action against institutions and their agents in the ZUS. The policy of immigrant territorial dispersion in the 1960s was rapidly abandoned by those in charge of settlement policies and replaced by a housing-market approach that called for full occupancy in the public housing projects. After the second oil shock, a new law passed at the end of the 1970s focused on access to home ownership rather than to subsidized public housing. Numerous large households belonging to unskilled or semi-skilled families – a majority of those were of immigrant origin – were then invited to occupy the vacant public units deserted by upwardly mobile employees and workers. One survey revealed that 600 youth from ninety households lived in one of these housing blocks (Vieillard-Baron 1999). More recent data say that 31 per cent of ZUS populations are under 20 years old (versus 24 per cent on average) (DIV 2006). Families with numerous children are located in the poorest segments of public housing, either because they are new arrivals without skills adapted for new economies or unemployed or single-parent households with numerous young children not in the labour market.

Colonialism adds another dimension to this specific context. During the Algerian war (1954–62), a large number of Algerians living in France were murdered. It is estimated that 200 Algerians died during the repression of a single area demonstration in 1961 in Paris. While the first generation remained silent about this institutional violence, some of their children recall this treatment in their demands for a political identity. Some in the second generation perceive their current social and economic situation, and the discrimination and violence they are subjected to at the hands of the police and the state, as closely linked to the legacy of colonialism. This generation and the following one use different modes of expression from their fathers generation, which had resorted to strikes to prevent discriminatory firings or conducted hunger strikes to get prayer rooms at their work place. Those active among second and third generations want to mark a rupture in repertoires of expression and to find their own. The new repertoires of action come from the neighbourhoods where they live. According to a witness of teenagers' joyriding activities in Lyon, 'chases with stolen cars were for the youth a way to somewhat cope with all the humiliations they and their parents had been going through....Their aim was to get at the cops who kept them from living quietly in their own world and to fight with them, one on one' (quote in Jazouli 1992, p. 22). Collective popular memory of police brutally repressing workers' movements in the nineteenth and early-twentieth centuries has currently been replaced by that of police forces clashing with these male youth in problematic urban peripheries. Around fifteen serious clashes of police and youth have occurred each year since the beginning of the 1980s in the high-risk zones.

Ethnicization and criminalization of marginalized youth

From October to December of 1983, the first March for Equality and Against Racism started off in Lyon with thirty participants and attracted hundreds as it circulated around France, finally ending in Paris. The march took place in a contradictory context of openness and hostility. Reported incidents of racist violence increased. The next two marches in 1984 and 1985 protested racist murders, 'colonial' police conduct and the unequal treatment of youth and their immigrant parents. Influenced by and reacting to the racist propaganda of the Far Right, the public did not grant these anti-racist movements legitimacy. Taguieff (1993) has shown that anti-racist postures frequently mirrored those of the racists, leading to a 'Nazification' of the enemy, essentializing it. Organized groups also fell apart due to internal divisions, localism and the cooptation of the issue by the Left in power via the creation of the national organization, SOS Racism (Body-Gendrot 2008, pp. 105–6).

Antagonism between the police and second-generation immigrant youth continued to fester. Numerous uprisings followed the death of Malik Oussekine, who suffocated from asthma while being chased by police during student demonstrations in 1986 on the Left Bank in Paris, the death in police custody of Aïssa Ihich in Mantes la Jolie in 1991 and the shooting by guards of a youth in Sartrouville in 1992. Also the deaths of police officers at the hands of youth helped root the on-going tensions between the police and youth in the ZUS (Body-Gendrot 1993). In 1990 disorder and arson rocked Vaulx en Velin in a *banlieue* of Lyon following the death of another youth during a dramatic police chase. After these events, covered by over 250 articles, public opinion began changing. Many French people realized that immigrant families would not return to their home countries and that integrating (i.e. assimilation) would take longer than with previous immigrant (frequently Catholic) waves, in part because the trauma of the Algerian war would continue impacting on French society in terms of hierarchization and exclusion. It seems that the more time passed following the Algerian war, the more its repressed history haunted French society and its institutions.

As the far right got more vocal, the colonial war was interpreted through a racial paradigm (with the French colons at the top and the 'unmeltable' or unassimilable Arabs at the bottom), translating into a narrative about why contemporary multiculturalism would not work in France (Stora 2002, p. 20). The French media fuelled the idea that rampant, wild violence, emanating from those idle, very visible males, threatened the peace of local communities and of French society in general. They also drew many comparisons with the American ghettos and emphasized the dangers of the Americanization of French society (no-go areas, drugs, gangs, anti-assimilationist identity politics or communitarianism, etc.). In a widely-circulated editorial titled 'Communitarianism, this is the enemy!', René Grossmann, the deputy mayor and president of the Strasbourg urban metropolitan area, gave his point of view following the attempted arson of a synagogue:

> Communitarianism substitutes disastrous allegiances for citizenship. It is likely to bring back a state of war on our national soil and to launch extreme forms of violence that would tear the French apart. It negates individual rights, jeers at the République and supports terrorism over democratic debate. The time of tribes has come. Civil peace and Republican citizenship are threatened. There is just a fine line between Sarajevo, a city where communities kill each other, and our French cities.[9]

However, the growing fear expressed by many French residents and fuelled by the media was not grounded in reality. In fact, documented offences, gangs, weapons possession, and homicides were far less frequent than those occurring in, for example, the large cities of the United States.[10]

Ethnic identity and racial profiling

It is important to note how these youth self-identify, in contrast to how they are perceived by the police, mainstream society and the media. Based on interviews that I conducted with violent youth at the request of the Ministry of Interior and currently at the National Commission of Civilian Police Review [CNDS], in France *bandes* of youth belong to the collective space of the *banlieues* (Body-Gendrot and Le Guennec 1998, p. 36). Their identification with one public housing project may override religious, racial or ethnic differences that are perceived as secondary. Ethnic differences are reconstituted *ad hoc*, meaning that whites may be part of a multicultural *bande* or vice versa. Such *bandes* are unlike gangs, as they form and split very rapidly. Intersecting factors of location, age, gender and socio-economic disparities and inequalities are crucial in the production of social and political cleavages, and in the formation of *bandes*, that cannot be ignored. Second, it is also crucial to specify what is behind the term *ethnic*. The conceptual obscurity of this concept cannot be denied. It is located between *race* (although the country is supposed to be race-blind) and *culture* (although the Republican model of social integration does not take distinct cultural 'communities' into account when conceptualizing the formation of the public sphere). The constant process of interactions between majority and minority groups (they meet daily and influence each other continuously) explains why ethnicity is no more fixed than the situations in which it is produced and reproduced. At certain moments, a salience of ethnicity may occur but its occurrence is discontinuous.

An innovative investigation of racial profiling in two transit stations (Gare du Nord and Châtelet-les-Halles) in Paris between October 2007 and February 2008 illustrates the difficulty in isolating ethnicity (Open Society 2009). Two researchers, F. Jobard and R. Levy from the French National Centre for Scientific Research, completed the study under the auspices of the Soros Foundation (ibid.). Trained monitors observed as the police checked identities, and then interviewed the people who had been stopped by the police. Five variables were tested: gender, age, clothing, possession of a backpack and skin colour. Out of 525 stops in four months (which is less than expected), clothing – hip-hop, punk, Gothic, tectonic – was the first marker for the police. Individuals in such clothing made up 10 ten per cent of the people at the stations, but 47 per cent of them were stopped.[11] As two-thirds of those wearing such clothing were visible minorities, those who appeared to be of Arab origin were stopped 7.8 times more often and those perceived to be black were stopped six times more often than 'whites' from that sample. Jobard concluded that clothing is a racialized variable, adding, however, that a young white male in hip-hop clothing was more likely to be stopped than a black male wearing a suit. Blacks form 43 per cent of the sample, but only 14.5 per cent of them wore hip-hop clothing. According to Levy, this minority of the minority is almost always stopped.

When presented with the study's findings, Marie Lajus, a spokesperson for the Paris police, explained that the police do not stop a representative sample of the population. Checks take place in areas where 'youth gangs come on trains from the suburbs in order to pick fights'.[12] No one who was stopped complained of racist or disrespectful treatment, with the exception of a small minority (3 per cent). The study recommended that, as in the UK, the police record the ethnicity of the person after the stops so that their behaviour could be monitored. However, as explained above, this recording of ethnicity would be against the law in France. It is unlikely that this research will open a breach, since, to date, institutional practices and the race-neutral optic of the state prevent a more informed treatment of racial profiling in France.

Institutional responses to ZUS resistance

After the trauma of Malik Oussekine, in the 1990s, the French police began to respond to the shifting nature of public opinion. From this time on, the police's attitude during demonstrations, car burnings, etc., was to show its strength in order not to use it. As one police chief remarked to me:

> We are not here to put delinquents in prison. They belong to our society. ... The police hierarchy must calm their men and, when confronted with fifty youth armed with iron bars, the only civic reaction for the police is to leave and not to treat the problem when it is hot; it would worsen the situation and make it impossible to redress later on. The police refuse to contemplate a Pyrrhic victory. (Body-Gendrot 2000, p. 237)

Nevertheless, this attitude does not necessarily trickle down to young officers who are tired of being humiliated, sneered at and physically attacked by disenfranchised youth.

During the internationally publicized urban unrest and rioting against police in the ZUS in 2005,[13] foreign police forces praised the French police's conduct. Disorder lasted for twenty-one consecutive nights, the largest and longest urban disorder event since the legendary Sorbonne student riots of 1968. The unrest began on 27 October 2005 in Clichy-sous-Bois, on the margins of Paris, after two youths, Zyed Banna and Bouna Traouré, died of electrocution when they ran into a power plant while fleeing police. On 8 November, President Sarkozy declared a state of emergency, but the unrest continued, spreading to 300 urban neighbourhoods in the country. TV coverage showed scores of burnt cars and damage night after night, but, when the riots finally ended, the only recorded deaths were the two 'accidental' ones which had started the unrest.

In the mid-1990s, when fear of crime was a serious concern among the whole population, more repression and risk management methods were introduced in police departments by the ruling Left government, culminating in 2002 when crime had become France's main concern. Since then, a new policy focused on zero tolerance for delinquents has given more leverage to police and prosecutors. Stricter rules for the judicial treatment of youth at risk were elaborated (Body-Gendrot 2005), and a new age of punitive populism,[14] characterizing the evolution of the last forty years in more affluent, individualistic and less tolerant Western countries, was formulated by Minister of the Interior Nicolas Sarkozy (elected President of the Republic in 2007). Punitive populism implies that a majority of people are supportive of tougher legislation – higher sentencing levels, restrictions on the freedom of ex-offenders and new powers for the police – casting their votes and spending their taxes in support of such laws.

After the 2005 disorders however, unlike the Kerner report in the US and the Scarman and MacPherson reports in the UK, no inquiry commission investigated the root causes of the rebellion and its links to the lack of prospects for the marginalized youth. It could be that the government are reluctant to invite the police to talk about their malaise. In the next section I will introduce a brief analysis of the relationship between disgruntled police, the state and the treatment of minorities. These relationships may explain why this broad complex of public neglect is a catalyst for low-intensity violence in France.

Police, discrimination and institutional insulation

Membership in the national police, a civilian force, reached 115,000 in 2009, a number that is to be reduced by 4,800 before 2011.[15] The reduction of 1900 jobs will affect mostly the rank-and-file police officers called 'peace keepers' (*gardiens de la paix*) (97,000 officers), supervised by lieutenants and officers (16,000), accountable to management and police chiefs (2000). The number of police adjuncts averaged 7500 in 2008, down from 10,000 five years earlier.[16] The three major missions of the national police are maintenance of order, investigation (by judicial police) and security. The CRS (*compagnies républicaines de sécurité*) has 14,500 officers who prevent and repress 'disorder'. They are considered to be elite operatives, usually chosen from among young recruits eager for action, although only 5 per cent of their work is actually in active operations. There are also the newly merged intelligence services, the DCRI (4000) and the border police (7200). Paris has its own special status and a police service made of 19,000 officers headed by a prefect accountable not to the Ministry of Interior, but to the government. The National Gendarmes have military status, but are now headed by the Interior Ministry, which oversees their budget and workforce. The 105,975 gendarmes with a hierarchy of 3500 brigades follow an army model.[17] Theoretically, the gendarmes cover 95 per cent of the national territory, where 50 per cent of the population resides, while the police cover metropolitan areas. Gendarmes also work 200 more hours a year than police.

Unlike members of American urban police forces who can easily get promoted if they are efficient, such is rarely the case with the status of the French public functionary. Thus it is understandable that, when assigned to marginalized areas to arrest petty delinquents, French police feel they are doing the 'dirty work' and immediately request a transfer. Police recruits are almost never selected from within communities similar to the high-risk urban zones. Ninety per cent of those coming from provincial localities have their first assignments in the Parisian suburbs. They are influenced by what they see continuously on television and are not familiar with the urban culture of the high-risk zones. It is difficult for them to distinguish among youth, most of whom wear hooded sweatshirts and hip-hop-style clothes, and to separate out actual offenders (Bellot and Thibau 2008). In 2007, an 86 per cent turnover of police chiefs, not to mention the rank-and-file, was observed in Seine-Saint Denis, the most sensitive area in France.[18] Turnover was much lower when the police were decentralized and recruits came from within the locality they policed, that is before 1941. At that time, police were recruited locally and accountable to local populations and their political representatives. But the downside of this system was that they were also accused of corruption and clientelism.

In the late 1990s, the Left enforced a policy of neighbourhood or 'community policing', which was unpopular among the police forces. Nicolas Couteau, the head of the General Union of the police, complained that community policing missions were unclear: 'too often a policeman is meant to be a therapist, a psychologist or a social worker.' Another union leader added that 'the contact with the populations does not consist in organizing soccer games. ... We are not here to meet social goals (*faire du social*)'.[19] A majority of policemen shared the idea that community policing was not real police work. They were professionals and had nothing to learn from populations, it was a waste of time. Residents' expectations were too diverse and incoherent. In brief, police chiefs did not commit themselves to the reforms and claimed that they preferred to receive clear-cut orders from their hierarchy rather than meeting the 'blurred' demands of civilians. There was also a deeper fear, that of balkanization, of becoming accountable to politically diversified mayors, some of them under pressure from politicized and organized groups. The police's shared motto was that citizens should never be considered partners of the police, much less their advisers (Mouhanna 2008,

p. 78). When community policing was implemented at the end of the 1990s, delinquency figures rose because more police in the field meant more crimes were reported; hence, it proved to be politically costly. After he became Interior Minister in 2002, Nicolas Sarkozy dismantled community policing.

Since 2006, police-community relations have theoretically been put back on the agenda after huge urban riots have been perceived as triggered by youth hostility to the police. Many complaints have been voiced about the repressive methods of the police. New units, UVEQ (unités de quartier), were created in 2009, each comprised of twenty-one police officers who patrol the high risk-risk zones from five p.m. to midnight. The number of units is projected to reach 100 in 2010. The weak number of minority policemen and the lack of minority representation among political decision-makers make it unlikely that reforms supporting a civilian-police partnership in marginalized multicultural localities will soon take place.

No representation

Although the Council of Europe has required since 1994 that the police develop a more accurate, respectful and sensitive vision of various ethnic and racial groups (Conseil de l'Europe 1994 pp. 15, 19), and in spite of the injunction of the French Ministry of the Interior in 1999 that the composition of police forces should be more reflective of the populations they serve, the institution has proven notably reluctant to open its ranks to second- and third-generation immigrants; it has chosen to assign this task to private security agencies and to municipal local forces. Foreign-born population constitutes 10 per cent of the total population of France (vs. 4.4 per cent in the UK and 11.1 per cent in the US) (Schain 2008, p. 3). An unofficial source estimated the number of rank-and-file minority policemen at 7 per cent in 2006, from less than 5 per cent five years earlier (Smolar 2006). Among 1800 police chiefs, the percentage is even less: only five are of North African origin, according to one interviewee. Forty-five per cent of police chiefs' parents were in the public sector, and 10 per cent were working class. Special training sessions were launched in 2006 to recruit more candidates from minority groups.

In other more decentralized countries, change is frequently triggered by pressures exerted by organized minority groups acting from the bottom up and by legitimized anti-discriminatory organizations which, under favourable circumstances, find political allies in the decision-making system. But in France, the national police is insulated from third-party advocates whose issues are not taken up by mainstream political parties, whether from the Left or from the Right. Since there is no channel by which the problem can be politically recognized, except through the League of Human Rights or the CNDS' yearly reports, for instance, the status quo persists. Schain explains that only 17 per cent of electoral districts (sending representatives to the National Assembly) have immigrant populations of more than 10 per cent, most of them in the Parisian region. These localities usually vote for the Right. 'Voter reaction to immigrant presence seems to provide a key to the realignment of the party system, as well as a powerful argument against pursuing a positive strategy to mobilize immigrant voters by national parties' (Schain 2008, pp. 115–17). In comparison with the British Labour Party, the French Left, itself deeply divided, would lose more votes lobbying for immigrants' rights than it would gain. Minorities in France suffer from a lack of political representation. This asymmetry of power generally characterizing minorities is here aggravated by the institutional privileges of the police, their lack of accountability and of adequate supervision.

Failures of internal and external supervision of police

When internal sanctions by the police against one of their own do occur, the public – and victims particularly – are not informed, which exacerbates the lack of transparency. Yet, according to official reports from Inspection Générale des Services [IGS], an internal disciplinary and investigative body for the whole public sector created in 1854, 40 per cent of sanctions targeting public employees apply to policemen, who make up only 8 per cent of public employees. Policemen can receive a warning, demerit, temporary suspension or advanced retirement (only 150 cases a year). These sanctions concern all kinds of misconduct, like losing a police ID or vandalizing a police car. The internal inspectorate for the police (Inspection Générale de la Police Nationale, IGPN) (also nicknamed *boeufs-carottes*) has registered a decrease in police violence since 2004.[20] Police unions are eager to point out that, out of four million police actions a year, only 1348 were examined by the IGPN, including 43 per cent for alleged or real physical abuse.[21]

It is obvious, in view of tensions between working-class populations and local police forces and the ministers of the interior over the course of the twentieth century (Berlière *et al.* 2008), that the latter have to walk cautiously when police reforms are discussed: an acknowledgment of 'institutional racism' as defined in the UK would be unacceptable for the powerful French police unions as defined by Judge MacPherson (1999). The fact that judges are reluctant to condemn policemen, the strong arm of the state, for their misconduct or acts of discrimination is not specifically French. However, unique to France is a tendency not to intervene either to redress institutional discrimination or to promote minorities' constitutional rights. For victims and their families, the judicial process may seem extremely long, sometimes taking several years, and gives them the feeling that the police are above the law. Most of the time, the case is closed or dismissed for lack of proof. Judges often privilege the police's version of the story. Police also benefit from lawyers, and from the ability of the police or judge to denouncing the plaintiff for obstruction or contempt. All these elements give police the last word and discourage citizens from taking the police to court.

Take, for example, a case that the National Commission of Deontology on Security (CNDS 2008) examined with regard to an incident in 2006. A witness of police abuse in the Toulouse airport filed a complaint after seeing two policemen beat an immigrant man who was about to be deported. The police accused the witness of 'slanderous denunciation' two days after the officers were summoned by the CNDS. As a result, a judge ordered the witness to write a letter of apology to the two police officers and to pay each of them 100 euros, despite the CNDS' ongoing investigation. In its annual report, the CNDS denounced unbearable pressures voluntarily exerted against witnesses in cases of police abuse, and called for the attention of the Justice Minister, who had been silent on the issue. In January 2008, the head of the national police informed the commission that its inspectors in charge had sparked an investigation of abuse in the police services.[22]

Police perspectives

The interviews we carried out during our two-year investigation display a large range of opinions, attitudes and judgements among rank-and-file policemen (Body-Gendrot and de Wenden 2003). Some disregard all immigrant residents as troublemakers, drug users and fundamentalists, while others who reluctantly admit to having racial biases claim that they would never engage in discriminatory behaviour (we did not find any officer who would admit to having discriminated against immigrants).

Numerous police officers noted that in the ZUS they feel despised by the population, which spits on them, stones their cars and insults them, while mainstream society seems generally indifferent to the police, except when it feels threatened, as was the case in November 2005. Professional police culture tends to divide its 'clients' between those who are legitimate (belonging to the mainstream) and those who are not and hence should be under surveillance. These are precarious populations living on welfare, the homeless, gypsies and second- or third-generation unemployed. In order to be efficient, the police are required by their superiors, elected officials and society at large to monitor potential delinquents. For them, making this distinction is a functional dimension of their work.

Policing problem areas means working fast and spontaneously due to unexpected and singular situations. According to police specialist Christian Mouhanna (2008), the institution has trouble stabilizing. Daily policing is painful work for rank-and-file police who have to cope with the aggressiveness and contempt of part of the population, expressed through verbal or physical violence. The gap between what is assigned to them and what they go through is obvious, so that officers feel isolated both from a restless population and from an administration constantly enforcing misunderstood reforms.

For the last twenty-five years, the French national police have been submitted to continuous reforms. The Ministry of the Interior saw hiring young police officers as an opportunity to carry out reforms. But in the field their inexperience is perceived as a weakness since some of the know-how, the networks of contacts, the empirical lessons allowing some perspective when confronted with events, incidents or crises are lost. It increases police officers' feeling of vulnerability. Numerous policemen feel 'harassed' by people, the media, politicians or their own chain of command. Police officers resent the state because it does not give them enough recognition and it pays them poorly; they resent members of parliament passing laws that are lenient on delinquents; they resent justice and judges they consider 'soft'; they resent the youth, which they find increasingly violent and less law-abiding.[23] The police feel instrumentalized by the political sphere. Bataille (1997) noted 'organizational problems of a public sector under pressure' due to the lack of resources and a loss of confidence in assigned missions, values and identity. Too much priority seems to be given to internal management rather than to public service, while too much pressure on young officers contributes to the exacerbation of tensions, especially those related to the ownership of public space.

Space at stake

Space is a decisive element of police strategy: an officer's duty is to control, assign to specific territories the homeless who lack the resources to go to private shelters and to limit those using public space to those who can justify their social presence. 'In these tough areas,' a police chief from a difficult area in Paris observes:

'residents want to see us, so I do all I can to make ourselves visible. They expect a dynamic approach, the deportation of ... the undesirable, so we do all we can to displace them: checking their I.D.s, we only have a few options in our repertoire, if not, they will stay where they are. Then we stop. This is the only police method: enforcing the rule of law'.

Both habitual and unpredictable situations turn the police force into an institution that assigns definitive and temporary status. Therefore, it is through their organization of the occupation of public space that the police assert their dominance.

A survey taken in 1982 confirms this point and reveals that policemen have their own typology of suspects: immigrants (45 per cent), youth (22 per cent), car drivers (6 per cent). Moreover the report says that, because immigrants are different, they are suspect: 'Policemen feel that immigrants distrust them: "they are very touchy ... ", "they speak behind your back and you do not understand, yet you are not supposed to be offended ...;" they probably think: "why am I always searched?"' (DGPN-DFPP 1983 n. 35).

Confronted by residents reproaching them for either being invisible or too visible, inefficient or too bothersome, and under surveillance and suspected by poor foreign families for all kinds of reasons, the police respond with suspicion and bitterness. Dominique Duprez and Michel Kokoreff, in their work on drugs, quote a rank-and-file policeman patrolling a public housing project at the periphery of Lille: 'Each time we arrest a youth from B., there will be problems. Some time ago, after we stopped one at the student dormitory his friends told us: "If you do not let him go, we will harass you all night long".... That is what happened, they torched cars all night long' (2000, p. 276).

The rhetoric of fear of crime tends to turn policemen into the wardens of Republican order. It raises disproportionate expectations in comparison with their resources and training. The youngest police officers, assigned to the most difficult neighbourhoods, are not prepared to confront unexpected problems. It explains the mutual misunderstandings between them (aiming to restore order, arrest trouble-makers and be respected for that role) and the residents in problem areas, who have diversified attitudes, some of them encouraging policemen when they stop trouble-makers, others expressing their outrage, while most remain indifferent.

Conclusion

In France, the lack of appropriate training and supervision of junior police officers sent to multicultural neighbourhoods is noticeable. The issue of authority, governance and control in such areas can be summarized by the assertion that 'low-status policemen end up dealing with low-status "clients" with a large level of personal discretion'. We can assume that one way some of these rank-and-file police mark their distinction is to resort to a 'confined violence', in the shadows where there are no witnesses (Jobard 2002, p. 212). Were there witnesses, would they be willing to face a judge and denounce racist practices? As 'usual suspects' themselves, would it be possible for them to file a legal complaint in the absence of third parties (such as public prosecutors) or of anti-discriminatory organizations monitoring abuse?

In other words, both delinquent policemen and delinquent youth are the leftovers of an indifferent mainstream society, political representatives and institutions that do not concern themselves with what happens at the margins and do not openly discuss discriminatory practices (Ocqueteau 2002, p. 210). Rank-and-file police often feel they are enforcing the 'dirty work' of control, surveillance and arrests in marginalized urban areas because other integrative institutions (family, educational, social, occupational) have neglected their duties. Proof of this neglect was revealed not just by the three weeks of disturbances in November 2005, but by the astounding silence of the state months after they took place. More than four years later, questions about the incident that triggered the riots are still unanswered.

The heart of the matter is that state officials do not know what to do with these problem areas and with their underprivileged youth. While the government focuses on finding long-term solutions, the media impose more and more short-term visions. The state can only manage to act technocratically (risk management) and mechanically. It has failed to recognize that in order to alleviate the marginalization that these populations of immigrant and French origins experience, the government must engage more effective, local *à la carte* solutions and support more actively visible minorities' rights to fair treatment.

Currently, policies strong in rhetoric and weak in resources seem unable to halt the intensification of racialization and repressive action within the state and society or to put an end to the cycles of urban violence in France.

Notes

1. 'Visible minority' is a much-used term in contemporary France. However, the term is contested given that the French population is officially divided only into French nationals and foreigners.

2. Polls show that the proportion of respondents saying that 'there are too many immigrés and foreigners in France' went down respectively from 51 and 42 per cent in 2002 to 44 and 38 per cent in 2004 (Body-Gendrot 2008, p. 107). Another poll showed that 77 per cent of the French think that 'Muslim French are "French like the others"' (CSA *Le Figaro*, 2003).

3. For instance, the 2000 Eurobarometer revealed that 58 per cent of European Union citizens surveyed 'tend to agree' with the statement that immigrants were 'more often involved in criminality than the average' (Sora 2001 p. 40). This was the majority opinion in twelve of the fifteen member states, and on average only 30 per cent of Europeans surveyed 'tended to disagree' with the claim.

4.   See Guillaumin's seminal *L'idéologie raciste: génèse et langage actuel* (1972) and René Gallissot's *Misère de l'antiracisme* (1985). See also Véronique de Rudder and Michèle Guillon's *Autochtones et immigrés en quartier populaire* (1987) and de Rudder's 'Le racisme dans les relations interinterethniques' (1991), while Daniele Lochak (1987, 1990) reflected on the concept of discrimination. In 1988, Pierre-André Taguieff published *La force du préjugé : Essai sur le racisme et ses doubles.* That same year, Balibar and Wallerstein (1988, p. 20) pointed out a major difference between France and the US regarding immigrant and minority integration: while Americans promoted the ethnicization of minorities, France, perceiving itself as an ethnically homogeneous country, promoted the ethnicity of majorities, a distinction which I later debated, showing that there were already visible convergences in the two countries' racialization logics (Body-Gendrot 1995).

5.   On theoretical debates, see Bulmer and Solomos (2004).

6.   See *La France raciste,* which included a chapter on the police (Wieviorka 1992)

7.   French Jews were required to mark their difference with a yellow star, which facilitated their persecution. One-third (70,000) of the French Jewish population was assassinated by the Nazis.

8.   *Le Monde,* 1 September 1973.

9.   *Figaro Magazine,* 15 June 2002, p. 36.

10.   Unlike in the US, the number of homicides in France is fairly small and has not increased much since 1991 (1.1 per 100,000). Homicides perpetrated by juveniles are unusual, less than 5 per cent, and by foreigners 15 per cent (Mucchielli and Spierenburg 2009, p. 149).

11.   *New York Times,* 30 June 2009.

12.   *New York Times,* 30 June 2009

13.   For an analysis of the 2005 disorders in English, see Body-Gendrot (2007).

14.   As defined by Garland in *The Culture of Control* (2001, pp. 145–6).

15.   *Le Monde,* 8[0] January 2009.

16.   *Le Figaro,* 3 June 2008.

17.   Ibid.

18.   *Le Figaro,* 3 June 2008, p. 8[0].

19.   *Le Monde,* 19 February 2003, p. 7.

20.   *Le Monde,* 14 June 2008, p. 3.

21.   Of course, in the absence of statistics on ethnicity, it is difficult to determine how frequently ethnic discrimination occurs.

22.   The CNDS can only be summoned by citizens via a parliamentary member or institution (Children's Defence, for instance). Currently the number of cases examined each year averages 170. While the commission has no power to redress harm, it has investigation and hearing powers and it issues recommendations, thus giving visibility to cases of misconduct (regarding juveniles, body searches or deliberately tight handcuffing, for instance). However, as it was created by the Left, the commission did not receive much support from governments on the Right. Its termination has been programmed by the government. A larger consultative body with appointed members should replace it in 2010.

23.   *Le Monde,* 19 February 2003, p. 7.

References

BALIBAR, ETIENNE 2005 'La construction du racisme', *Actuel Marx*, no. 38, pp. 11–28
BALIBAR, ETIENNE and WALLERSTEIN, IMMANUEL 1988 *Race, Nation, Classe: Les identités ambiguës*, Paris: La Découverte
BATAILLE, PHILIPPE 1997 *Le racisme au travail*, Paris: La Découverte
BELLOT, MARRIANICK and THIBAU, ANGELIQUE 2008 'Police and discrimination, an investigation by Radio Program Surpris par la nuit', *France Culture*, 25 June

BERLIÈRE JEAN MARC, DENYS, CATHERINE, KALIFA, DOMINIQUE and MILLIOT, VINCENT (eds) 2008, *Métiers de police: Être policiers en Europe, XVIIIe–XXe siècles*, Rennes: Presses Universitaires de Rennes

BODY-GENDROT, SOPHIE 1993 *Ville et violence*, Paris: Presses Universitaires de France

—— 1995 'Models of immigrant integration in France and in the United States: signs of convergence?', in M. P. Smith and J. Feagin (eds), *The Bubbling Cauldron and the Urban Crisis*, Minneapolis: University of Minnesota Press, pp. 244–62

—— 2000 *The Social Control of Cities? A Comparative Perspective*, Oxford: Blackwell

—— 2005 'Deconstructing youth violence', *European Journal on Crime, Criminal Law and Criminal Justice*, vol. 13, no. 1, pp. 4–26

—— 2007 'Police, justice and youth violence in France', in T. Tyler (ed.), *Legitimacy and the Criminal System: International Perspectives*, New York: Russell Sage, pp. 243–76

—— 2008 'Racist victimization in France', in George Anthonopoulos and John Winterdyk (eds), *Racist Victimization in the World*, Willowdale, ON: De Sitter, pp. 89–111

BODY-GENDROT, SOPHIE and LE GUENNEC, NICOLE 1998 *Mission sur les violences urbaines*, Paris: La documentation française

BODY-GENDROT, SOPHIE and WIHTOLD DE WENDEN, CATHERINE 2003 *Police et discriminations raciales: le tabou français?*, Paris: Editions de l'atelier

BONNAFOUS, SIMONE, HERSZBERG, BERNARD and ISRAEL, JEAN-JACQUES (eds) 1992 'Sans distinction de ... race', *Mots*, vol. 33, December

BULMER, MARTIN and SOLOMOS, JOHN (eds) 2004 *Researching Race and Racism*, London: Routledge

COMMISSION NATIONALE DE DEONTOLOGIE DE LA SECURITE (CNDS) 2008 *Rapport 2007*, Paris: La documentation française

CONSEIL DE L'EUROPE 1994 *Formation de la police concernant les relations avec les migrants et les groupes ethniques: Directives pratiques*. Strasbourg: Les Editions du Conseil de l'Europe

DE RUDDER, VERONIQUE 1991 'Le racisme dans les relations interethniques', *LHomme et la Société*, 4

DE RUDDER, VERONIQUE, with GUILLON, MICHELE 1987 *Autochtones et immigrés en quartier populaire*, Paris: L'Harmattan

DELEGATION INTERMINISTERIELLE A LA VILLE (DIV) 2006 *Zones urbaines sensibles: un enjeu territorial de la cohésion sociale*, Paris: Delégation interministérielle à la ville

DIRECTION NATIONALE DE LA POLICE NATIONALE (DGPN-DFPP) 1983 Les policiers, leurs métiers, leur formation, Paris: La documentation Française

DUPREZ, DOMINIQUE and KOKOREFF, MICHEL 2000 *Les mondes de la drogue*, Paris: Odile Jacob

GALLISSOT, RENE 1985 *Misère de l'antiracisme* , Paris: Arcantère

GARLAND, DAVID 2001 *The Culture of Control*, Chicago, IL: University of Chicago Press

GUILLAUMIN, COLETTE 1972 *Lide'ologie raciste: genèse et langage actuel*, Paris-La Haye: Mouton

—— 1994 '"Racisme", vocabulaire historique et critique des relations inter-ethniques', *Pluriel-Recherches*, vol. 2, pp. 67–70

HALL, STUART 1997 'Old and new identities, old and new ethnicities', in Anthony D. King (ed.), *Culture, Globalization and the World-System*, Minneapolis: University of Minnesota Press, pp. 31–68

JAZOULI, ADIL 1992 *Les années banlieue*, Paris: Le Seuil

JOBARD, FABIEN 2002 'Les violences policières', in Laurent Mucchielli and Philippe Robert (eds), *Crime et sécurité: Lé'tat des savoirs*, Paris: La Découverte, pp. 206–14

—— 2003 'Research note: counting violence committed by the police: raw facts and narratives', *Policing & Society*, vol. 13, no. 4, pp. 423–28

LOCHAK, DANIELE 1987 'Réflexions sur la notion de discrimination', *Droit social*, 11

―――― 1990 'Les discriminations frappant les étrangers sont-elles licites?' *Droit social*, 1; trans. in G. Noiriel (ed.) *Immigrants in Two Democracies: French and American Experiences*, New York: New York University Press, 1992

MACPHERSON, SIR WILLIAM OF CLUNY 1999 *The Stephen Lawrence Inquiry*, London: Her Majesty's Stationery Office.

MOUHANNA, CHRISTIAN 2008 'Police: de la proximité au maintien de l'ordre généralisé?', in Laurent Mucchielli (ed.) *La Frénésie sécuritaire*, Paris: La Découverte, pp. 77–87

MUCCHIELLI, LAURENT and SPIERENBURG, PIETER 2009 *Histoire de lhomicide en Europe*, Paris: La Découverte

OCQUETEAU, FREDERIC 2002 'Réflexions de méthode au sujet de l'examen des violences policières', *Cahiers de la sécurité intérieure*, vol. 49, pp. 207–13

OPEN SOCIETY JUSTICE INITIATIVE 2009 *Police et minorités visibles: les contrôles didentite' à Paris*, New York: Open Society Institute

POLI, ALEXANDRA 2001 'Les jeunes face au racisme dans les quartiers populaires', in Michel Wieviorka and Ohanna Johanna (eds), *La différence culturelle*, Paris: Balland, pp. 198–205

SCHAIN, MARTIN 2008 The Politics of Immigration in France, Britain, and the United States, New York: Palgrave Macmillan

SMOLAR, PIOTR 2006 'Une lente amélioration dans la police', *Le Monde*, Jan 23

SORA 2001 'Attitudes towards minority groups in the European Union', European Monitoring Centre on Racism and Xenophobia, Vienna

STORA, BENJAMIN 2002 *Histoire de la guerre d'Alge'rie*, Paris: La Découverte

TAGUIEFF, PIERRE-ANDRE (ed.) 1988 *La force du préjugé: Essai sur le racisme et ses doubles*, Paris: La Découverte

―――― 1993 *Face au racisme*, Paris: La Découverte

VIEILLARD-BARON, HERVE 1999 *Les banlieues: Des singularités françaises aux réalités*, Paris: Hachette

WIEVIORKA, MICHEL 1992 *La France raciste*, Paris: La Découverte

ZAUBERMAN, RENEE and LEVY, RENE 2003 'The French State, the police and minorities', *Criminology*, vol. 41, no. 4, pp. 1065–100

The Bosnian police, multi-ethnic democracy, and the race of 'European civilization'

AnnJanette Rosga

Abstract

In many social science accounts of the role of law enforcement organizations in relation to race and racism, police are positioned as the *agents* of racialization projects, directly or indirectly carrying out the state's work of demarcating insiders from outsiders along racial or ethnic lines. This paper will argue that in post-war Bosnia-Herzegovina the Bosnian police themselves have been the targets of a massive racialization project – one undertaken by police reformers from the international community. Furthermore, by entering the fray with Anglo-American paradigms of ethnicity and identity, and by imposing reforms governed by such paradigms, they only differently 'ethnicized' the Bosnian police rather than helping them to heal extant divisions. In turn, these imposed solutions trapped internationals and Bosnians alike in a situation in which the presence or absence of appropriate ethnic demographics became, for too long, one of the main proxy measures for democratic policing practice.

Introduction: a wolf/bear thing

To understand is to translate.

George Steiner
After Babel

In this collection of studies we have been asked to consider the role of police in racializing projects in the nation-states where each of us has conducted research. My specific site is Bosnia-Herzegovina [BiH] circa 2002–2005,[1] where a massive police reform campaign had been underway for nearly a decade as part of an internationally led 'peacekeeping and state-building [exercise]' since the war ended in 1995 (Doyle 2007, p. 231).

However, applying the concept of 'racializing projects' to Bosnia-Herzegovina immediately risks inviting one's readers to draw signifying links between Anglo-American concepts of race and the axes of difference along which the Balkan Wars were fought. This is partly because the phrase 'racialization project' is hybridized from a series of terms that Michael Omi and Howard Winant define most clearly in their history of 'racial formation in the United States',[2] and partly because the concepts of race and ethnicity are so often used interchangeably in the English language. The risk of conflating Anglo-American concepts of race/ethnicity with identity categories used in Bosnia-Herzegovina is even greater, however, because its 1992–1995 war is routinely described as an 'ethnic conflict'.

This is not to say the translation will not work, or that the concept of 'racializing project' has no place in a discussion of policing in post-war Bosnia-Herzegovina. However, in order for such a discussion to be useful rather than misleading, one must take great care with one's terms. Goran (a pseudonym), an interpreter for the UN's International Police Task Force [IPTF] in BiH, told me a story that beautifully illustrates the translation problem with which this paper must contend.

Before his job with the IPTF, Goran was an interpreter for the UN protection forces during the war. He described an experience interpreting in the middle of a conflict zone where electricity had gone out. The power line ran from one side of the conflict to another and negotiators were unable to agree on how to restore it. Goran's position as an interpreter, understanding both BCS[3] and English, enabled him to understand something none of the negotiating parties grasped: that while one party believed the refusal to repair the downed electric line was due to wilful intransigence and a general refusal to negotiate with despised foes, there was actually a matter of military secrecy at issue which the negotiator could not discuss. When Goran realized what was really going on, he 'broke role' (a term interpreters use when they say things other than what their employers intend to speak *through* them) and advised the person he was interpreting for to negotiate in a different manner:

> I suggested to this guy "Maybe you should ask that person [to open up access to this one part of the front line to repair the electricity]". Once he has said his part [the military security part], maybe you

should stress that we are not interested in that part at all, etc. Because once we cleared that problem there was no problem any more to actually get out in the field and get [the electricity] back up.

When I asked Goran how he'd figured out the real source of the problem, he said:

I figured out [that] it was a lack of explaining to the other side that we are not endangering them. Because they were all the time seeing us as some sort of danger and we were not even realizing that we are a danger. Then we figured out that they are feeling us as some sort of danger and eliminated this potential danger. ... Sometimes it's figuring out what is actually the problem. ... Let's say I communicate to you through an interpreter and you to me, and I already suppose that you know some of the stuff I'm speaking about. Sometimes this is a problem that ... I'm thinking about the bear and you are thinking about the wolf. Sometimes it's hard to understand because when I'm speaking about the bear I think that you *realize* that I'm speaking about the bear and all the time *you* are thinking about the wolf. It comes down to that. Sometimes we have to figure out that we have a wolf/bear thing.

In other words, to speak of the police role in racializing projects in Bosnia-Herzegovina is to run a high risk of 'having a wolf/bear thing'. Anglo-American concepts of 'ethnicity' and 'ethnic groups' have so thoroughly suffused accounts of the 1990s Balkan conflicts, and have had such far-reaching consequences for the quotidian practices of post-war police reform, that no discussion of current-day policing in BiH can proceed without an examination of the differences between 'ethnicity' and the terms in BCS that it glosses.

Part I of this paper will examine these differences briefly. Part II will describe the 'ethnic' dimensions of post-war governance structures in Bosnia-Herzegovina. Parts III and IV will confront a second translation challenge that is raised by the consideration of law enforcement's role in racializing projects in Bosnia-Herzegovina.

Police are, as I have argued elsewhere, 'metonymic' for the state (Rosga 1999, p. 168–9). If, as Andreas Wimmer asserts in *Nationalist Exclusion and Ethnic Conflict* (2002), the modern state is 'captured' inevitably by nationalism, then so too are police as the state's most visible representatives. As such, when the police role in racializing projects is typically discussed, police are positioned as the *agents* of racialization to the citizen-subjects of the nation.[4] They perform the state's work of demarcating insiders from outsiders, criminals from victims, citizens from 'illegals', and those who are doing the right things from those who – dangerously – are not.

Part III of this study will explore how international reformers positioned police as central to ethnically reintegrating the country after the war, and how Bosnian police experienced this positioning. Finally, in Part IV, the study turns to a discussion of how Bosnian police themselves manifested their position in the larger racialization project. I argue that, contrary to the more typical depiction in social science accounts, for a key period lasting several years after the Bosnian war (and perhaps continuing today) the police have been *themselves* the targets of a massive racialization project – one undertaken by police reformers from the international community – as much as they have been agents of any such project by the Bosnian state.

Part I: translating ethnicity

The war that brought Bosnia-Herzegovina to the world's attention had many causes. In contrast to Wimmer's (2002) suggestion (that nations are founded upon and always-already 'captured by' nationalism), in *Balkan Tragedy*, one of the most careful and thorough reviews of 'the Yugoslav Crisis',[5] Susan Woodward is particularly insistent that Yugoslavia's 'descent into territorial war and ethnic violence ... was never inevitable' (Woodward 1995, p. 3).

Woodward identifies two main views of the wider Balkan conflict that became consolidated in explanatory accounts of the war in BiH. In the first view, held predominantly by US officials:

> the war was an act of aggression by Serbs against the legitimate government of a sovereign member of the United Nations [first Slovenia, then Croatia]. ... This view ... had become the basis ... for the identification of a more general pattern in the post-cold war period of what American officials called rogue or renegade states, headed by 'new Hitlers' ... who defied all norms of civilized behavior and had to be punished to protect those norms and to protect innocent people. (Woodward 1995, p. 7)

The second view foregrounded the 'ancient ethnic hatreds' thesis, a theory that was more common in Canada and Europe:

> The argument was that communist regimes had kept their populations in a deep freeze for forty years, repressing ethnic identities and freedoms. Freedom throughout the region had restored to countries their national histories of the precommunist era, which ... included ... enduring and venomous animosities between ethnic groups that had exploded into new cycles of revenge when the repression lifted. (Woodward 1995, pp. 7–8)[6]

Even if an ethnicity-based account of the war were to provide us with helpful explanatory frameworks, important dimensions of meaning are lost and others misconstrued when the English word 'ethnicity' is used to translate what in BCS is termed *'nacija'* (pl. *nacije*) or *'narod'* (pl. *narodi*). These terms are occasionally translated into English as 'nation' or 'people', but none of the three words alone conveys the full meaning of either term in BCS. *Nacija* combines elements of territorial geography, national identity, patrilineal descent, and religious/cultural heritage and traditions. *Narod* is often used interchangeably with *nacija*, but in practice is more associated with officialdom than used in everyday speech.[7]

Among the key differences between the concepts of ethnicity and ethnic group as they are often used in English and *nacija/narod* are how, in the latter, family groups can have living historical memory of mixed *nacije* affiliations, and/or of having 'switched' allegiances from one *nacija* to another for political, social or economic reasons – in addition, possibly, to religious conviction. While this can also be said of members of religious groups in 'the West', the concept of ethnicity usually connotes an identity group into which one is born rather than one which can be chosen.

A further difference, from the point of view of many among the English-speaking police and other security sector reformers I interviewed, is that even to one another, Serbs, Muslims and Croats are often physically indistinguishable. (While some Bosnians claim they can identify another's *nacija* on sight, they most commonly identify each other by surname and/or by differences in their BCS language use.) According to several of the US police trainers I spoke with, these facts, coupled with the expectations they arrived with (having heard the country's war described as a conflict between 'ethnic groups'), were confusing.

According to some Bosnian police I interviewed, many of the international reformers who arrived to provide technical assistance in the wake of the war had difficulty grasping the particularly intimate nature of the conflicts. The 'ancient ethnic hatreds' account of the war led many international police, for instance, to expect that Bosnians had lived across clearly demarcated ethnic divides for centuries. This expectation was not irrational. The former Yugoslavia had been constituted as a federation of six semi-autonomous republics (Slovenia, Croatia, Bosnia-Herzegovina, Macedonia, Montenegro and Serbia), all but one of which (Bosnia-Herzegovina) was populated by a demographic majority of the *narod* matching the territorial republic. Thus the majority of people living in Croatia were of the *Croat narod*; the majority of Serbians were of the *Serb narod*; etc. The exception to the rule was Bosnia-Herzegovina.

Figure 1. *Ethnic majorities in Bosnia and Herzegovina by Opstina [Munici-pality], 1991 census*
Source: University of Texas at Austin (http://www.lib.utexas.edu/maps/bosnia/
ethnic_majorities_97.jpg [accessed 20 October 2008])

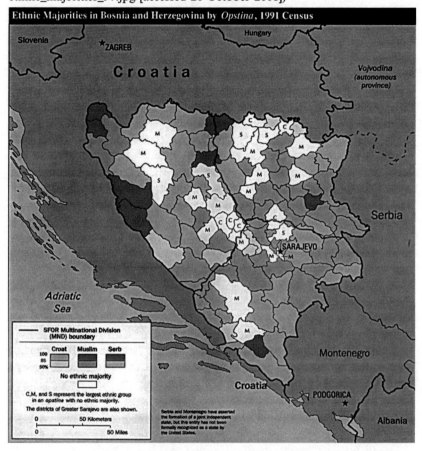

Yet, before the war, Bosnia-Herzegovina's composition was highly mixed, though there were different majorities in different areas (see Figure 1). Mixed marriages between Muslims and Serbs, Serbs and Croats, Croats and Muslims were not unusual. For Bosnia-Herzegovina to have the kind of clearly demarcated *narodi* divisions that the other former Yugoslav republics had, it had to be – as the phrase was coined for the conflict – 'ethnically cleansed'.

Furthermore, ethnicity-based explanations for the war deceptively suggest agreement *among* Bosnians on definitions for given 'ethnicities' – the term 'ethnic group' implies a certain clarity to the grouping. In fact, it was, at least at times, the very *absence* of such boundary-clarity over which the war was fought. Among Bosnians themselves, 'ethnicity'-based accounts fracture into at least two mutually contradictory versions of reality. The 'Muslim version' (overgeneralized to be sure) asserts that individuals, families and communities who identify themselves as Muslim have always considered themselves more culturally than religiously Islamic. The majority of Muslims in BiH before the war tended toward secularism (Bringa 1995). Nonetheless, many Muslims own that they have (and the more nationalist among them say they have always had) a collective sense of self that is distinct from the *nacije* claims of their neighbours and family members who identify as Croatian or Serbian. For some of these Muslims, the active practice of Islam is a vital part of their identity; for others, less so.

In the respectively generalized Croat and Serb versions of reality, 'Muslim' signifies a religion, not an ethnicity. Each group harkens back even further to a shared south Slavic origin, but now the more nationalist among them contend that all the Muslims of BiH belong to either the Serbian or Croatian *narod*. In this view, it was the height of hypocrisy and betrayal for the mostly secular Muslims to have embraced an independent *nacija* identity on the basis of a religion that everyone knew they seldom practised.[8]

Those in BiH who identified themselves as Serbs or Croats were in effect identifying with a set of geopolitical boundaries belonging to neighbouring republics (Serbia and Croatia). Muslims identifying neither as Serbian nor Croatian, who might formerly have chosen to speak of themselves as Yugoslav, were suddenly without a geopolitical entity to call their own. Many began to call themselves 'Bosnian,' for the boundaries of the republic in which they lived, but the war produced too many conflicting claims to that title, so a new term emerged to distinguish Bosnian Muslims from Bosnian Serbs or Bosnian Croats: Bosniak.

To complicate matters still further, most Bosnians (people living within the geographical boundaries of Bosnia-Herzegovina) who identify with the Croat *nacija*, as well as most Croatians, are Catholic by religious heritage; most who identify as belonging to the Serb *nacija* are Eastern Orthodox. This apparent isomorphism of ethnicity with religion seemed to fuel certain Serb (and later, some Croat) military units' claims that their own actions in BiH were taken in national self-defence against Muslim fundamentalists.

Part II: 'This *is* still Europe': ethnicity under the Dayton Peace Accords

The transformation of Bosnia-Herzegovina from a republic into a nation-state occurred with a referendum in favour of independence from the Socialist Federal Republic of Yugoslavia on 1 March 1992, following similar declarations by both Slovenia and Croatia. Although 'an overwhelming majority of Bosnian Muslim (Bosniak) and Croat citizens had voted in favor of an independent and multiethnic state',

Bosnian Serb paramilitary groups, teaming up with Yugoslav National Army units, coordinated a siege on multiple towns throughout Bosnia and surrounded the city of Sarajevo (Doyle 2007, p. 233). The ensuing war lasted more than three years and consisted of multiple 'Yugoslav and Bosnian Serb operations ... designed to divide Bosnia and establish ethnically 'pure' Bosnian Serb territories' (Doyle 2007, p. 233). While early on, 'the main Croat political party, Croat Democratic Union (HDZ) ... and most Croats had supported the idea of a unified Bosnia ... [they later] fought for the glory of Herceg-Bosna, a separate Croat territory in areas bordering Croatia, envisioned as an ethnically pure addition' to that newly independent nation (Doyle 2007, p. 234).

By the end of the war, nearly half the people in the country – 'between 1.4 and 2 million, out of a total 4.36 million' had been forced to flee their homes (Pavkovic 2000, p. 168) and most of the country's regions had been rendered, and still remain, largely homogenous by *nacija*. The region known as Herceg-Bosna is populated mainly by Croats, and the territories cleansed by Serbian military and paramilitary groups into predominantly Serb populations were consolidated into a region known as the Republika Srpska [RS]. The resultant nation-state of Bosnia-Herzegovina was subdivided in 1995 by the Dayton Peace Accords [DPA] into two primary political entities: the RS and the Federation of Bosnia-Herzegovina [FBiH; also known as the Muslim-Croat or Bosniak-Croat Federation]. According to the DPA, which instituted an 'ethnically' tripartite presidency, the RS would remain Serb-ruled, while the Federation was subdivided into ten 'cantons' or municipalities. Eight of these were defined in the new country's constitution as either Bosniak- or Croat-majority, while only two were designated 'mixed' (see Figure 2).[9]

Under the DPA, each political entity retained separate police forces and judicial systems, and each ethnic army had separate chains of command (Doyle 2007, p. 235).

The DPA was envisioned by its international framers, including lead negotiator, US envoy Richard Holbrooke, as a transitional document designed to help Bosnians reintegrate the divided population and gradually combine the separate entities into a unified nation-state (Holbrooke 1999). It provided for 'temporary' governance of the country by a central supervisory structure known as the 'Office of the High Representative' [OHR], but as of June 2009 – more than fourteen years after its creation – the OHR has an 'indefinite' mandate permitting it to oversee the governance of Bosnia-Herzegovina.

Among the key political obstacles standing in the way of a truly independent and effective Bosnian state is the structural integration of the country's 'ethnically' divided police forces. Because the resistance to integration has fallen persistently along DPA-imposed inter-entity

Figure 2. *Bosnia-Herzegovina and its post-war entity-divisions*
Source: United States Central Intelligence Agency, 2008 (http://www.lib.utexas.
edu/maps/cia08/bosnia_herzegovina_sm_2008.gif [accessed 20 October 2008])

lines, and because the DPA is seen to have 'entrenched rather than healed ethnic divisions' (Bilefsky 2008), it is possible to perceive political leaders' resistance to the structural integration of police forces as a problem either of ongoing ethnic conflict among police officers, or of ongoing ethnic tensions throughout the country maintained and inflamed by the entities' separate police forces. However, within the narrowly framed windows it provides (Sarajevo 2002, 2005), my research suggests that additional dynamics may be at work.

In several dozen interviews I did with Bosnian police officers of all *nacije* in BiH, I frequently heard some variant on the theme that international community [IC] members[10] who began inundating the new-born nation in 1995 to 'experiment' with democratic reforms came

utterly unprepared and ill-informed about the officers' lives and the
experiences they had lived through. As one officer said to me:

> Don't take it personally. I don't want to [disparage] your project. But
> I think that hundreds of people are getting their Ph.D. and other
> degrees thanks to this experiment. For a very simple reason, because
> they use ... your country is [intending to use] us as an example [of]
> how they should act if they, God forbid, [find] themselves in a
> situation like this. So for them this is an excellent opportunity to
> practice. We have a little bit strange mentality, that's a fact, but this
> *is* still Europe at the same time. To act here like [you are] in some
> African country, without insulting any African ountry, but you
> cannot have that attitude to us.' (Interview with male police officer,
> age forty-four, fifteen years on the force).[11]

In my own interviews with IC reformers,[12] it was easy to see how this
occurred. So much of the inter-group hostility that police officers read
about prior to their arrivals in BiH resembled things they knew – or
thought they knew – about race riots, police imposition of racially
discriminatory laws and prejudices our societies had 'overcome'. Thus,
it was easy to assume that 'ethnic' in BiH meant the same thing that
'ethnic' means in the US, UK, France, Germany or Denmark.

This is not to say that it makes *no* sense to use a phrase like 'ethnic
hatred' to characterize the conflict that splintered the former
Yugoslavia. Such a claim would be patently absurd. Indeed, the
predominant categories available, particularly from the perspective of
the US or UK, of race and ethnicity and, thereby of inter-group
conflict along racial/ethnic lines, may have obscured more than they
illuminated. As Woodward asserts:

> [B]y giving in to an ethnic account of the conflict and defending only
> one nation in a multinational context, proponents of the aggression
> theory abandoned the *non*-ethnic understanding and constitutional
> mechanisms necessary to protect that group (and all citizens in
> general) against discrimination, expulsion, and death on the basis of
> their ethnicity/nationality. (Woodward, 1995, p. 14)

As will be discussed in the next part of this paper, the 'ethnic account'
produced largely ethnicity-focused solutions. The United Nations
police reform programme centred on the belief that by ethnically
re-integrating the police force – 'making police officers from different
ethnic groups go through the same training, both inside and outside
the police academies, an esprit de corps would gradually develop'
(Celador 2005, p. 367). In turn, they thought, this would build
confidence among citizens and encourage those who had been expelled

to return to their old neighbourhoods and villages. In sum, the entirety of BiH could be (re-)multi-ethnicized with a reintegrated police force leading the way.

> [p]olice officers would no longer see the world through the mindset of membership of a particular ethnic group but would adopt the "master identity" of a police officer, representing the interests of the Bosnian state. (Celador 2005, p. 367)

As should be clear by now, these best-laid plans were not brought to satisfactory fruition. The above reviewer, Celador, concluded (for a host of reasons beyond the scope of this paper to discuss):

> The success of the UN minority police recruitment policy is debatable ... although the police are no longer part of the problem, they still cannot be regarded as part of the solution. Compared with the war and the immediate post-conflict phase, the police are no longer perpetrating or condoning large-scale violations of human rights. There are, nevertheless, occasions where they are failing to deal effectively with cases involving minority returnee victims. (Celador 2005, pp. 367, 373)

More generally, Celador agrees with many other commentators, among them active participants in police reform like Graham Day, who have asserted 'that the emphasis on minority recruitment is not an end in itself but an essential first step in breaking down structural barriers to a professional nonethnically prejudiced local police service' (Day 2000, p. 159).

Part III: racialization and the police, or, My mind is not set up for that'

In BiH, during the 1992–1995 war, many police became armed combatants in the conflict. A significant number carried out orders directly related to, or complicit with, ethnic cleansing campaigns throughout the country. Following the war, many combatants who had never been police officers attempted to present themselves (with their weapons and uniforms) as police officers, dramatically swelling the post-war ranks of law enforcement agencies in BiH. Because so many thousands of refugees had been forced from their homes in 'ethnic cleansing' campaigns, most international efforts to assist BiH with its post-war recovery focused in some way on supposedly reparative strategies of ethnic reintegration. At the very centrepiece of these efforts was the International Police Task Force [IPTF] established as part of the United Nations Mission in BiH [UNMIBH].

Among the UNMIBH's key duties as part of its police reform mandate was the ethnic integration of the Bosnian police forces. Thus, from 1995, when the war ended in BiH, until the close of UNMIBH's mission in December 2002, the Bosnian police were the targets of a massive racialization project undertaken by the international community. In the larger multi-agency effort to encourage refugees to return to the homes they had been 'ethnically cleansed' from during the war, UNMIBH made the 'ethnic' integration of the nation's police forces one of its central tactics. The theory was twofold: first, integrating the police would mean that 'minority' officers would be working in regions from which people of their 'ethnicity' had been driven. This would theoretically draw refugees back as the police would serve as citizen-magnets, their presence indicating that it was safe to go home. Second, widespread human rights training to ensure that the police treated all ethnicities equally would accompany the integration of police forces. Thus, the integrated police in each region of the country would *in fact* work to protect returning refugees.

As Celador and others have amply documented, this strategy has not been fully successful for many reasons. A full recounting of the ongoing failure of refugee-return programmes in BiH cannot be provided here, but two reasons for the inaccuracy of UNMIBH's assumption about refugee returns bear mentioning. First, many of the officers who were recruited to work in regions dominated by *nacije* different from their own did not, in fact, *live* in those regions. Instead, they commuted from considerable distances, opting to remain in their original homes. Whether this is primarily due to a resistance to ethnic integration, fears of ethnicity-related violence, or to other unrelated concerns is not a question that has been objectively evaluated. There is clearly evidence among officers for both ethnicity-related and non-ethnicity-related decisions against re-locating (Celador 2005, pp. 366–7).

Second, for reasons beyond those of present-day safety, many refugees are reluctant to return to areas they were forced from during the war. As one Bosnian refugee explains:

> We have everyday problems with the electric power and water. Roads are bad. There is no job to find and that is our greatest problem. Bosniacs do not touch us, but it is felt that we are not welcome. ...
> Only those who have no other solution return here. (Quoted in Celador 2005, p. 28)

In 2002 and 2005, as noted above, I interviewed several dozen Bosnian police officers about their impressions of the international community's police reform efforts. I also observed several police training sessions led by the United States International Criminal

Investigative Training and Assistance Program [ICITAP], interviewed trainers and ICITAP administrators, toured the newly established law enforcement academies in Sarajevo and Banja Luka, and talked at length with staff and trainers from the UN IPTF and the UNMIBH Civil Rights division.

From this research, a number of findings emerged.[13] First, in contrast to what many international reviewers have reported, I found little if any evidence of persistent 'inter-ethnic' conflict within the police force. This may well be specific to (a) the location in which I conducted most of my interviews – Sarajevo, the city in BiH with the longest and most vehemently asserted claims to valuing diversity; and/ or (b) the particular officers with whom I spoke. However, I talked with police who ranged in experience on the force from five to twenty-six years, and who expressed a wide range of opinions about any number of political issues. In only a small handful of interviews did I have the impression interviewees were presenting a deliberately skewed picture of their experiences as a way of presenting either themselves or BiH in a particular light.

The fact that I conducted all of my interviews in Sarajevo seems far more significant. News accounts in the international and Bosnian press all suggest that the police who are most resistant to full integration are those who work in the Republika Srbska [RS]. However, even there, when I observed training at the Banja Luka academy, the tension I heard expressed along *nacije* lines was far greater among civilians than among police.[14] Thus, I am somewhat at a loss to explain the disjuncture between my own findings and claims by reviewers like Celador, who writes: 'In BiH there have been a high number of cases where minority police officers have faced antagonism and discrimination in their contacts with work colleagues from the majority group' (Celador 2005, p. 369).

Celador's source for this claim is a 'confidential interview' with an 'UNMIBH official', so it is difficult to evaluate. When I asked officers about inter-ethnic tension on the force, they consistently denied it was much of an issue. For example, a relatively young female officer who had joined the force after the war (the force was all-male until post-war reforms required 10 per cent female membership) said, 'I'm also not one who has noted that there are any special tensions. My mind is not set up for that. In my opinion, it is all in the aspect of how you've been raised in your home. I simply do not think about it. Maybe there is some, but I do not notice'.

Of course this could be a kind of 'I don't see race' racism at work, but my sense is that such a reading would be misapplying a US lens to the officer's comment. I base this on the fact that so many officers said similar things – regardless of their *nacija* identity. They also *never* brought the issue up themselves, and often the younger officers seemed genuinely surprised when I did. Older officers would sometimes roll their eyes as if to say, 'Oh, *that* question again,' as though it were all too typical coming from an American. Then they would begin to lecture me on all the things that were of more urgent concern for police in BiH, like a lack of equipment or resources.

This is not to say that differences of *nacija* were absent from police talk; rather, they were somehow invisibly (or inaudibly) omnipresent. In some sense, they were so taken for granted as to be unnecessary to articulate at all. A horribly violent war had been fought along *nacije* lines, so *of course* there were lingering hatreds, resentments and fears. But no 'ancient ethnic hatreds' thesis could ever effectively incorporate the very real, corporeal fact that Bosnians had, until immediately prior to this war, lived side-by-side in a state of almost entirely mixed and *inter-nacije* harmony. As one police officer described this:

> In the same building where me and my friend grew up, we were attending the same school, elementary and the same high school [and college]. More or less we got married [and had our children] at the same time. Our parents belong to the same social class. I am Serbian and he is Serbian. Not only did he leave the city at the beginning of 1992 [when the siege of Sarajevo began] and do horrible things. He never even gave me any hint what he was going to do and that these things were going to happen to me, as a friend. The only realistic reason that I could figure out why he didn't tell me is that my wife is a Muslim. Maybe that stopped him.

Stories like this one recurred multiple times in my interviews with Bosnians, police and civilian alike. For many, the war forced them to *choose* a *nacija,* because their actual heritage was mixed between Croatian, Serbian and Muslim. Another common story I heard was one in which someone of mixed *nacija* had changed her or his surname solely to avoid being identified with a *nacija* at odds with whatever group was in power locally.

Part IV: 'We have the feeling that we are monkeys'

It is not that what outsiders were calling 'ethnic differences' were not vividly real to Bosnians, nor that police were not still grappling with the after-effects of an ethnicized war. It was more that the particular valences of how the war was being understood by outsiders (and reflected back to them) seemed to have no 'sticking' power. They did not recognize themselves in the mirror being held up to them by the 'international community'.

And why was this the case? Because in that mirror, *racism* – and in particular, inter-ethnic violence – was the sign *par excellence* of their society's barbarism. They understood that the international community was saying to them that to be unable to exist in multi-ethnic harmony was in fact to be uncivilized, and to be uncivilized was to be un-European. For example, a fifty-year-old male officer who had been on the force some twenty-five years said:

> This might sound hard, maybe I shouldn't say this, but I feel [the] need to say it. Someone who's coming from a country where they hit people with a stick cannot come in front of me and teach me about human rights. ... Many who came to Bosnia were having opinions about us that we are totally uncivilised. I think that you could see for yourself that we are after all people with a high level of civilisation.

So many of the officers made reference to these countries where police allegedly beat people with sticks (Pakistan, India or African nations) that my interpreter started laughing at one point and broke role to comment:

> He is hoping for the European Union police to be more challenging because they can learn more from the European country police than from some other countries.[15] [laughs] They are all making the same remarks about the Pakistani police who are still having the sticks ...

Another male officer (aged forty-three, working as a police officer for seventeen years) said,

> I was always open to the IPTF. I was interested in what they practice in their countries. ... [But] sometimes you have a feeling that they are just implementing the interest of their own countries. ... I attended [some] courses [where] we have the feeling that we are monkeys [to them]. That was very painful for the people, especially those who had some police background and education.

Thus, the way *racism* mostly appeared (in the sense usually articulated in Euro–American social science theory) in my interviews with Bosnian police was not in how they talked about one another. It appeared in how they talked about the internationals who had descended upon them.

Based on my interviews with internationals, Bosnian officers were not entirely mistaken about how outside reformers perceived them.[16] For one thing, most UNMIBH officials I spoke with were adamant that every police officer working during the war became a combatant for one side or another, and it was thus reasonable to suspect him of having participated in war crimes. In contrast, many Bosnian police officers told me that while, yes, several of them did (sometimes voluntarily, sometimes out of a sense that they had no other choice) take up arms in the conflict, just as many attempted to carry on *policing* – whatever that might mean – to the best of their abilities.

> One [segment of the police] was fighting directly in the battlefield, in the lines. The second part, which I was belonging to, was ... trying as police to provide to the citizens of the city, as best they could, normality and safety. We had thousands of armed people. We had traumatized people – very hard cases. ... And altogether it was very tough to keep even this minimum of safety. But what you cannot doubt is that in Sarajevo, considering all these conditions ... as police, we were honestly doing our best. The fact is that, fortunately for us – and we all feel like this – no other city would behave so good in such crazy conditions. (Male officer, aged forty-four years, fifteen years on the force)

Thus, not only did many of the Bosnian officers wish to position themselves as better trained and more 'civilized' than their putatively superior monitors from non-European nations, some wanted it known that their policing was probably better in quality than *any* other nation's would have been under similarly challenging circumstances. One Bosnian officer described his experiences with US IPTF advisors:

> The majority of them says that ... the police in their country are much more making mistakes and abusing the rights. And even [the High Representative, who has governing authority over BiH] has said that the condition in Bosnia [by 2000] was better maintained than in England for the last fifty years.

In sum, Bosnian officers were far more acutely attuned to how they were being 'racialized' by international reformers than to any potential role they might be playing themselves in ethnicizing or nationalist projects of the Bosnian state.

Conclusion

Much of the research on the role of police in racializing projects positions them as agents of the state in that process. However, in the case I have presented here, in post-war Sarajevo, Bosnian police were themselves a racialized project of international reformers. That is, for the most part, the racializing *agency* did not rest in Bosnian police hands. It is important to remember that during the time these interviews were conducted, this was (perhaps only) possible given that there *was* no independently functioning Bosnian state on whose behalf the police could be serving clearly as agents. Thanks to the ongoing oversight of the Dayton-imposed OHR, while Bosnians go through the motions of practising democratic statehood, they remain literally subject to an external authority. This will continue to be the case until various conditions are met, among them further integration of police agencies between the two entities of RS and FBiH.

For this reason, even if the mission of fully integrating the police forces along *nacije* lines had been fulfilled by the end of 2002 – even if police officers could indeed have been said to have adopted a 'master identity' of police officers rather than viewing 'the world through the mindset of ... a particular ethnic group' – it would still be difficult to say that they 'represent[ed] the interests of the Bosnian state' (Celador 2005, p. 367). What would the interests of this state *be*, ethnically speaking? In the ideal world envisioned by UNMIBH and other international reformers, presumably, the state's ethnocratic interests would be to maintain a peaceful, democratic, multi-ethnic society with transparently functioning, ethnically integrated and human-rights-respecting police forces at all necessary jurisdictional levels (cantonal, entity, federal, etc.).[17] However, as mentioned above, some argue that by framing the solution to the problem of nationalist violence in BiH in terms of a legalized multi-ethnic political structure and enforced multi-ethnic policing, the international community consolidated and further entrenched ethnic divisions in the country.

My argument focuses less on how ethnic, or *nacije,* divisions were affected – in fact, or by perception – and more on the epistemological set-up into which all the players (locals and internationals alike) were effectively trapped. As the comments by Bosnian officers made clear, they felt positioned – and they positioned themselves – on a kind of racially marked evolutionary scale of singular dimension: civilization. On that scale, policing that embodies ideals of European masculinity (reasoned, cosmopolitan) represents civilization, while policing prac-tised by Pakistanis and Indians who hit people with sticks (as opposed to the more orderly application of force with batons, presumably) represents the barbarism of the world's still-developing peoples. The internationals used this same scale and imported its developmental teleology, however unintentionally, with them in much of their training curricula.

To understand policing in BiH now requires us to reject dominant colloquial and social scientific framings of ethnicity. Only then might we begin to understand the war in Bosnia on its own terms, without over-determined discussions about 'ethnic conflict' eclipsing all other frames. Under such conditions, perhaps spaces might be created in which police and civilians alike could approach the fraught task of imagining – and building – a peaceful nation across *nacije* lines.

118   *AnnJanette Rosga*

Notes

1.   The interviews discussed in this paper took place almost entirely in Sarajevo, Bosnia-Herzegovina, (with a few exceptions in Banja Luka) during approximately one year of ethnographic fieldwork in 2002 and a short follow-up visit in 2005.
2.   Omi and Winant use the term 'racialization' to 'signify the extension of racial meaning to a previously racially unclassified relationship, social practice or group. . . . "Racialization" is grounded in historically constructed theories of race and denotes superiority or inferiority' (Omi and Winant 1986, p. 64). Their related phrase 'racial formation' captures how concepts of race in the US are implicated in structural and cultural dimensions of social life (Omi and Winant 1999, p. 15).
3.   BCS refers to Bosnian-Croatian-Serbian, the hyphenated language formerly known as Serbo-Croatian. After the war, it became important to many former Yugoslavs to refer to their native tongues by a sub-region-specific name (e.g. Bosnian, Croatian, Serbian) and to insist that these were indeed separate *languages.*
4.   Examples of this depiction of the uni-directionality of racialization projects abound. Implicitly, these same depictions often represent police as more-or-less ethnically homogenous – in their interests and in the effects of their actions, if not in their actual demographics. See, for example, Edward Escobar (1999) on the history of Mexican American racial identity in Los Angeles, California, as related to police characterizations of them; and Chan and Mirchandani (2001, p. 117) on the 'racialization and gendering of street gangs' in Canada. In both these works, police are the primary agents in the processes by which racialized categories are mobilized.
5.   Other excellent accounts include Glenny (1996); Malcolm (1996); Silber and Little (1997); and Pavkovic (2000).
6.   Whether sociobiological or historical materialist, both varieties of explanation accept as given that the groups at war with one another in Bosnia-Herzegovina have been so for centuries in ways that have not changed in any meaningful way. They both assume an unchanging essence in the identity categories 'Serb', 'Croat', and 'Muslim', rather than, for instance, emphasizing how present-day political leaders may have manipulated public storytelling about various groups to serve particular – and very current – social and political interests (a theory of ethnicity clearly favoured by Woodward – one that Ronnie Lipschutz calls 'instrumental' [Lipschutz 1998, p. 55]).
7.   See, for example, Bringa:

> Prior to the war in Bosnia-Herzegovina (April 1992) its population officially consisted of three *narodi* distinct in terms of religious affiliation but not of geography, language or social life. Affiliation with one of the three religious doctrines, Roman Catholic, Serbian Orthodox, and Sunni Islam, corresponds to membership in a Bosnian *nacija* or official *narod.* Thus, Catholics are Croats, Serbs are Orthodox, and Muslims are members of the 'Muslim' *narod* (Bringa 1995, p. 10).

Following Bringa (1995, p. 21–2), I privilege the term *nacija* over *narod* because it was the one used most frequently in daily conversation during the year I lived in Sarajevo.
8.   Though it is worth noting that under Tito's communist rule, which lasted nearly a decade after his death in 1980, all religion was banned, so the fact that neither Croats nor Serbs have living memories of their Muslim neighbours worshipping in mosques cannot necessarily be equated with an absence of religious identity or feeling.
9.   Major cities tend to be somewhat more 'ethnically' mixed. Sarajevo remains a richly diverse city, though Muslims are now estimated to make up its largest *nacija* group by far.
10.   I retain the term 'international community' or 'IC' because it was so pervasively used in BiH. It refers to actors from the UN and/or other international governmental and nongovernmental organizations [IGOs and INGOs respectively] who arrive in the wake of conflicts or other humanitarian crises.

11.   I carried out interviews either in English (many Bosnians who live in Sarajevo or Banja Luka are fluent or near-fluent in English) or a mixture of BCS and English. Quotations from interviews included in this paper retain certain grammatical errors in English because correcting such errors risks the possibility of altering the speakers' intended meanings more than translation already does.

12.   I also interviewed approximately four dozen employees of UN, US government, and OCSE/ODIHR affiliated agencies involved in Bosnian police reform.

13.   The Bosnian officers expressed a fairly balanced combination of appreciation for the assistance they had received from the UN, the US and other countries; thoughtful reflections on 'democratic policing' in comparison with policing and training before the war under Communist rule; and incisive criticisms of aspects of international assistance and reform. This paper disproportionately reflects their criticisms due to the collection's thematic focus.

14.   Reference to civilian claims comes from participant-observation ethnographic fieldwork in BiH. I lived in Sarajevo (renting from and partially co-habiting with an elderly Bosnian woman), travelled throughout BiH, and taught classes at the University of Sarajevo for ten months in 2002.

15.   This mention of European Union police referred to the fact that the UNMIBH IPTF, terminating in December 2002, was to be taken over in 2003 by a European Union Police Mission.

16.   From the internationals' perspective, it didn't help Bosnian officers appear more 'civilized' to refer to their Pakistani, Indian or African colleagues as stick-wielding thugs. However, projecting barbarism onto others in order to make oneself appear more civilized by comparison is inextricable from much of Western civilization – see, for example, Said (1994); Goldberg (1993); Balibar (1990); Bhabha (1990); Delacampagne (1990). It is tricky at best for anyone framed as 'racist' or 'barbaric' to escape that frame – see Rosga (2001).

17.   Some indication of what a newly self-governing Bosnian state's interests might be for its police forces, and within them the relative positioning of interests one might define as ethnocratic, can be found in an 'unofficial declaration' signed by the reigning political leaders of Bosnia-Herzegovina in late 2007. This document asserts 'full and unconditional agreement' to reform the country's police forces according to three European Commission principles:

1.   All legislative and budgetary competencies for all police matters must be vested at the State level;
2.   No political interference with operational policing;
3.   Functional local police areas must be determined by technical policing criteria, where operational command is exercised at the local level (OHR 2007).

All of these precede 'agreement and acceptance' that 'the overall reform aims at establishing a functional, multiethnic and professional police' force. At the time the declaration was signed, it seemed a hopeful indicator of progress toward structural integration of the country's law enforcement agencies. However, more recent events suggest otherwise. These include accusations by the Serb signatory of the Declaration, Milorad Dodik, that efforts to integrate the police are part of a conspiracy to annihilate the RS as a semi-autonomous entity (Bilefsky 2008; 2009) – accusations the OHR has long denied (OHR 2005).

References

BALIBAR, ETIENNE 1990 'Paradoxes of universality', in David Theo Goldberg (ed.), *Anatomy of Racism*, Minneapolis, MN: University of Minnesota Press, pp. 283–94
BHABHA, HOMI K. 1990 'Interrogating identity: the postcolonial prerogative', in David Theo Goldberg (ed.), *Anatomy of Racism*, Minneapolis, MN: University of Minnesota Press, pp. 183–209

BILEFSKY, DAN 2008 'Fears of new ethnic conflict in Bosnia', *New York Times*, December 14, http://www.nytimes.com/2008/12/14/world/europe/14bosnia.html (accessed 10 July 2009)
––––– 2009 'Bosnia Serbs and envoy are at odds on powers', *New York Times*, June 20, http://www.nytimes.com/2009/06/20/world/europe/20bosnia.html (accessed 10 July 2009)
BRINGA, TONE 1995 *Being Muslim the Bosnian Way: Identity and Community in a Central Bosnian Village*, Princeton, NJ: Princeton University Press
CHAN, WENDY and MIRCHANDANI, KIRAN 2001 *Crimes of Colour: Racialization and the Criminal Justice System in Canada*, Peterborough, ON: Broadview Press
CELADOR, GEMMA COLLANTES 2005 'Police reform: peacebuilding through "democratic policing"?' *International Peacekeeping*, vol.12, no.3, pp. 364–76
DAY, GRAHAM 2000 'The training dimension of the UN Mission in Bosnia and Herzegovina (UNMIBH)', *International Peacekeeping*, vol. 7, no. 2, pp. 155–68
DELACAMPAGNE, CHRISTIAN 1990 'Racism and the West: from praxis to logos', in David Theo Goldberg (ed.), *Anatomy of Racism*, Minneapolis, MN: University of Minnesota Press, pp. 83–8
DOYLE, MICHAEL 2007 'Too little, too late? justice and security reform in Bosnia and Herzegovina', in Charles T. Call (ed.), *Constructing Justice and Security After War*, Washington, DC: United States Institute of Peace Press, pp. 231–70.
GLENNY, MISHA 1996 (1992) *The Fall of Yugoslavia*, New York: Penguin Books
GOLDBERG, DAVID THEO 1993 *Racist Culture: Philosophy and the Politics of Meaning*, Oxford: Blackwell
HOLBROOKE, RICHARD 1999 (1998) *To End a War*, New York: The Modern Library
ISAJAW, W. 1974 'Definitions of ethnicity', *Ethnicity*, vol. I no. 2, pp. 111–74
LIPSCHUTZ, RONNIE 1998 'Seeking a state of one's own: an analytical framework for assessing ethnic and sectarian conflicts', in B. Crawford and R. Lipschutz (eds), *The Myth of 'Ethnic Conflict': Politics, Economics, and 'Cultural' Violence*, Berkeley, CA: University of California International and Area Studies Digital Collection, no. 98, pp. 44–77
MALCOLM, NOEL 1996 (1994) *Bosnia: A Short History*, New York: New York University Press
OFFICE OF THE HIGH REPRESENTATIVE 1997 'Peace Implementation Council Bonn conclusions, Bosnia and Herzegovina 1998: self-sustaining structures', Bonn: Germany, 10 December, http://www.ohr.int/print/?content_id=5182 (accessed 10 June 2009)
––––– 2005 '5 common misconceptions about police restructuring', 17 March, Sarajevo: Bosnia-Herzegovina, http://www.ohr.int/ohr-dept/rule-of-law-pillar/prc/default.asp?content_id=34263 (accessed 5 June 2009)
––––– 2007 'Declaration on honouring the commitments for implementation of the police reform with aim to initial and sign the Stabilisation and Association Agreement', Sarajevo: Bosnia-Herzegovina, 29 October, http://www.ohr.int/print/?content_id=40748 (accessed 3 June 2009)
––––– 2008 'Press conference by the High Representative Miroslav Lajčák following the Peace Implementation Council Steering Board session in Brussels on 26–27 February 2008' http://www.ohr.int/ohr-dept/presso/pressb/default.asp?content_id=41353 (accessed 10 June 2009)
OMI, MICHAEL and WINANT, HOWARD 1986 *Racial Formation in the United States: From the 1960s to the 1980s*, New York: Routledge and Kegan Paul
––––– 2001 'Racial formation', in Steven Seidman and Jeffrey C. Alexander (eds), *The New Social Theory Reader*, New York: Routledge, pp. 371–83
PAVKOVIC, ALEKSANDAR 2000 (1997) *The Fragmentation of Yugoslavia: Nationalism and War in the Balkans*, New York: St. Martin's Press
ROSGA, ANNJANETTE 1999 'Policing the state', *Georgetown Journal of Gender and the Law*, Inaugural Issue, Summer, pp. 145–71
––––– 2001 'Deadly words: state power & the entanglement of speech and violence in hate crime', *Law and Critique*, vol. 12, no. 3, pp. 223–52
SAID, EDWARD W. 1994 (1978) *Orientalism*, New York: Vintage Books

SILBER, LAURA and LITTLE, ALLAN 1997 (1995) *Yugoslavia: Death of a Nation*, New York: Penguin Books

STEINER, GEORGE 1975 *After Babel: Aspects of Language and Translation*, New York, Oxford University Press

WIMMER, ANDREAS 2002 *Nationalist Exclusion and Ethnic Conflict: Shadows of Modernity*, Cambridge: Cambridge University Press

WINANT, HOWARD 1999 'Racism today: continuity and change in the post-civil rights era', in Paul Wong (ed.), *Race, Ethnicity, and Nationality in the United States*, Boulder, CO: Westview Press, pp. 14–24

WOODWARD, SUSAN L. 1995 *Balkan Tragedy: Chaos and Dissolution After the Cold War*, Washington, DC: The Brookings Institution

Counting bodies: crime mapping, policing and race in Colombia

Eduardo Moncada

Abstract

How do internationally informed, technology-driven efforts to democratize the police and citizen security policies in developing countries intersect with pre-existing racial dynamics and discourses? This question is relevant to scholars of both race and security in developing countries, given the current global diffusion of US policing reforms into distinct racial and political contexts. I analyse the intersection between the adoption of crime-mapping technology in urban Colombia and dynamics and discourses regarding the Afro-Colombian population. I find that efforts to democratize the police can paradoxically displace important questions about race from citizen security policy discussions and generate seemingly 'objective' findings that fuse with subjective assumptions regarding the links between criminality, violence and race.

Introduction

How do efforts to democratize the police and citizen security policies in developing countries intersect with pre-existing racial dynamics and discourses? At a time when citizen security is a major concern in Latin America and the region faces multiple democratic deficits, including longstanding forms of racism, the lack of research on the intersection between these phenomena is surprising. I use the adoption of crime-mapping technology in Cali – Colombia's third most populous city and home to the largest urban population of Afro-Colombians – as a 'heuristic case'[1] (Eckstein 1975, p. 104) to develop a provocative hypothesis. In the absence of a broader political project that explicitly recognizes racial discrimination's potential contribution to violence, crime mapping can both displace important questions about race from citizen security policy-making and generate seemingly 'objective' findings that fuse with subjective assumptions regarding the links between criminality, violence and race. This case study has potentially broader implications, given that Cali's groundbreaking citizen security policies are used as models throughout the region and it has one of Latin America's largest urban populations of people of African descent.

State-directed crime mapping in Colombia has gone through three phases. The first phase took place at the national level starting in the 1980s with the general mapping of urban crime and violence related to the narco-trafficking cartels and the civil war. Cali's pioneering incorporation of traditional crime mapping technologies and practices into the city's security policy-making process in the early 1990s constitutes the second phase. Crime mapping during this phase informed local state efforts to address socioeconomic and political inequities that mapped onto longstanding racial fault-lines. The third phase is Cali's continued reliance on crime mapping but without a political framework that recognizes the potential role of racial discrimination in fostering crime and violence. Crime mapping during this third period devolved into an exercise in 'counting bodies' that deracialized security analyses and policies and fused with pre-existing racial dynamics and discourses.

This study builds upon the rich literatures on race relations in Latin America (e.g. Graham et al. 1990; Wade 2001; Appelbaum, Macpherson and Rosemblatt 2003; Hooker 2005; Wade 1997, 2006) and specifically in Colombia (e.g. Arocha 1992; Wade 1993; De Friedemann 1993; Wade 1995; Van Cott 1996; Restrepo 1998; Urrea and Quintín 2000; Urrea and Ortiz 1999; Barbary, Ramirez and Urrea 2002; Appelbaum 2003; Restrepo and Rojas 2004; Urrea and Barbary 2004). It considers the implications that state responses to worrisome security conditions pose for historical racial dynamics and discourses in the Americas. The paper also contributes to the burgeoning literature on the politics of police and citizen security reform (e.g. Ungar 2002; Arias 2006; Bailey and Dammert 2006; Hinton 2006; Tulchin and Ruthenburg 2006; Eaton 2008; Moncada 2009) by examining how seemingly objective policing technologies can undermine the very efforts to democratize security institutions. The analysis may also inform ongoing efforts to democratize the police and citizen security policies in Brazil, Venezuela and other Latin American countries with sizeable populations of African descent and equally complex race relations and security conditions.

Hypothesis

The privileged role of crime mapping in Cali's citizen security policy-making provides a heuristic case for hypothesis-building to inform future research on what the global diffusion of technology-driven efforts to combat crime and violence implies for racial dynamics and discourses in the developing world. My analysis considers how the political environment in which crime mapping is deployed by the state shapes policy analysis, findings and their interpretation by elites with the political resources to influence how the state responds to insecurity. The resulting hypothesis proposes that, in the absence of a political project of inclusion that recognizes how racial discrimination contributes to crime and violence, crime mapping may both displace important questions about race from citizen security policy discussions and generate seemingly 'objective' findings that fuse with subjective assumptions regarding the links between criminality, violence and race.

A political project that privileges racial inclusion increases the probability that racial discrimination will not be eclipsed as a potential contributing factor to crime and violence by the 'impartial' findings of efforts to map the spatial distribution of criminality and its proximate causal variables. Crime mapping has the potential to inform and guide comprehensive state responses to insecurity if political leaders recognize the complex links between racial marginalization and criminality. Absent this recognition, however, crime mapping can devolve into a narrow exercise in 'counting bodies' that fosters coercive state responses. A political project of racial inclusion can also affect how crime mapping's findings are interpreted by broader elements of society. The absence of a political focus on racial discrimination may result in the use of 'objective' findings to justify subjective racial discourse. Before analysing Cali's crime mapping experience, I briefly identify the main elements of crime mapping, and then outline Colombian racial dynamics into which crime mapping was inserted at both the national and urban levels.

Crime mapping: place and pitfalls

An integral element of the current wave of citizen security reform across the developing world is the democratization of the police (Call 2002; Ungar 2006), which in part entails technological development linked to shifts in policing strategies. Police use of crime mapping technology began in 1994 with the New York City Police Department [NYPD]. This initiative, today known as CompStat, was intended to develop officers' knowledge of micro-level crime dynamics (Eterno and Silverman 2006). Crime mapping relies on the use of Geographic Information Systems [GIS] to produce detailed depictions of crime at varying spatial levels, from entire cities to individual neighbourhoods. These maps in turn rely on the constant collection and analysis of reported criminal activity. Crime mapping also identifies correlations between a variety of contextual variables and criminal activity in specific geographies, including the time a criminal act takes place (i.e. specific hour, day, week and month), demographics of the victimizer and victim, potential motive(s), type(s) of weapon used and the presence of alcohol or other potential artificial catalysts.

Despite the subsequent drop in crime in New York City and the widespread emulation of the CompStat model, crime mapping has raised significant concerns (Greene 1999). The increased reliance on statistical indicators as a measurement of police effectiveness and security can generate a counterproductive tendency among police officers to focus on reducing such indicators at any cost (Eterno and Silverman 2006, p. 223), including improper or illegal practices. Between 1992 and 1996, citizen complaints against the NYPD increased by over 60 per cent (Greene 1999, p. 176). Racial minorities are frequently the targets of these excessive policies, as crime mapping often establishes a correlation between specific racial populations and criminal activity – either as perpetrators or as residents of high-crime neighbourhoods (Ibid., p. 176). In brief, crime mapping can play an important role in informing state efforts against crime and violence, but it can also introduce pitfalls that may antagonize relations between the state – principally its security forces – and racial minorities.

National and urban racial contexts in Colombia

One-quarter of the Latin American population is of African descent. Of Colombia's 41.5 million residents, 4.2 million are Afro-Colombian and 1.4 million are indigenous, constituting 10.6 and 3.4 per cent of the total national population, respectively (DANE 2005). Regional fragmentation along racial and ethnic lines have characterized Colombia since its national independence and inhibited the emergence of a cohesive national identity.

Van Cott (1996, p. 526) finds that Colombian intellectuals associate racial and ethnic heterogeneity with weakness. Colombian society therefore employs a discourse that projects a racially and ethnically homogenous – and thus harmonious – nation-state composed principally of *mestizos* (mixed Amerindian-European) (Barbary 2001, p. 90). This 'deracialized'[2] intellectual discourse facilitates the continued exclusion of Afro-Colombians from traditional positions of power by masking racism and curbing the full potential of race as a potentially powerful 'collective action frame' (Tarrow 1994, ch. 7).[3] The Afro-Colombian population generally experiences unequal access to basic social services and remains mired in the low-income service and informal sectors of the economy (World Bank 2005). Afro-Colombians thus express a generalized sense of what they characterize as a 'lack of opportunities' (Ibid., p. 6).

Afro-Colombians have realized some important national-level political gains in recent years. A new national constitution in 1991 recognized Colombia as a culturally and ethnically diverse nation (Barbary 2001, p.85; Barbary, Ramirez and Urrea 2002, p. 75; Oslender 2004, p. 35). National legislation in 1993, better known as 'Law 70', legally recognized the collective land rights of the Afro-Colombian communities in the western Pacific region of the country (Arocha 1992; Wade 1995; Restrepo 1998). These procedural gains, however, have not always been upheld in practice, nor have they empowered Afro-Colombians to address additional concerns in the political arena (Barbary 2001, p. 91; Oslender 2004).

At the urban level, Colombian cities underwent rapid growth in the mid-twentieth century,[4] and today slightly more than 70 per cent of both the general Colombian and the Afro-Colombian populations reside in urban areas (Barbary, Ramirez and Urrea 2004, p. 76). One-quarter of the Afro-Colombian population resides in the south-western Valle del Cauca, one of the country's thirty-two departments. The capital of the Valle del Cauca is Cali, where approximately 26 per cent (539,000) of the city's total population of just over two million is Afro-Colombian (DANE 2005). With over 12 per cent of the country's Afro-Colombian population (Barbary, Ramirez and Urrea 2004, p. 80), Cali has the country's largest urban population of people of African descent.

Migratory flows to Cali, unlike those of Bogota and other major Colombian cities, have historically been diverse in composition, drawing from the Pacific coastline, the highland plateaus of neigh-bouring districts and the southern portion of the country's main coffee-growing territory (Barbary and Hoffman 2004, p. 119). Afro-Colombians have migrated to Cali since the 1950s. Yet, the spread of the armed conflict to the country's Pacific region – whose population is predominantly Afro-Colombian – intensified migration to Cali throughout the 1990s (Ibid.). Migrants from the Pacific region now constitute 18 per cent of Cali's total migrant population, and of the Pacific migratory flow over 80 per cent is Afro-Colombian (Ibid., p. 144). The majority of Cali's Pacific migrants reside in the impoverished western fringes of the city (Barbary 2004, p. 176), including three administrative divisions – called *comunas* – that together constitute an area known as the Aguablanca District, depicted in Figure 1 with shading.[5]

Cali's sharp population growth since the mid-twentieth century taxed the city's capacity to provide adequate housing, which led migrants to settle on the city's outskirts. Aguablanca eventually became home to some of the city's poorest residents. The spatial concentration of a low-income population coupled with relatively deficient or absent public service provision has historically provided

Figure 1. *Map of Cali and the Aguablanca District*

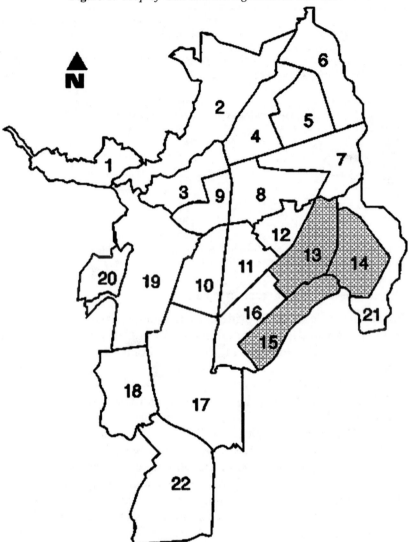

ample fuel for clientelism. Extant supplies of local housing and public services are the result of piecemeal efforts that include the self-help of local residents, charitable donations and periodic public investment during elections (Alvarez et al. 1990; Machado and Ocoro 2004, p. 23). Table 1 indicates that approximately 40 per cent of Cali's Afro-Colombian population resides in Aguablanca,[6] with Afro-Colombians constituting 50 per cent or more of the total residents in Comunas 14 and 15. Table 1 also provides initial insights into the area's security dynamics.

Table 1. *Demographics and violence in Cali (2000–2007)*

	Cali	District of Aguablanca	Comuna 13	Comuna 14	Comuna 15
Total population	2,075,380	454,559	171,646	154,076	128,837
Total Afro-Colombia population	539,598	209,097	65,225	78,578	64,418
Afro-Colombian %	26	46	38	51	50
	Homicides as % of annual city total				
2000		20			
2001		22			
2002		20			
2003		25			
2004		24			
2005		21			
2006		28			
2007		30			

Sources: Demographic data for Cali and Aguablanca: Urrea and Botero. N.D. P. 3, Table 1. Homicide data: Observatorio Social. 2003–2007 and author's calculations

Urban (in)security and crime mapping

Based on Table 1, it is evident that – on average – Aguablanca accounted for one-quarter of all homicides in Cali between 2000 and 2007. Nearly 20 per cent of the city's homicides took place in Aguablanca in 2000, and by 2007 the figure was at 30 per cent. Between 1993 and 2000, over 55 per cent of all homicide victims in Cali were youth between the ages of ten and twenty-nine (Machado and Ocoro 2004, p. 16). Of the 1,250 homicides committed against youth under the age of eighteen in Cali between 2000 and 2007, 43 per cent occurred in Aguablanca (Observatorio Social 2006, pp. 19–20). Being young *and* black – two of the defining demographic features of Aguablanca – is a particularly dangerous combination in Cali, where the mortality rate for black youth between the age of fifteen and nineteen is more than twice that of non-black youth (Urrea and Botero undated, p. 5, fig. 2). How has the periodic evolution of crime mapping in Cali intersected with the racial dynamics in Aguablanca?

Phase I: war on drugs and counter-terrorism

The first phase of crime mapping in Colombia was not a micro-level analysis but instead a national-level effort to chart the extent of the narco-trafficking cartels' urban activities and the incursion of the civil war into the country's major cities. This initial phase set the context for Cali's subsequent adoption of traditional crime-mapping technologies and practices. National-level crime mapping revealed that the socioeconomic and political marginalization of populations living in peripheral urban areas – such as Aguablanca – facilitated the recruitment efforts of drug cartels, leftist insurgencies and right-wing paramilitary forces among disenchanted youth.

Financial assistance provided by the United States to the Colombian military and police as part of its 'war on drugs' supported efforts to map the operations of drug trafficking cartels based in Cali and the country's second largest city, Medellin. Drug-related urban violence was a major concern in Colombia starting in the 1980s and through the early 1990s. The national government was also under intense pressure from the United States to make gains against the cartels, given their export of narcotics to the lucrative North American market. Efforts to plot the cartels' activities mainly informed military and police operations, as did the mapping of the urbanization of the country's historically rural civil war as insurgents and paramilitaries penetrated urban peripheries. In Cali, for example, the M-19 insurgency made significant inroads via Aguablanca and other peripheral parts of the city. The national-level mapping of narcotrafficking and the civil conflict revealed how the poor socioeconomic conditions in the urban periphery facilitated the consolidation of power by several violent, non-state actors. This in turn provided the context in which Cali adopted traditional crime-mapping technologies and practices.

Phase II: urban violence and racial fault lines

Arguably, nowhere in Latin America has the process to democratize the police been as extensive and complex as in Colombia. Cali was the first Colombian city to undertake a comprehensive citizen security-reform project, within which the democratization of the police was a central element.[7] While Cali is known for the powerful 'Cali drug cartel' that controlled a major portion of the cocaine that was trafficked around the world up until the late 1990s, it is paradoxically also renowned in international public health, security and development circles for its preventive citizen security policies between 1992 and 1994. Then Mayor Rodrigo Guerrero executed a series of projects focused on addressing the societal roots of crime and violence in peripheral areas of the city long ignored by the traditional political and socioeconomic elites. These initiatives were grouped under a broader programme known as Development, Security and Peace, or 'Desepaz' in Spanish. Interviews with Guerrero, members of his staff and several consultants to the programme reveal that crime mapping was foundational for Desepaz.[8]

Crime mapping during this second phase was integral for the visualization and analysis of crime and violence at the aggregate city level and the micro level of individual neighbourhoods. Weekly meetings were held between the mayor and members of his staff, the police and other local government functionaries in rooms where the walls were covered with maps of Cali and pushpins were used to identify criminal hot spots. More importantly, data generated by crime mapping was the foundation for Desepaz's efforts to address socio-economic and political inequities that mapped onto racial fault lines. Desepaz is today recognized as *the* regional model for a preventive approach to crime and violence throughout Latin America (Ayres 1998, p. 20).

Table 2 provides an overview of Desepaz's policies. The individual programmes grouped under the five strategic objectives included targeted efforts in specific geographic areas of the city – especially Aguablanca – to reduce socioeconomic inequality, dissuade at-risk youth from using violence to resolve conflict, as well as broader city-wide efforts to increase citizens' awareness about violence through the public dissemination of crime data. Desepaz's efforts in Aguablanca were based in part on the logic that racial and cultural divergences had resulted in the fracturing of society in Cali, which in turn had contributed to the concentration of criminality and violence in Aguablanca.[9] Guerrero's ability to openly address racial and cultural fault lines historically considered unmentionable among the city's elite was due to the fact that he himself was drawn from this powerful elite social network. Before becoming mayor, Guerrero directed a major charitable foundation in Aguablanca whose funding came from a group of large private sector firms that had been major economic and political forces in Cali since the early twentieth century. As one of Desepaz's first consultants to work directly with black at-risk youth in Aguablanca indicated, Guerrero's approach to citizen security and his focus on Aguablanca alarmed Cali's socioeconomic and political elites. But Guerrero's own elite background enabled him to 'effectively manoeuvre past these political obstacles'.[10]

Yet, Desepaz all but disappeared after Guerrero left office in 1994. Subsequent mayors displaced the initiative from its central role in combating crime and violence to the periphery of local government by dismissing the majority of its staff, cutting its financial budget and providing it with little direction. Lack of participation and support from key sectors of civil society and the private sector and the legacy of corruption perpetuated by years of drug trafficking and violence contributed to its withering. The single reform from Desepaz's initial years that has persisted over several mayoral administrations is crime mapping. Yet, how have political leaders' failures to explicitly consider how racial discrimination contributes to violence impacted crime mapping's role in policy-making and elite discourse?

Table 2. *Desepaz's citizen security policies (1992–94)*

Strategic objectives				
Systematic research on violence	Institutional development	Education and communications for peace	Socioeconomic equity	Youth
Programmes				
Epidemiological study of violence through crime mapping	Weekly inter-institutional security meetings	Weekly meetings between local government and community members	Construction of new schools	Cultural activities for at-risk youth
Bi-annual public opinion survey on the police and judiciary	Education and housing provisions for the police	Cultural activities in exchange for the surrendering of toy guns	Teacher training programmes	Sports competitions
	Increased access points for citizen denouncement of crime	Public relations peace and conflict resolution training for community leaders	Public service programmes in Aguablanca	Micro-business training for at-risk youth
	Information technology for the judiciary		Housing for impoverished families	

Source: Guerrero (1999, pp. 4–9)

Phase III: counting bodies

There are two ways in which the third phase of Cali's crime-mapping experiment intersects with pre-existing racial dynamics and discourses. First, it produces deracialized policy discourses regarding the origins of and appropriate responses to violence in places like Aguablanca. An exploration of the security policy discourse and analysis based largely on crime mapping in Cali reveals the predominance of what one local scholar calls a 'focus on counting bodies' without an equal degree of attention to the racial and related political power dynamics that may shape these numbers.[11] Second, crime mapping generates seemingly 'objective' findings that fuse with subjective preconceptions regarding the links between criminality and race.

Deracialized policy discourse and analysis

I rely on semi-structured interviews with mayors, policy-makers and security consultants in Cali conducted during several field research trips between 2006 and 2009 to assess the relationship between crime mapping and policy discourse and analysis. I also analyse publications on crime generated by Cali's Secretariat of Government and Citizen Security between 2003 and 2007. The Secretariat is responsible for both designing and executing the majority of the city's citizen security initiatives.

Aguablanca has long been an epicentre of violence in Cali. Expressions and sources of violence in Aguablanca are multiple and complex. According to a recent study, 'there are gangs, social cleansing organizations, and militias in most of the area's neighborhoods who have organized themselves to address the problem of 'security' by dominating territories and restricting local residents' mobility and possibilities to associate with each other' (Machado and Ocoro 2004, p. 15). Marked inequality and poverty contribute to an overall context conducive to violence as both a means to obtain material resources and a mechanism through which to resolve conflict (Ibid.).

Yet, the fact that a significant portion of the area's population is Afro-Colombian would also be expected to generate debate and discussion among the city's political and policy-making circles about how racial dynamics and discrimination may be a contributing factor to the area's security dilemmas. Atehortua et al.'s (1998) ethnographic study of violence and exclusion in Aguablanca finds that social stigmatization of the area's black youth leads to feelings of disempowerment and consequently the use of violence to gain attention, respect and self-satisfaction. Machado and Ocoro's (2004, p. 20–8) interviews and focus groups with youth from a predominantly Afro-Colombian neighbourhood in Aguablanca also reveal a sense of racial discrimination as a catalyst for the use of violence as a way to gain social status. Community leaders in Aguablanca who work with at-risk youth concurred that young Afro-Colombians hesitate to venture outside of their neighbourhoods because non-blacks often assume that they are readying to commit a crime.[12] As one black youth interviewed by Urrea and Quintín (2001, p. 1, translation by author) states:

> People are very racist ... people think that all blacks are thieves and begin to look at us suspiciously. Especially the whites ... When we go to the city center in Cali to buy our clothes, they see us ... as blacks and they think to themselves, "No! This one is going to rob me", and that hurts.

Racial tensions also feed state-sponsored violence. A former consultant to Desepaz who worked on conflict resolution with youth gangs in Aguablanca during the early 1990s indicated that the city's police harassed and 'disappeared' several of the young black males with whom he worked, based on their race and place of residence alone. He and his staff were 'constantly harassed by the police' and told to 'stop wasting their time' trying to incorporate young blacks into mainstream society. The consultant eventually abandoned his work in Aguablanca, as he and his team experienced intense police pressure and threats of violence.[13] Another Afro-Colombian community leader that works with at-risk youth in Aguablanca indicated that police assigned to the area 'don't assume that they're here to protect the residents of Aguablanca, but that instead they're here to stop [us] from committing crimes against people in the rest of the city'.[14] This assumption leads the police and the state to privilege repressive practices versus more preventive approaches to crime and violence.

Despite indications that racial discrimination contributes to insecurity in Aguablanca, interviews with public officials in charge of the city's citizen security policies reveal a uniform discourse where race and racial discrimination are largely absent. There is instead a neutral discourse focused on the technical aspects of mapping criminal activity that sidesteps the contentious issues of race and racism in the urban context. Policy-makers and security consultants thus use crime mapping primarily to identify proximate variables, such as the presence of alcohol or the time of day a crime was committed.

Nonetheless, one local Afro-Colombian political leader stressed that violence in Aguablanca is much more complex in origin than establishing a link between alcohol and crime. As the studies noted above indicate, some acts of violence in Aguablanca stem partly from longstanding resentment and suppressed frustration with the pervasive mechanisms of racism that facilitate socioeconomic marginalization among a large and young population. The local state's privileging of crime mapping without consideration for race constrains the political space available to local community actors to debate and discuss how racial discrimination feeds violence and the necessary steps to reduce discrimination.[15] The director of a conflict resolution organization in Aguablanca indicated that, after the Desepaz experience in the early 1990s, the local city government has consistently refused to acknowledge the potential for racial discrimination as a macro-level factor associated with crime and violence. 'The state prefers to assume that Aguablanca's security dilemma is reducible to organized youth gangs and the appropriate response is thus more police and more coercion'.[16]

The failure to address race is further evident in the analyses of criminal activity published by the Secretariat of Government between 2003 and 2007, specifically the annual reports on crime based on crime mapping (Observatorio Social 2003–2007). These publications are generated by the Secretariat's Social Observatory, whose institutional mission is to 'define local [citizen security] public policies' (Observatorio Social 2004, pp. 1–2). The Social Observatory's data analysis is the foundation for weekly citizen security policy evaluation and development meetings held between the mayor, their staff, the police and other state security agencies.[17]

The reports consistently rank various neighbourhoods in Aguablanca, including several that are predominantly Afro-Colombian, as among the most violent in the city measured by number of homicides. Aguablanca is thus classified as a 'high priority' area for local state intervention each year. Yet, part of the logic behind labelling Aguablanca as a 'high priority' is evident in the 2003 report, which argues for targeted state intervention in Aguablanca and several other areas of the city that together account for 50 per cent of the city's total number of homicides in order to *'lower the city's overall homicide rate'* (Observatorio Social 2003, p. 17, emphasis added). Aguablanca is in part considered a 'high priority' not because of its particular violent dynamics, but because of what these dynamics imply for the overall number of deaths by homicide in the city. This logic mirrors what Eterno and Silverman (2006, p. 223) identify as a focus on the reduction of quantitative indicators without equal attention to macrolevel causal forces. How does this focus shape the state's citizen security policies?

Specific recommendations to lower levels of violence in Cali based on crime mapping prioritize technocratic measures that privilege the proximate factors associated with homicides. The 2003 report (Observatorio Social 2003, pp. 18–21), for example, called for targeted intervention in Aguablanca and other high-violence areas of the city through campaigns to encourage people not to carry firearms and restrict the periods of time during which stores and entertainment venues can sell alcohol, among others. The Social Observatory's spatial analysis of patterns of violence in 2004 led it to argue that the application of restrictive measures, such as curfews for youth and the restriction of alcohol sales in Aguablanca, had contributed to a slight reduction in the city's overall homicide rate (Observatorio Social 2004, pp. 21–5). In 2005, the institution noted that the Cali had reached its goal of limiting homicides to 'four a day' partly by focusing its intervention on weekends – which crime mapping indicated was the period of time with highest concentrations of violence (Observatorio Social 2005, pp. 25–6). In 2006 and 2007, the Social Observatory focused on lack of educational opportunities and drug addiction as key determinants of violence among youth in Aguablanca and other parts of the city, but made no mention of how these factors interrelate with racial discrimination and socioeconomic marginalization based on race (Observatorio Social 2006, p. 56; Observatorio Social 2007, p. 57). In brief, an analysis of the analyses that inform and guide state security policy-making reveals not a single reference to the potential role of racial dynamics for criminality and violence.

Objective findings and subjective interpretation

How has the 'objective' data generated by crime mapping fused with subjective assumptions regarding the link between criminality, violence and Afro-Colombians? To answer this question, I conducted interviews with several of Cali's past and present elites. A focus on elite discourse is particularly important, given that these are powerful interests with the resources to influence local state response to crime and violence.

The constant diffusion of statistics on criminal activity in Cali and the seemingly perpetual identification of Aguablanca as a 'high priority' with regards to crime and violence has become a mechanism to further crystallize what some elites frame as an insurmountable cultural division between Cali and Aguablanca as the 'other' city that has emerged inside of it. Aguablanca has historically existed at the periphery of both the city's concrete spatial expanse and the imagination of the city's socioeconomic elites. This dual marginalization has not translated into absolute abandon of the area by the city's elites; rather it is the target of public and private philanthropic and community development projects, some of which are financed by several of the city's most powerful private sector firms and families.

Nonetheless, private sector leaders responsible for these projects carefully balance a two-pronged discourse regarding Aguablanca and criminality. They profess the need for increased community development in Aguablanca to prevent delinquency. But they also argue that the cultural and racial differences between Aguablanca's predominantly Afro-Colombian population and the city's majority *mestizo* population explain the concentration of crime and violence in Aguablanca. Despite its geographic isolation, Aguablanca's reputation for criminality and violence as documented by the state is seen as a major hindrance for Cali's overall political and economic development by local elites. Aguablanca, in other words, constrains Cali's ability to become 'modern'.

Previous migratory flows into Cali are depicted as positive by leading socioeconomic elites because they consisted of industrious individuals who arrived with 'four pesos in their pockets'[18] and ultimately succeeded in establishing businesses and settling into a middle-class lifestyle. According to one agroindustrial elite, these early migrants helped make Cali a 'paradise where security was never an issue'.[19] The current, predominantly Afro-Colombian migratory in-flows are seen in a very different light. Contemporary migrants are viewed as arriving with 'empty pockets' to 'make demands on the city' and not contribute to its overall development.[20] How has crime mapping contributed to this conceptual divorce between Cali and Aguablanca and, more importantly, to the perceptions and assump-tions that elites have of their neighbours in the city's outskirts?

Aguablanca's consistent ranking among the top security priorities in the Cali has further crystallized the divorce between it and the rest of the city in the discourse among the city's elites.[21] Elites repeatedly pointed to the high number of homicides in Aguablanca reported in local media outlets based on the data provided by the Social Observatory as further evidence that this is simply a world apart from the city proper. A recent opinion column in the city's main newspaper, for example, used the high degree of 'insecurity' in Aguablanca to argue that Cali would otherwise be a 'manageable' city if it were not for Aguablanca, which it characterized as the 'prototype of informality, disorder, poor management, unemployment, and *insecurity* that provides little and demands everything in return' (*El País* 3/19/2008, emphasis added).

During an interview with a representative of one of the city's major commercial business associations, the representative noted that despite living his entire life in Cali, he had never once been to Aguablanca. In further discussion about the conditions of crime and violence in Aguablanca, he echoed the sentiment that 'Cali will never prosper as long as Aguablanca is a part of the city'. Finally, he repeatedly noted how 'studies produced by the local government' show how Aguablanca 'is the most violent part of the city', further justifying the fact that he would likely never visit Aguablanca because 'it's a jungle over there'.[22]

An interview with a member of a well-known family from the agroindustrial sector – a key economic sector that relies heavily on the Afro-Colombian influx for manual labour – provides a particularly insightful look at elite discourse concerning Aguablanca, race and criminality. This elite also heads a semi-formal organization supported by the private sector that works with the public sector to address crime and violence in the city – partly by supplementing the crime mapping efforts of the Secretariat of Government and Citizen Security. In addition to reaffirming the discourse that describes the current migratory inflow as 'needy' and overall 'negative' for the city, he specifically indicated that 'criminality began to increase in Aguablanca once Afro-Colombians began migrating heavily to the area' starting in the mid to late 1980s.

He also indicated that the private sector's efforts in Aguablanca will likely never support a broad political project focused on the racial or socioeconomic roots of crime and violence. Instead, the private sector focuses on macro-level security issues that emphasize building the coercive capacity of the police, increased coordination between the city and the national military and combating kidnappings of business owners. Echoing the commercial sector representative's depiction of Aguablanca as a savage and separate part of the city, he noted that his 'charity trips' to this area to deliver food and other basic needs are for him like 'traveling to the Congo' – again invoking the perception that the criminality and violence in Aguablanca constrain Cali from developing into a modern metropolis.[23]

Toward an alternative crime mapping: conclusion and future research

How do efforts to improve citizen security and democratize the police in developing countries interact with historical racial dynamics and discourses? I identify two potential implications through a case study of crime mapping's introduction into Latin America via the city of Cali, with its sizeable Afro-Colombian population. Because crime mapping is a critical element of the current global diffusion of policing reform models across the developing world – including several Latin American countries with their own large populations of peoples of African descent – this analysis and its findings provide a preliminary step toward hypothesis and theory development of both scholarly and policy relevance.

Cali's adoption of crime mapping has paradoxically both deracialized policy analysis and fused with subjective assumptions regarding the links between race and criminality among the city's political and socioeconomic elites. Interviews and archival analysis reveal a surprising lack of consideration for how racial dynamics contribute to crime and violence despite the fact that Aguablanca – an epicentre of violence in Cali – is home to a large portion of the city's Afro-Colombian population. Policy-makers and analysts instead focus on easily quantifiable and proximate variables correlated with crime and violence that in turn produce findings and recommendations that circumvent the issue of race in a city where one-quarter of the population is black.

Yet, the seemingly 'objective' findings generated by crime mapping and related analyses are also used as evidence to confirm 'subjective' assumptions among elites that link Afro-Colombians with criminality. The constant diffusion of crime data and labelling of Aguablanca and its Afro-Colombian neighbourhoods as 'high priority' security concerns are used by elites to validate their arguments that the cultural divide between Afro-Colombians and the 'rest' of the city's population is a detriment to Cali's overall development and modernization. Information generated by crime mapping enables elites to develop racially charged discourses regarding historical migrations to Cali, wherein the previous migrants are depicted as industrious and 'civil' while the current Afro-Colombian migrants are painted as a drain on the city's finances and culturally prone to violence.

What are the potential alternatives to the current use of crime mapping in Cali? Community leaders in Aguablanca argue for a return to the broader political project within which crime mapping was adopted in Cali in order to create the political space necessary to discuss how racial discrimination contributes to crime and violence. Increased public participation in the policy-making process is also a major demand, as Aguablanca's community leaders profess little understanding of how crime mapping works, despite the fact that it repeatedly generates categorizations of their neighbourhoods as among the most violent in the city that feed into perceptions of Afro-Colombians as somehow 'naturally' inclined toward delinquency and violence.[24] More broadly, community leaders worry that crime mapping is being used by political incumbents and policy-makers to justify a policy of 'carrots and sticks', where the state's focus is on repression and socioeconomic conditions. As one leader noted, 'We see socioeconomic inequalities as important factors when it comes to violence, but these inequalities are themselves products of the larger force of racism.'[25]

This leads us to consider potential future avenues of research. While I focus on the implications of citizen security reforms for race in this study, race in Colombia and most of Latin America overlaps significantly with class in both material reality and common discourse. Future research might explicitly consider how the intertwining of race and class in Latin America shapes the incentives for policy-makers and the police when it comes to policy choices regarding citizen security. Under what conditions does the interrelation between race and class increase or decrease the probability that political incumbents will favour crime mapping and other approaches designed to produce 'objective' scientific findings over research methodologies more likely to produce nuanced understandings of how race and class are associated with criminality? More broadly, comparative analysis might interrogate how divergences in pre-existing dynamics between race and class both across and within cases shape political discourse and public opinion on criminality and violence.

Finally, the growing diffusion of citizen security reforms across Latin American countries with their own sizable populations of peoples of African descent and complex racial histories underscores the importance of increased debate and discussion between policy-makers and scholars of race and security as part of broader efforts to address these important and increasingly intertwined issues.

Notes

1.   A heuristic case study is purposely chosen to develop a theoretical framework or hypothesis that is potentially generalisable.
2.   The concept of deracialization has been used by scholars of US city politics to categorize political campaigns by racial minorities – mainly African-Americans and Latinos – that remove race as a defining feature of the political image and platform in order to build multiracial and multiethnic political coalitions that increase the probabilities of winning an election. As the case of the official discourse concerning racial diversity in Colombia demonstrates, however, deracialization is a political tool available to those who already hold public office to advance particular depictions of social harmony. For an overview of the concept of deracialization in the context of US city politics, see Perry (1999).
3.   The country's indigenous population has nevertheless managed to realize important political gains that exceed those of the Afro-Colombians. Hooker (2005) finds that that the disparity in political gains result from the indigenous population's ability to claim an ethnic identity distinct from the national culture, something which the Afro-Colombian population has had more difficulty achieving.
4.   Colombia's urban population grew at a pace of 5.6 per cent annually between 1951 and 1964 (Barbary and Hoffman 2004, p. 118).
5.   Cali is divided into twenty-one comunas.
6.   By 1999, Aguablanca and a few smaller politically defined parts of the city housed nearly 70 percent of the city's Afro-Colombian population (Barbary et al. 1999).
7.   The interests involved in the political debate and policy-making process regarding security in Colombia broadened considerably following the wave of decentralization that began with the popular election of city mayors in the late 1980s. Efforts to create a more participatory and decentralized democracy through the 1991 constitution converted citizen security in Cali and other cities into a major *local* political issue, as city mayors were made legally responsible for security.
8.   Author interviews of Rodrigo Guerrero, Cali, Colombia, on 7 August 2008; former Cali Peace Councilor (1), Cali, Colombia, on 30 July 2008; former Peace Councilor (2), Cali, Colombia, on 8 August 2008; former Peace Councilor (3), Washington, DC, on 18 September 2008; former Director of Desepaz (1), Cali, Colombia, on 30 July 2008; and former Director of Desepaz (2), Cali, Colombia, on 12 August 2008.
9.   Author interview of Rodrigo Guerrero, Cali, Colombia, on 7 August 2008.
10.   Author interview with former Desepaz consultant (1), Bogota, Colombia, on 24 August 2008.
11.   Author interview of Professor of Sociology at the Universidad del Valle, Cali, Colombia, on 31 August 2008.
12.   Author interviews with Director of Asolibertad, Cali, Colombia, on 30 June 2009 and with Director of the Centro Empresarial Juvenil de Aguablanca on 30 June 2009.

13.   Author interview with former Desepaz consultant (1), Bogota, Colombia, on 24 August 2008.
14.   Author interview with Director of Asolibertad, Cali, Colombia, on 30 June 2009.
15.   Author interview with Afro-Colombian political leader from Aguablanca (1), Cali, Colombia, on 14 November 2008.
16.   Author interview with Director of Asolibertad, Cali, Colombia, on 30 June 2009.
17.   Author interview with Director of the Social Observatory, Cali, Colombia, on 8 June 2006.
18.   Author interview with the Executive President of a major philanthropic foundation, Cali, Colombia, on 13 November 2008.
19.   Author interview with representative from the Agroindustrial Sector and Director of a private sector commission on security in Cali, Cali, Colombia, on 21 November 2008.
20.   Author interview with the former president of an economic group based in Cali, Cali, Colombia, on 21 November 2008.
21.   This is despite the fact that parts of the heart of the city where both formal commercial businesses and informal workers are concentrated have also historically had high levels of crime and violence.
22.   Author interview with representative from a Cali-based commercial business association, Cali, Colombia, on 15 August 2008.
23.   Author interview with representative from the agroindustrial sector and director of a private sector commission on security in Cali, Cali, Colombia, on 21 November 2008.
24.   Author interview with Director of Comite Empresarial Juvenil de Aguablanca, Cali, Colombia, on 30 June 2009.
25.   Author interview with Director of Asolibertad, Cali, Colombia, on 30 June 2009.

References

ALVAREZ, ADOLFO, *et al.* 1990 'Evaluación del programa de obras de aguablanca', Memo, Cali, Colombia: Foro Nacional por Colombia
APPELBAUM, NANCY P. 2003 *Muddied Waters: Race, Region and Local History in Colombia, 1846–1948*, Durham, NC: Duke University Press
APPELBAUM, NANCY P., MACPHERSON, ANNE S. and ROSEMBLATT, KARIN A. 2003 *Race and Nation in Modern Latin America*, Chapell Hill, NC: University of North Carolina Press
ARIAS, ENRIQUE DESMOND 2006 *Drugs and Democracy in Rio de Janeiro: Trafficking, Social Networks, and Public Security*, Chapell Hill, NC: University of North Carolina Press
AROCHA, JAIME 1992 'Los negros y la nueva constitución colombiana del 1991', *América Negra*, vol. 3, pp. 39–54
ATEHORTUA, ADOLFO, BAYONA, JOSÉ, and RODRÍGUEZ, ALBA 1998 *Sueños de Inclusión*, Cali, Colombia: CINEP
AYRES, ROBERT L. 1998 *Crime and Violence as Development Issues in Latin America and the Caribbean*, Washington, DC: World Bank
BAILEY, JOHN and DAMMERT, LUCÍA (eds) 2006 *Public Security and Police Reform in the Americas*, Pittsburgh, PA: University of Pittsburgh Press
BARBARY, OLIVIER 2001 'Segmentación socioracial y percepción de discriminaciones en Cali', *Desarrollo y Sociedad*, pp. 89–149
BARBARY, OLIVIER and HOFFMANN, ODILE 2004 'La Costa Pacífica y Cali, Sistema de Lugares', in Olivier Barbary and Fernando Urrea (eds), *Gente Negra en Colombia: Dinámicas Sociopolíticas en Cali y el Pacífico*, Medellín, Colombia: Editorial Lealon, pp. 113–56
BARBARY, OLIVIER, RAMIREZ, HECTOR FABIO and URREA, FERNANDO 2002 Identidad y ciudadanía afrocolombiana en la región pacifica y cali: elementos estadísticos y

sociológicos para el debate de la "cuestión negra" en colombia', *Estudios Afro-Asiáticos*, vol. 24, no. 3, pp. 75–121

CALL, CHARLES 2002 War transitions and the new civilian security in Latin America', *Comparative Politics*, vol. 35, no. 1, pp. 1–20

DE FRIEDEMANN, NINA 1993 *La Saga del Negro: Presencia Africana en Colombia*, Bogotá, Colombia: Pontificia Universidad Javeriana

Departamento Administrativo Nacional de Estadísticas (DANE) 2005 Colombia: Una Nación Multicultural, Bogotá, Colombia: DANE

EATON, KENT 2008 'Paradoxes of Police Reform: Federalism, Parties, and Civil Society in Argentina's Public Security Crisis', *Latin American Research Review*, vol. 43, no. 3, pp. 5–32

ECKSTEIN, HARRY 1975 'Case study and theory in political science', in Greenstein Fred and Polsby Nelson (eds), *Strategies of Inquiry*, Reading, MA: Addison-Wesley, pp. 79–137

El País 2008 'Inmigración decontrolada', March 19 p. 11

ETERNO, JOHN and SILVERMAN, ELI 2006 'The New York City Police Department's CompStat: dream or nightmare?' *International Journal of Police Science and Management*, vol. 8, no. 3, pp. 218–31

GRAHAM, RICHARD, *et al.* 1990 *The Idea of Race in Latin America, 1870–1940*, Austin, TX: University of Texas Press

GREENE, JUDITH A. 1999 'Zero tolerance: a case study of police and practices in New York City', *Crime and Delinquency*, vol. 45, no. 2, pp. 171–87

GUERRERO, RODRIGO 1999 'Programa Desarrollo, Seguridad y Paz: Desepaz en la Ciudad de Cali', Paper presented at the Inter-American Development Bank's Conference on Municipal Programs for the Prevention of Violence, Rio de Janeiro, 29–30 July

HINTON, MERCEDES S. 2006 *The State on the Streets: Police and Politics in Argentina and Brazil*, Boulder, CO: Lynne Rienner Publishers

HOOKER, JULIET 2005 'Indigenous inclusion/black exclusion', *Journal of Latin American Studies*, vol. 37, pp. 285–310

MACHADO, MARILYN and OCORO, ANNY 2004 *Exploración de las Percepciones de Jóvenes, Familias y Agentes Institucionales y Comunitarios Sobre la Violencia en Dinámicas Locales de Conflicto Urbano en Cali*, Cali, Colombia: Alcaldía de Santiago de Cali

MONCADA, EDUARDO 2009 'Toward democratic policing in Colombia? Institutional accountability through lateral reform', *Comparative Politics*, vol. 41, no. 4, pp. 431–49

Observatorio Social 2003 *El Homicidio Cali*, Colombia: Alcaldía de Santiago de Cali

―――― 2004 *Informa Anual de Delitos de Mayor Impacto Social*, Cali, Colombia: Alcaldía de Santiago de Cali

―――― 2005 *Visión Cali*, Cali, Colombia: Alcaldía de Santiago de Cali

―――― 2006 *Visión Cali*, Cali, Colombia: Alcaldía de Santiago de Cali

―――― 2007 *Informe Enero-Octubre 2007*, Cali, Colombia: Alcaldía de Santiago de Cali

OSLENDER, ULRICH 2004 Geografias de terror y desplazamiento forzando en el pacifico colombiano: conceptualizando el problema y buscando respuestas, in Eduardo Restrepo and Axel Rojas (eds), *Conflicto e (in)visibilidad*, Cali, Colombia: Editorial Universidad del Cauca, pp. 35–52

PERRY, HUEY L. 1999 'Deracialization as an analytical construct in American urban politics', *Urban Affairs Quarterly*, vol. 27, no. 2, pp. 181–91

RESTREPO, EDUARDO 1998 'La construcción de la etnicidad: comunidades negras en Colombia', in María Lucia Sotomayor (ed.), *Modernidad, Identidad y Desarrollo*, Bogotá, Colombia: ICAN, pp. 341–59

RESTREPO, EDUARDO and ROJAS, AXEL (eds) 2004 *Conflicto e (in)visibilidad: Retos de Los Estudios de la Gente Negra en Colombia, Popayán*, Colombia: Editorial Universidad del Cauca

TARROW, SIDNEY 1994 *Power in Movement: Social Movements, Collective Action, and Politics*, Cambridge: Cambridge University Press

TULCHIN, JOSEPH S. and RUTHENBURG, MEG (eds) 2006 *Toward a Society Under Law: Citizens and Their Police in Latin America*, Washington, DC: Woodrow Wilson Center Press

UNGAR, MARK 2002 *Elusive Reform: Democracy and the Rule of Law in Latin America*, Boulder, CO: Lynne Rienner Publishers

UNGAR, MARK 2006 'Crime and citizen security in Latin America', in Eric Hershberg and Fred Rosen (eds), *Latin America After Neoliberalism: Turning the Tide in the 21st Century*, New York: North American Congress on Latin America, pp. 171–92

URREA and BOTERO undated 'Violencia Social, Racismo y Violación de Derechos Humanos: La Situación de los Jóvenes Negros en la Ciudad de Cali', unpublished manuscript

URREA, FERNANDO and BARBARY, OLIVIER 2004 *Gente Negra en Colombia: Dinámicas Sociopolíticas en Cali y el Pacífico*, Medellín, Colombia: Lealon

URREA, FERNANDO and ORTIZ, CARLOS HUMBERTO 1999 'Patrones sociodemo-graficos, pobreza y mercado laboral en Cali,' working paper for the World Bank, Cali, Colombia

URREA, FERNANDO and QUINTÍN, PEDRO 2000 'Segregación urbana y violencia en Cali', paper presented at 'La societé prise en otage. Sratégies individuelles et collectives face à la violence. Réflexions autour du cas Colombien', Marseille, France, 23 November

—— 2001 'Ser hombre, negro y joven: construcción de identidades masculinas entre sectores populares excluidos en Cali', in A. Valencia (ed.), *Exclusión Social y Construcción de lo Público en Colombia*, Bogotá, Colombia: Cidse-Cerec, pp. 159–97

VAN COTT, DONNA LEE 1996 'Unity through diversity: ethnic politics and democratic deepening in Colombia', *Nationalism and Ethnic Politics*, vol. 2, no. 4, pp. 523–49

WADE, PETER 1993 *Blackness and Race Mixture: The Dynamics of Racial Identity in Colombia*, Baltimore, MD: Johns Hopkins University Press

—— 1995 'Cultural politics of blackness in Colombia', *American Ethnologist*, vol. 22, no. 2, pp. 341–57

—— 1997 *Race and Ethnicity in Latin America*, Chicago, IL: Pluto Press

—— 2001 'Racial identity and nationalism: a theoretical view from Latin America', *Ethnic and Racial Studies*, vol. 24, no. 5, pp. 845–65

—— 2006 'Afro-Latin studies: reflections on the field', *Latin American and Caribbean Ethnic Studies*, vol. 1,no. (1), pp: 105–24

WORLD BANK 2005 *The Gap Matters, Poverty and Well-Being of Afro-Colombians and Indigenous Peoples*, Washington, DC: World Bank

Concept, category and claim: insights on caste and ethnicity from the police in India

Anasuya Sengupta

Abstract

Drawing upon contemporary conceptual understandings of race and
ethnicity, this essay examines their relevance to ways in which the
meaning and effects of caste are transformed within the everyday Indian
state. Ethnographic insights from the police in Karnataka demonstrate
the continuum of analytical concept, social category and political claim:
different moments along this continuum allow for specific individual and
institutional constructions of identity. Analysing caste and ethnicity in
this fashion pushes further the porous boundaries of affinity and
identification with concept, category and claim, i.e. with the politics of
participation, representation and inter-relations. 'Training' processes to
engender change and lessen discrimination by the police, therefore, need
to use this complexity as a starting point, and root their methodologies in
the notions of 'dignity', rather than 'diversity', critiqued for being flawed
in its assumptions of difference and multiculturalism, and its inability to
invoke a sense of social justice.

The rich
will make temples for Siva.
What shall I,
a poor man,
do?
...
Listen, O lord of the meeting rivers,
things standing shall fall,
but the moving ever shall stay.

Basavanna, twelfth-century Veerashaivite poet from Karnataka
(Ramanujan 1973, p. 19)

Four men sat at a table, eating a meal, with servers bustling around
them, ready to refill their glasses or their plates. Three men crouched in
a corner, looking hungry, but steadfastly ignored by both diner and
server. Visible signs of caste discrimination are still not uncommon in
parts of rural India; uncommon to this scenario, however, was the fact
that it was an enactment by a group of junior policemen, an
improvization on different forms of social injustice. In the discussion
that followed, one of the young actors seemed surprised by his own
intensity of feeling as he described his frustration at being ignored: he
felt angry, he said, but also helpless. A few of his colleagues nodded in
understanding, others simply looked unsurprised and unmoved. A
particularly cynical observer – as it turned out, a lower caste head
constable – came up to me later to ask, '*ee aata yella adas bahadu,
nijavagalu namma novana artha maadkonthara?* (They can play these
games, but do they really understand our pain?)'

This improvization by police officers from Karnataka (South India)
was part of an ongoing 'training' project begun in 2001; a UNICEF
(India) partnership with the Karnataka State Police [KSP].[1] As
someone working with this project from its inception until 2007, it
was an opportunity for me to engage with the local police on a routine
basis, and a personal challenge to live in the liminal spaces of the
insider/outsider activist/researcher.[2] The partnership was an attempt to
use 'gender sensitization training processes' to create a greater
responsiveness of the police towards violence against women and
children, but it was clear to me, and the rest of the team,[3] that issues of
identity, power, violence and discrimination could not be neatly
contained within that official description, not only for police actions
in public, but equally so for police actions within the state itself. The
candour of the head constable who approached me at the end of the
training programme was hardly unexpected. Given the horrific
instances of caste-based violence that continue to occur across India,
his lack of faith in our attempt to shift perceptions and understandings
of caste oppression was understandable. At the same time, it would
have been disingenuous of him to deny the inaction – or worse,
complicity – of the police in many of these instances, and interestingly
he accepted this without much protest during our conversation; the
training process was focused, after all, on generating a greater sense of
responsibility for the police's role in combating social injustice. More
interesting, however, was what he left unsaid. It is likely that as a
lower-caste entrant to the police department, he was promoted to head
constable well before many of his upper-caste colleagues and is seen by
them to be 'unfairly' advantaged and privileged within the system,

thereby embodying the contradictions and possibilities inherent in the Indian state: a site that offers rich ethnographic evidence of the ongoing mutability, as well as the continued immutability, of different aspects of caste and other social identities.

The implications of police policy, perceptions and behaviour on the common citizen are self-evident. In this essay, therefore, I choose to begin from the perspective of the common police officer. I argue that it is critical to understand how the police in Karnataka – and possibly elsewhere – are involved in complex and specific individual and institutional manoeuvres with and around caste, religion and ethnicity, as well as gender and age. Indeed, the meanings and understandings of these identities and social institutions are themselves transformed within the everyday state, while they simultaneously mediate the public workings of formal state structures (Sengupta 1998). A transient moment of theatrics may have led to an acknowledgement of caste discrimination by upper-caste police officers, but far more complicated encounters occur within the everyday state that reflect both a continued observance of certain social hierarchies, as well as a dramatic recasting of identity politics and positions, made possible through a range of institutional mechanisms and informal man- oeuvres. The examination of these encounters contributes towards the understandings of caste in its multiple forms, and its particular manifestations within the Indian state. Most significantly, I believe it is necessary to draw upon the rich theoretical languages of race, caste and ethnicity and to extend them, to posit the experiences and understandings of social identities within the state as held upon a continuum of *analytical concept, social category* and *political claim*: from rigid hierarchies of pollution and purity to fluid contestations of power and position.

This essay uses a background of the formal institutional structures of the police in India to reveal significant insights on the politics of identity within the state, embodied and engaged with by police officers themselves. Mapping out such complexity – and the mobility as well as mutability of notions of caste and ethnicity, including language – has implications for any kind of 'training' process with the police, particularly those dealing with issues of discrimination. Without it, the potential for any kind of individual and structural change process is diminished. It is clear that the experience with the Karnataka police offers a vocabulary that is different from that of 'diversity', critiqued as being flawed in its assumptions of race, racialization, difference and multiculturalism (Prashad 2003; Ahmed 2007). Drawing on these experiences, I conclude this essay with some insights on training methodologies rooted in the notions of 'dignity' rather than 'diversity', which use a language that straddles the analytic and the applied, the spaces 'between' English and Kannada, urban and rural, global and local.

Status hierarchicus: the police in India and Karnataka

The civil police in Karnataka currently comprises 57,720 persons, while with the armed and reserve police the number goes up to 89,292.[4] This is a force that polices a State with a population of close to 53 million (Census of India 2001) through 876 police stations. Across India, the strength of the civil and district armed reserve police consists of 1,182,058 officers and 12,548 police stations.[5] The structures of the present Indian police can be traced historically to a peculiar combination of an already existing rural police system and a British model, set up in the mid-nineteenth century, based on the Royal Irish Constabulary (Bayley 1969). With the governance of two-fifths of the sub-continent passing from the control of the East India Company to the Queen in 1858, a slew of legal codes and legislations were enacted for British India, including the Code of Civil Procedure in 1859, the Indian Penal Code in 1860, the Code of Criminal Procedure in 1861 and, finally, the Police Act of 1861. The Act established a police structure that is virtually intact in contemporary India: a three-tier system comprising the constabulary, the supervisory ranks (Sub-inspector and Inspector) and the Deputy Superintendent and Superintendent of districts as 'superior' officers (Raghavan 1989, p. 11), along with a Deputy-Inspector General who supervised a range (a set of districts), and the Inspector-General who oversaw the police department and reported to the provincial government.

The Acts that governed the British model continue to be the core legal tenets invoked by the Indian police, while the three-tier structure also continues with some modifications, including the expansion of the senior levels with the creation of posts such as the Additional Director Generals and Director Generals of police. In Karnataka, for instance, the State police are headed by the Director General and Inspector General of Police, while two other Director Generals support him (see Figure 1 for the organizational structure). The entire police department is under the control of the Ministry of Home Affairs at the provincial level, and the head of the department is supervised by the Home Secretary and the Chief Secretary, the senior-most civil service officer (both of the Indian Administrative Service, or IAS, recruited through a set of all-India examinations).

An important consideration in understanding the Indian police is the nature of federal and provincial relations around policing. Under Article 246 of the Constitution of India, which distributes legislative powers between the Parliament and the State legislative assemblies, the police, public order, courts and other allied institutions come within

Figure 1. *The formal structure of the Karnataka Police*

Director General and Inspector General of Police [DG-IG]

{In charge of the State Police Force}

↓

Director Generals of Police [DG]

{In charge of the branches of Corps of Detectives [CoD], Fire and Home Guards, Housing}

↓

Additional Director Generals of Police [Addl. DGP]

↓

Inspector Generals of Police [IGP]

{In charge of a zone, which comprises a few ranges}

↓

Deputy Inspector General of Police [Dy. IGP]

{In charge of a range, which comprise a group of districts}

↓

*Superintendent of police [SP]

{In charge of the district}

↓

Additional Superintendent of Police [Addl. SP]

↓

*Deputy Superintendent of Police [Dy.SP]

{In charge of a sub-division in the district}

↓

Inspector of Police [PI]

{In charge of a police station}

↓

*Sub-Inspector of Police [SI]

{In charge of a smaller police station}

↓

Assistant Sub-Inspector of Police [ASI]

{Staff of the police station}

↓

Police Head Constable [HC]

{Staff of the police station}

↓

*Police Constable [PC]

{Staff of police station}

Note: * Levels of recruitment

the ambit of State or provincial authority. This implies that the Government of India, i.e. the central government, has authority over central policing institutions like the Central Bureau of Investigation [CBI], the Intelligence Bureau [IB], and the Central Paramilitary Forces [CPFs], but the civil police – the 'face' of the local police and thereby, in obvious ways, of the everyday state – is an institution governed at the State level, with local police Acts that complement the all-India structures and procedures.

Some of the complicated nature of these 'multiple but interdependent' centre–State relations manifests itself in recruitment processes and in the sharing of police 'intelligence' across the country (Arnold 1986; Subramanian 2007, p. 22). While the senior-most officers of the Indian police – consisting of Assistant Superintendents and above – are recruited through the same all-India process as IAS officers, to a cadre known as the Indian Police Service [IPS], the bulk of the civil police is recruited within the province or State, at the levels of constable, sub-inspector and deputy superintendent of police. The all-India civil service, which includes the IAS (for administrators or 'civil servants') and the IPS (for the police),[6] is considered far more prestigious than the State-level service, and obviously the levels at which an officer is recruited within the State police also command varying degrees of status and respect, and not only in a formal institutional sense.

While Sir Charles Napier – generally considered to be the colonial architect of the present police structure – knew of Robert Peel's model for England of the Metropolitan Police, the system set up in India was based on what was considered efficacious in Ireland, already a space of considerable conflict and disorder for the British in the nineteenth century (Verma 2005). This certainly has implications for the ways in which the independent Indian state struggled, and continues to struggle, with shifts not only in police structures but also cultures. Bayley makes the critical point that the police legacy of the British to independent India went beyond its structure: not only did they bequeath 'perceptions, attitudes and predispositions toward the police' to both the public and the policy-makers, but also a 'concept of "proper" police duties' that continues to follow what was considered 'proper' under the British (Bayley 1969, pp. 49–50).

What is 'proper' in the contemporary understandings of the civil police is obviously contested at different levels of the structure, but the rigid hierarchy and 'discipline' of the system is a ubiquitous trope, invoked with both pride and prejudice, the latter particularly at the lower echelons of the police. As a trainee Sub-Inspector said to me, to the applause of the rest of his cohort: 'The problem is that if a senior officer says a crow is white, I must repeat, "Yes, sir, a crow is white".' Interestingly, senior officers tended to view internal caste politics as the 'biggest problem' for the effective functioning of the police system, while the violence and oppression of the hierarchy itself was the issue most discussed by junior officers.[7] Sometimes the two were conflated: 'what is the use of talking to us about discrimination in society?' asked an Inspector bitterly, during the course of a residential workshop that was part of the KSP–UNICEF training project, 'what is our police but another form of the caste system?'

'Interrogating' the police: caste, ethnicity and other politics

When the Portugese arrived in India in the late fifteenth century, they found a complex system of social stratification they called 'casta': 'lineage', 'breed' or 'race'. Insofar as it can even be seen as a unitary whole, the Indian caste system is structural in the empirical sense of defining actual groups of people and supplying norms which guide their interaction, but it is also ideological and provides systems of meanings through which these defined groups can interpret the world and their roles in it (Harriss 1982). Much of this meaning was provided by the ancient system of differentiation known as *varna*, where society is divided into four categories: Brahmins (the priestly caste); Kshatriyas (the warrior caste); Vaishyas (the merchant caste); and Sudras (the caste of agriculturalists or labourers). Outside the *chaturvarna* system were the 'untouchables' or Dalits. However, in the reconstructions of caste hierarchies over time, the 'system' would become effectively five-fold, while encompassing a complex range of hierarchies that included the categorizations of *jati* or 'community'.[8] Gupta, in fact, asserts that the process of 'interrogating' caste implies understanding it as discrete categories with multiple hierarchies, as each caste tends to overvalue itself in relation to others (Gupta 2000). Regional diversities in the caste hierarchies made it possible for groups to undergo 'Sanskritization', while constitutional innovation created the Scheduled Castes and Tribes, and electoral politics seemed to reinforce the dominance of caste, not dilute it.[9] According to Kaviraj, historically there has been a sort of class-effect of caste, whereby 'caste has taken over some of the political functions of class' (1997, p. 18), although the opposite has also occurred: amongst the metropolitan middle class, for instance, caste tends to be an idiom for status distinctions along class lines (Fuller 2000). Religion, according to Kaviraj, has been the other 'traditional identity' to undergo a process of transformation (1997, p. 30). He argues that this has been more due to modern politics than the modern industrial or capitalist economy, where the intensification of sectarian politics has been accompanied by a decline in traditional religiosity.

Karnataka, specifically, possesses what can be seen as a comparatively cohesive society within the Indian context (Manor 1989). Manor argues that although it has a significant Muslim population estimated at 11.64 per cent (Census of India 1991), Hindu–Muslim clashes have been relatively rare, while it has one of the smallest Scheduled Tribes [ST] populations in the sub-continent – 0.8 per cent in his estimate (Manor 1989, p. 322). While this is true in part, his assessment needs to be re-visited, both in terms of the religious conflicts of the past two decades, as well as in the escalation of caste and 'backward class' (a category that includes the Muslims) politics, with its roots in the reorganization of the state in 1956.[10] In addition, the first majority government of the conservative Hindu Bharatiya Janata Party [BJP] to rule in any State of South India was elected in mid-2008; this complicates the political landscape further. Caste politics in Karnataka is a jostling for socio-political power between the two 'dominant castes' (Srinivas 1987) and their sub-castes: the Vokkaliga and the Lingayat. The current BJP government in Karnataka is perceived to be strengthened by Lingayat solidarities, whereas most earlier governments were seen as reflecting Vokkaliga interests (Manor 1989). As is apparent from Table 1, both groups are numerically significant, along with the Scheduled Castes [SC] or Dalits.[11] However, there has been a considerable if uneven rise in local activism by Scheduled Caste groups from the 1970s, but particularly over the past decade, which has implied some reconfiguration of the local constellations of socio-economic and political power (Karanth 2004).

In an essay on the 'ethnicity of caste', Reddy refers to Kancha Illaiah's concept of the 'global mobility' of caste, asserting that her concern is with the means of its movement from more local to less local contexts, and with the vehicles that transport it across these terrains: aspects of the discourse of race, in conjunction with that of

Table 1. *Estimates of the important caste/community groupings in Karnataka*

Caste/ Community	Percentage of population as per the Chinnappa Reddy Commission Report (1988)	Percentage of population as per the Test Survey (1989)
Scheduled castes	16.7182	18.5439
Lingayatha/ Veerashaiva	15.3389	18.4232
Vokkaliga	10.8086	12.9590
Kuruba	6.2753	8.3165
Muslim	11.6744	6.4556
Brahmin	3.4558	1.8349
Scheduled tribes	6.7254	0.3732

Source: Thimmaiah (1993, pp. 138–40)

human rights. (2005, p. 545).

This notion of mobility resonates with analyses of race and racialization that consider it a process – a set of discursive practices which continually produce and regulate 'race' as an analytical concept and social category (Solomos and Back 1996; Knowles 2003; Solomos 2003; Murji and Solomos 2005). However, drawing upon Berreman's call to compare caste and race, so that it would yield insights 'not only into caste in India, but into a *widespread type of relations between groups*' (Reddy 2005, p. 546, emphasis in original), Reddy sees these relations as comprising both a 'type' with given attributes and a process through which relations are constituted. She thereby reaffirms ethnicity as a critical descriptor of identity that goes beyond any ontological understandings of both 'race' and 'caste':

> My use of the term "ethnicity" in this context therefore is meant simply to highlight two important and intimately related features of caste in contemporary India: its fluidity, in contrast to its presumed doctrinally-given rigidity, and therefore its capacity to strategically deploy established, essentialized notions of itself in a movement that seeks less to undermine caste than to restore dignity to re-claimed caste identities. (Reddy 2005, p. 547)

While accepting Reddy's premise for using ethnicity to transcend the binary of local/global and the dyad of black/white, I would argue that examining caste within the Karnataka State Police demonstrates that it is precisely the assertions of doctrinally given rigidity – and its complicated manifestations in experience – that also give rise to its mobility and strategic deployment. If 'global-ity' and 'local-ity' are be seen as geographies of 'representation' and 'participation' respectively, then this complex of rigidity and mobility of caste and ethnicity, and their discursive affinities with 'race', are most clearly demonstrated through the ways in which caste is claimed and manoeuvred institutionally. This is based on social categories of status, hierarchy and discrimination, but the state offers more: caste and ethnicity within the Indian police are a matter of participation, in the sense of embodied claims to certain identities and categories, but also representation, in the sense of larger strategic claims – symbolic and material – to what these identities and categories signify for relative power and mobility within and without the state. From this perspective, there are both local and global issues at stake.[12]

Reddy's definition of ethnicity, therefore, offers grounding for individuals participating in a complex world, at the same time as creating strategic solidarities for representation in that world (Reddy 2005, p. 546). However, in extending this to examining caste, ethnicity and religion within the state, it is clear that there are slippages between the analytical concepts of caste, the social categories of caste, *jati* and religion, and the political claims made on behalf of each. For instance, in Kannada – the official language of the State of Karnataka – the word for caste is *jati*, yet *jati* is a far more all-encompassing word than caste as we understand it in English and academic-speak (Chatterjee 1993; Kaviraj 1997). In a survey I conducted for UNICEF in 2007 with police officers in a north Karnataka district on their motivations for joining the police, the socio-demographic data asked for both caste (*jati*) and religion (*dharma*); most Muslim officers wrote 'Muslim' under the category *jati* and 'Islam' under the category *dharma*. This is not only a self-referential process, and not only about Kannada: in a conversation with a Hindu officer about a Hindu–Muslim conflict situation he had been involved with, he made an oblique reference to a fellow officer who happened to be Muslim, saying '*avvaru aa caste, artha aitha, madam, aa caste*' ('he is that caste, do you understand, Madam, that caste').[13] When I asked him to clarify what he was referring to, he said, with some discomfiture, that he meant 'Muslim'. Whether this implies a tendency to claim a certain kind of assimilation or not on the part of either Hindu or Muslim officers, it is clear that references to ethnicity help signal a shift in the meaning of caste, brought about by the operation of caste along with language and religion in the political arena; often this connotes differences in bargaining power and life chances of groups rather than hierarchical distinctions of status (Béteille 2000, pp. 171–2). However, while Béteille argues against seeing ethnicity as the substantialization of caste, since it has a misleading implication of homogeneity, Fuller sees a process in which a 'vertical social system' defined by hierarchical relationships is decaying while castes are becoming like 'horizontally' disconnected ethnic groups (Fuller 2000, p. 22). Part of the reason for these seemingly contradictory assessments, I would argue, is the way in which representation, through the process of reservations, is understood within the contemporary Indian state.

Possibly the earliest documented history of struggle against social discrimination in Karnataka, the twelfth-century *vachana* movement (literally 'that which is said') was against caste and gender oppression, exemplified by poets such as Basavanna – quoted at the beginning of this essay – and Akka Mahadevi (Ramanujan 1973; Manasa 2000). While this was a pre-modern socio-literary phenomenon, it continues to have implications for the cultural politics of the *Lingayat* community. A different trajectory in the colonial period, in which the *Vokkaliga*, *Lingayat* and Muslim communities created groupings of solidarity against a Brahmin monopoly, led to Karnataka also having one of the longest histories of policies of reservations – or affirmative action – in modern India, going back to the late nineteenth century (Manasa 2000). This has extended into the post-independent, reorganized State of Karnataka as well. In the Karnataka police, reservations have been standardized according to a vertical and horizontal 'matrix' from 2002, drawing upon caste-based reservation policies from 1995 and linguistic and rural/urban reservation policies from 2001 (Government of Karnataka 2002). It is a fairly comprehensive policy of about 50 per cent reservations over all, and covers most ethnic categories in the state: as one senior Brahmin police officer told me, 'the only groups who don't have reservations in the police today are Brahmins, Jains, non-converted Buddhists, Vaishyas and Christians'. However, to use an example from the police recruitment manual, there is still a 50 per cent quota for those with 'general merit': if there is a vacancy of 30 posts, 15 posts are for general merit candidates, and 5 for SC, 1 for ST, 1 for Category I (Backward Classes or BC), 5 for Category IIA (Other Backward Classes; OBC), and 1 each for Categories II B (mainly Muslim), III A (mainly Vokkaliga) and III B (mainly Lingayat) (Ibid, p. 11). This vertical roster is then again classified against the horizontal roster of categories that include women, ex-military personnel and rural candidates.

These caste and community categorizations – in decreasing perceived socio-economic deprivation, and thereby also in decreasing order of opportunities of promotion through affirmative action within the state – are constantly being debated and re-negotiated publicly, through claims of differing caste ancestries and experienced socio-economic oppression.[14] Within the police, the politics of caste and ethnicity are equally dynamic, but played out somewhat differently from that in civil society. While there is no existing data to demonstrate the levels of actual representation of different castes and communities, there is a tacit acceptance that *Lingayats* and *Vokkaligas* are numerically dominant within the police as well, with a growing number of SC/ST officers through the reservations process, while Muslims are numerically insignificant except in areas with a dense concentration of Muslim communities. In addition, in order to ensure representational power through transfers and promotions, there are informal cliques for each category. As a woman Deputy Superintendent [DySP] explained, 'I am left out because I am a woman, and I don't want to join these II A, II B, IIIA, IIIB clubs'.

The language used within the department naturally reflects bureaucratic control and vocabulary in other ways. Dalits are always called 'SC' within the department, including by officers who are Dalit officers themselves, and never Dalits or the names of their individual sub-castes (such as *Holeya* or *Madiga*). While this is also manifest in popular usage across the country, police officers themselves appeared to have distinct rules of movement between 'official' and 'social' or political nomenclature. While talking to different officers, terms like 'Dalit' or '*Vokkaliga*' would be invoked with reference to personal identity and pride – 'participation' – whereas, rather obviously, the official nomenclature of 'SC' or 'III A' would be used for staking political and institutional claims for 'representation'. Indeed, it was seemingly through a deliberate use of 'Dalit' rather than 'SC' in a particular conversation with an officer that I gained his confidence, and thereby a more personal appraisal of caste politics from his perspective.

What is somewhat counter-intuitive in the politics of representation within the state is the rising level of positional and political power for SC officers. This is in terms of both an actual shift engendered by the reservations policy that also affect promotions – thereby allowing SC officers to rise faster through the system than other communities – but also in terms of their increasing power as perceived by other ethnic groups, who then demonstrate their anger in subtle and not-so-subtle ways. As a retired Deputy Superintendent of Police in a north Karnataka district told me, 'I may have retired as a DySP, but my colleagues couldn't forget I was Dalit ... some of them would not sit in the same jeep as me'. This kind of discrimination, however, did not seem as apparent in urban Karnataka; a woman Dalit Assistant Sub-Inspector said she had never faced problems as either an SC or a woman in her career of over thirty years. In fact, she recast the language of 'casteism' in a fascinating move: upset that she had not got promoted to the rank of Sub-Inspector, she responded, when I asked her about discrimination, '*Yaava casteism? Casteism nijavagalu iddare, nanage promotion sikkthaithu*' ('What casteism? If there was truly casteism, I would have got my promotion!')

The more obvious politics of caste and ethnicity, however, are exemplified by the processes of transfers and the actual authority of officers in different positions; these are forms of 'control' over the police department that tend to be immediately established by new governments. In the first two months of the new BJP government coming to power in Karnataka, for instance, over four hundred transfer orders were given for officers from Sub-Inspectors to Additional Director Generals. Some of them were multiple sets of orders for the same officers, since there is always resistance to positions that are not seen as 'important' or 'good', euphemisms for relative power and authority, as well as money-making potential. While corruption has always tended to accompany the transfer processes within the Indian state (see Wade 1982; de Zwaart 1994), and different governments with different caste and community constituencies have also manoeuvred their ethnic preferences, what was particularly significant about the transfer processes in 2008 was the manner in which there was both obvious acceptance and resistance within the police department. The transfers involved shifting officers who had been in a largely *Vokkaliga*-dominated government of the

BJP and Janata Dal coalition, which was later were headed by the Governor, under President's Rule (imposed in November 2007), to what was ubiquitously perceived as a *Lingayat*-dominated department. As officers at different levels told me, the most significant moves were the appointments of *Lingayat* officers to the positions of the Commissioner of Police, Bangalore, bypassing strict seniority in the process, as well as the officer in charge of State Intelligence, a position which is commonly seen as being the most critical position in the police department, even more than that of the nominal head (the Director General and Inspector General); he is considered to control the 'hotline to the Chief Minister'. In fact, the nodal officer for State Intelligence is normally the rank of an Additional Director General of Police; in this case, the position was downgraded to Inspector General to conform to the existing rank of the *Lingayat* officer.

Similarly, at lower levels of the system, there might be fairly uniform representations of different caste and community groupings, but what is significant is their relative status and authority. Throughout my fieldwork, I observed that the most important positions in a police station, apart from that of the Inspector or Sub-Inspector, are the police 'writer' (who documents the cases) and the officers in charge of intelligence gathering, courts summons and warrants. These are all considered powerful and lucrative roles for station-level officers. Depending on the inclinations of the Inspector, these positions are normally given to officers of his/her own caste and community, while others are given less important and often more arduous duties.

Gupta contends that with the rise of democratic politics, there has been a collapse of the caste system that has led to the competitiveness of caste politics (2005). Similarly, Fuller finds that contemporary understandings of caste are 'above all a denial, most explicitly in the public domain, of the existence or continuing significance of caste in its "traditional" form' (2000, p. 21). The ethnographic insights from the Karnataka police shared in this essay complicate this analysis by acknowledging the competitive and fluid nature of caste categories and political claims while retaining the hierarchies of status and difference connoted by 'traditional' concepts of caste.

Dignity, not diversity: possibilities of change

The complexity of caste and community politics within the police, coupled with the nature of its hierarchies of authority and control, would seem like a strange place to begin for a training process on 'gender sensitization' and police responsiveness to violence against women and children. However, in retrospect, it seems like the only place *to* start, since it would have been conceptually and pragmatically limited to focus on issues of gender and age without engaging with other social relations as experienced and understood by the predominantly male police force (Government of Karnataka 2007). Women, in fact, are only about 2 per cent of the current strength, though attempts are being made to recruit in greater numbers and make the proportion at least 10 per cent.

The Gender Sensitisation and People-Friendly Police Project, as the Karnataka State Police–UNICEF partnership is called, works with small groups of forty to forty-five police officers over a three-day period on issues of violence against women and children and police responsiveness. From 2003–2007, over 7,000 police officers have participated in these workshops and review sessions. The first two years after the project's inception in 2001 were spent exploring existing police training processes and models for gender sensitization in India and elsewhere, and creating our own framework. We found that many training models relied heavily on theoretical literature in English and 'lecture' styles of training, neither of which seemed effective for junior-level police officers uncomfortable with English and bored by lectures. More importantly, these training modules did not explicitly address forms of discrimination other than violence on women, although many of them, particularly those from outside India, were based on assumptions of 'diversity'. It was clear from the pilot workshops we conducted, that there could be no shift in police officers' attitudes and behaviour without addressing the ways in which they themselves perceived and claimed their own positions of identity and power, as well as understood their own experiences of oppression. We soon recognized that 'dignity' was a powerful entry point, precisely because it was, as one woman police officer put it, experientially potent: 'I know when my dignity is violated, though I may not know what my rights are.' This, then, allowed us to focus on particular forms of discrimination and violence against women and children and police responsiveness to them.

Working towards structural change in a context of complex social identities and inter-relations, therefore, required a methodology that did not fall into the conceptual traps of 'diversity'. As Sara Ahmed writes:

> This model of cultural diversity reifies difference as something that exists "in" the bodies or culture of others, such that difference becomes a national property: if difference is something "they are", then it is something we "can have". (Ahmed 2007, p. 235)

Diversity then becomes a managerial imperative, based on individuating difference, rather than working towards undermining structural inequalities (Ahmed 2007). Prashad is equally dismissive of the concepts of diversity and multiculturalism, finding them inherently racist in their assumptions that people can 'respect "culture" as if it were a thing without history and complexity' (2003, p. 81). He goes on to say, '[s]ocial interaction and struggle produce cultural worlds, and these are in constant, fraught, formation' (Ibid.).

Without having recourse to these conceptual insights at the beginning of our project, we managed, through a process of what could be called feminist praxis, to create training methodologies that focused on the readily understood language of 'dignity' rather than the problematic concept of 'diversity'. 'Diversity' is not just analytically difficult to translate; words such as *maryade or gaurava* – Kannada for self-respect and pride – have a much greater emotive currency and instinctual appeal than 'diversity'. More significantly, 'diversity' tends not to appeal either to an individual or a systemic sense of social justice, both of which were critical drivers of our training methodologies (Benschop 2001; Ahmed 2007). Still, we were conscious of the limitations to this approach throughout the training project. There is a danger in hoping that singular moments of experience will dramatically shift police officers' behaviour and modes of discrimination. The improvisation referred to at the beginning of the essay may have signalled a powerful process of reflexivity in some police officers, but as the head constable averred, it may stay in the realm of '*aata*' or game, rather than in actual action at the police station. Yet, there were some stories of individual and institutional responses that came out of this process, that offer possibilities of structural change.

The vocabulary of 'dignity' created strategic opportunities for simple feats of analytical reflexivity. When police officers raised the hoary maxim of 'women are women's worst enemies' to abdicate male and police responsibility, we would offer the conceptual and pragmatic similarities between the patriarchies of the police station and the household, a process that met with surprising success. Using examples of discrimination based on caste and community – often personal stories from the police officers themselves, including some of those shared in the previous section – allowed us to explore 'dignity' not just as an analytical concept for individual comfort, but as a shared experience of empowerment, with the emancipatory potential of both participation and representation. Understanding what dignity means in a personal context could be used to move between 'participation' and 'representation': how much more significant is the loss of dignity, whether physically or psychologically inflicted, for others, for more vulnerable, less powerful individuals and communities? One of the project's most empathetic trainers is a Muslim officer whose motivation for joining the police force was intrinsically linked to his own experience of discrimination: as a young boy, he had accompanied his uncle, injured in a communally tinged fight, to the local police station, but both of them were made to wait for hours before their complaint was heard. He did not wish for this to happen to anyone else, he said; he wanted to be a police officer who served as a role model for his community, but also as a purveyor of justice to all.

For women officers, obviously, caste and ethnicity were even more inextricably linked to their gender identities. Not only did they face difficulties within their personal and professional lives as women, they were simultaneously having to negotiate the complex landscape of political claims within the system. While there were obvious instances of empathetic policing from women officers in cases of violence, using 'dignity' as a framework also helped emphasize that gender-just policing was neither the sole responsibility, nor necessarily the intention, of women officers. In fact, unsurprisingly, some women officers were known to be dismissive of women complainants, claiming that their stories of abuse were far less egregious than those they themselves had experienced, so they should go back home and 'adjust', the ubiquitous term for suffering violence silently. Even here, using the personal as professional while also moving beyond it when required helped establish a sense of support for junior-level officers without allowing them to abdicate their institutional and individual responsibilities towards citizens.

It seems clear that specific experiences and perceptions of and about caste, ethnicity and other social relations within the Karnataka police lie along the continuum of analytical concept, social category and political claim: different moments along this continuum allow for specific individual and institutional constructions of identity. In other words, analysing caste and ethnicity within the everyday Indian state pushes further the porous boundaries of affinity and identification with concept, category and claim, i.e. with the politics of participation, representation and inter-relations. Though the training project on gender sensitization is still a work in progress, its successes so far have been based on acknowledging hierarchies of discrimination, while working with the fluidity of concept, category and claim. As Basavanna said in the twelfth century, 'things standing shall fall, but the moving ever shall stay' (Ramanujan 1973, p. 19).

Acknowledgements

I would like to thank this journal's anonymous reviewers, Paul Amar, Barbara Harriss-White, Vijayendra Rao, Pradeep Chibber and colleagues in the South Asia Colloquium at Berkeley for their comments on this paper.

Notes

1.   A clear distinction is drawn here between the 'state' and a 'State': the 'State' refers to the constituent units of the Indian federation, in this case the province or State of Karnataka; these are further divided into administrative units known as 'districts'. The term 'state' is used technically for public authorities, or the state apparatus as a set of political, administrative and coercive institutions and organizations, headed and co-ordinated by an executive authority, the government (based on Skocpol's 'state-centred' definition [1985]).

2.   The conceptual and ethical dilemmas, coupled with the realities of such ethnographic research, have been extensively explored elsewhere, including in Gunaratnam (2003) and Young (2004). Marks (2005), in particular, looks at these issues while studying the police in a multi-racial society such as South Africa. Feminist critiques of knowledge production have long problematized the notion of 'objectivity' and affirmed the partial and situated nature of research (Haraway 1991; Harding 1991, 2004; Ali 2006).

3.   The project is officially called the Gender Sensitisation and People-Friendly Police Project (Karnataka State Police–UNICEF); it began in Bangalore in 2001 out of informal discussions between senior police officers and UNICEF members of staff, and went on to become a State-wide training project in 2002. I was part of the project from its inception, jointly coordinating it till 2004, when I became sole coordinator, working with the Additional Director General of Police (Recruitment and Training), the designated Nodal Officer for the project, as well as the Programme Officer (Child Protection), UNICEF Hyderabad, along with colleagues who are variously activists in child rights, sexual rights and activism around queer politics, and community mobilization for rural development. I resigned from the project in 2007, to continue with my doctoral dissertation on the police, and to enable interviews that might have been difficult to do, from an ethical perspective, while still working on the project.

4.   Collated from the *Annual Report of the Police Department for the year 2007*, Karnataka State Police, Government of Karnataka (2007).

5.   Collated from *Data on Police Organisations in India*, a report put together by the Bureau of Police Research and Development (BPR&D), Government of India, as of 1 January 2005 (Government of India 2001).

6.   The All-India services are so classified because officers serve in both the Central and the State governments; they include the IAS, the IPS and other such services like the Indian Forest Service. Government of India, or Central Government services include, amongst others, the Indian Foreign Service, the Railways and Customs and Excise.

7.   For the purposes of this essay, by junior officers I mean here Deputy Superintendents and below; while with the senior officers, I mean Assistant Superintendents and above.

8.   In fact, as mentioned earlier, British India re-invoked the *varna* system during the census process in order to make 'sense' of this complexity (see Dirks 2001); it would be misleading, however, to overstate this argument to the extent that Dirks does, in claiming that 'caste' was entirely a colonial construction.

9.   Both Kothari (1964) and Srinivas (1987) have demonstrated the mutability of the caste system, the latter by theorizing the process of adopting cultural characteristics through which castes achieve upward mobility ('Sanskritization') and the former through his detailed work on the electoral politics in India.

10.   Religious conflict has included both Hindu–Muslim clashes, but also increasingly, discrimination against the negligible proportion of Christians in the State; in September 2008, for instance, there was violence in Mangalore and elsewhere in Karnataka, with the desecration of church property by right-wing Hindu groups and threats against practising Christians (see, for instance, The Times of India, Bangalore, 16 September 2008).

11.   I have put down Thimmaiah's projected estimates and the test survey results of the 1989 Chinappa Reddy Commission Report, as it clearly demonstrates the unreliability of data and the differences of order depending on what criteria are used (see Thimmaiah [1993] for details). Such 'defective data' are politically sensitive and can do 'considerable injustice'

(Thimmaiah 1993, p. 140). However, they give an estimate of the relative importance of these groupings.

12.   While this is intuitively understood, I am currently working on a more analytical exposition of these notions in my forthcoming doctoral dissertation, tentatively entitled 'Bringing the police back in: policing and the state in India'.

13.   Frequently in India, in common parlance, but particularly with those who inhabit the state and use technical or bureaucratic terms, people mix English and the local language(s); this combination of Kannada and English, therefore, is unsurprising. Most of my conversations and the workshops conducted during my time with the Gender Sensitisation and People-Friendly Police Project (2001–2007) and interviews after my resignation in 2007 slipped in and out of English, Kannada and, occasionally, Urdu or Hindi. However, there is a language division based on position, status and class: these conversations were conducted primarily in Kannada with the junior officers, and primarily in English with the senior officers.

14.   See, for instance, the attempt of Kodagu Gowdas from the district of Kodagu (formerly known as Coorg) to move their classification from Category IIIA to IIA claiming both a different caste ancestry from the Vokkaligas, and a greater level of economic deprivation ('Kodavas seek change in BC category', The Hindu, 26 November 2004).

References

AHMED, SARA 2007 'The Language of Diversity', *Ethnic and Racial Studies*, vol. 30, no. 2, pp. 235–56

ALI, SUKI 2006 'Racializing research: managing power and politics?', *Ethnic and Racial Studies*, vol. 29, no. 3, pp. 471–86

ARNOLD, DAVID 1986 *Police Power and Colonial Rule: 1859–1947*, Oxford: Oxford University Press

BAYLEY, DAVID H. 1969 *The Police and Political Development in India*, Princeton, NJ: Princeton University Press

BENSCHOP, YVONNE 2001 'Pride, prejudice and performance', *International Journal of Human Resources Management*, vol. 12, no. 7, pp. 1166–81

BÉTEILLE, ANDRÉ 2000 'Caste in contemporary India', in C. J. Fuller (ed.), *Caste Today*, Oxford: Oxford University Press, pp. 150–79

CENSUS OF INDIA 2001 http://www.censusindia.gov.in/ (accessed 28 September 2008); Government of India 1994 Census of India 1991, New Delhi: Registrar General and Census Commissioner

CHATTERJEE, PARTHA 1993 *The Nation and its Fragments: Colonial and Post Colonial Histories*, Princeton, NJ: Princeton University Press

DE ZWAART, FRANK 1994 *The Bureaucratic Merry-Go-Round: Manipulating the Transfer of Indian Civil Servants*, Amsterdam: Amsterdam University Press

DIRKS, NICHOLAS B. 2001 *Castes of Mind: Colonialism and the Making of Modern India*, Princeton: Princeton University Press

FULLER, CHRISTOPHER J. 2000 'Introduction: caste today' in C. J. Fuller (ed.) *Caste Today*, Oxford: Oxford University Press, pp. 1–31

GOVERNMENT OF INDIA 2001 *Data on Police Organisations in India*, New Delhi: Bureau of Police Research and Development

GOVERNMENT OF KARNATAKA 2002 *Police Recruitment Test: Manual of Recruitment of Police Constables*, Bangalore: Directorate of Police Recruitment

——— 2007 *Annual Report of the Police Department for the Year 2007*, Bangalore: Office of the Director General and Inspector General of Police

GUNARATNAM, YASMIN 2003 *Researching Race and Ethnicity: Methods, Knowledge and Power*, London: Sage Publications

GUPTA, DIPANKAR 2000 *Interrogating Caste: Understanding Hierarchy and Difference in Indian Society*, New Delhi: Penguin Books
────── 2005 'Caste and politics: identity over system', *Annual Review of Anthropology*, vol. 21, pp. 409–27
HARAWAY, DONNA 1991 'Situated knowledges: The science question in feminism and the privilege of the partial perspective', in D. Haraway, *Simians, Cyborgs and Women: The Reinvention of Nature*, New York: Routledge, pp. 183–202
HARDING, SANDRA 1991 *The Science Question in Feminism*, Milton Keynes, UK: Open University Press
HARDING, SANDRA (ed.) 2004 *The Feminist Standpoint Theory Reader*, New York: Fetter Lane
HARRISS, JOHN 1982 *Capitalism and Peasant Farming: Agrarian Structure and Ideology in Northern Tamil Nadu*, Bombay: Oxford University Press
KARANTH, G. K. 2004 'Replication or dissent? Culture and institutions among 'untouchable' Scheduled Castes in Karnataka', *Contributions to Indian Sociology*, vol. 38, pp. 137–63
KAVIRAJ, SUDIPTA (ed.) 1997 *Politics in India*, New Delhi: Oxford University Press
KNOWLES, CAROLINE 2003 *Race and Social Analysis*, London: Sage
KOTHARI, RAJNI 1964 'The Congress 'System' in India', *Asian Survey*, vol. 4, no. 12, pp. 1161–73
MANASA 2000 'Karnataka and the Women's Reservation Bill', *Economic and Political Weekly*, vol. 35, no. 43/44, pp. 3849–53
MANOR, JAMES 1989 'Karnataka: Caste, class, dominance and politics in a cohesive society', in Francine Frankel and M. S. A. Rao (eds), *Dominance and State Power in Modern India: Decline of a Social Order*, Oxford: Oxford University Press, pp. 322–61
MARKS, MONIQUE 2005 *Transforming the Robocops: Changing Police in South Africa*, Durban: University of Natal Press
MURJI, KARIM and SOLOMOS, JOHN (eds) 2005 *Racialisation: Studies in Theory and Practice*, Oxford: Oxford University Press
PRASHAD, VIJAY 2003 'Bruce Lee and the anti-imperialism of kung fu: a polycultural adventure', in, *Positions*, vol. 11, no. 1, pp. 51–90
RAGHAVAN, R. K. 1989 *Indian Police: Problems, Planning and Perspectives*, New Delhi: Manohar Publications
RAMANUJAN, A. K. 1973 *Speaking of Siva*, New Delhi: Penguin Books
REDDY, DEEPA 2005 'The ethnicity of caste', *Anthropological Quarterly*, vol. 78, no. 3, pp. 543–84
SENGUPTA, ANASUYA 1998 *Embedded or Stuck: the study of the Indian state, its embeddedness in social institutions and state capacity*, University of Oxford: M.Phil. thesis, unpublished
SKOCPOL, THEDA 1985 'Bringing the State Back In: Strategies of Analysis in Current Research', in Peter Evans, Dietrich Rueschemeyer and Theda Skocpol (eds.), *Bringing the State Back In*, Cambridge: Cambridge University Press
SOLOMOS, JOHN 2003 *Race and Racism in Britain*, Basingstoke, UK: Palgrave
SRINIVAS, M. N. 1987 *The Dominant Caste and Other Essays*, Oxford: Oxford University Press
SUBRAMANIAN, K. S. 2007 *Political Violence and the Police in India*, New Delhi: Sage
THE TIMES OF INDIA 2008 'Rage Runs in Mangalore', 16 September 2008
THIMMAIAH, G. 1993 *Power Politics and Social Justice: Backward Classes in Karnataka*, New Delhi: Sage
VERMA, ARVIND 2005 *The Indian Police: A Critical Evaluation*, New Delhi: Regency
WADE, ROBERT 1982 'Corruption: where does the money go', *Economic and Political Weekly*, vol.17, no. 40, p. 1606
YOUNG, ALFORD A. JR 2004 'Experiences in ethnographic interviewing about race: the inside and the outside of it' in Martin Bulmer and John Solomos (eds), *Researching Race and Racism*, London: Routledge, pp. 187–202

Index

Page numbers in *Italics* represent tables.
Page numbers in **Bold** represent figures.

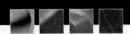
International Feminist Journal of Politics

EDITORS:
Sandra Whitworth, *Department of Political Science and School of Women's Studies, York University, Canada*
Catherine Eschle, *University of Strathclyde, UK*
Teresia Teaiwa, *Victoria University of Wellington, New Zealand*

International Feminist Journal of Politics is a unique cross-cultural and international forum to foster debate and dialogue at the intersection of international relations, politics and women's studies. Developed by a team of leading feminist scholars, this journal brings together some of the most influential figures in the field to build a global critical community of writers and readers.

This journal features research on women, gender relations and sexuality from the perspectives of:

- International relations
- Political theory
- Globalization studies
- International political economy
- Comparative politics
- Peace research
- International law
- Development studies
- Political geography
- Cultural studies

As well as the main section of the journal featuring full-length articles, it also offers a special 'Conversations' section, which publishes interviews with leading scholars and practitioners, conference reports and film readings. The book review section regularly features review articles as well as individual book reviews.

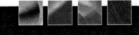

Routledge
Taylor & Francis Group

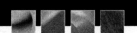

Ethnicity & Health

EDITORS:

Karl Atkin, *University of York, UK*
Hannah Bradby, *University of Warwick, UK*
Seeromanie Harding, *MRC Social & Public Health Unit, Glasgow, UK*

Ethnicity & Health is an international academic journal designed to meet the world-wide interest in the health of ethnic groups. It embraces original papers from the full range of disciplines concerned with investigating the relationship between 'ethnicity' and 'health' (including medicine and nursing, public health, epidemiology, social sciences, population sciences, and statistics). The journal also covers issues of culture, religion, gender, class, migration, lifestyle and racism, in so far as they relate to health and its anthropological and social aspects.

The journal aims to:
- Deal with practice and policy in a thoughtful and critical way.
- Present empirical material in a way that considers theoretical issues in addition to implications for policy and practice, given the contested nature of both 'ethnicity' and 'health'.
- Address the methodological problems that face both qualitative and quantitative studies in multi-cultural societies.

Ethnicity & Health is directed at the international community. Its audience includes academics, health and social care practitioners, those who train practitioners, and those in the policy and voluntary sectors.

For further information please visit: **www.tandf.co.uk/journals/ceth**.

> 2008 Impact Factor: 0.939
>
> Rankings: 1/9 (Ethnic Studies), 6/7 (Medical Ethics)
>
> © 2009 Thomson Reuters, 2008 *Journal Citation Reports®*

To sign up for tables of contents, new publications and citation alerting services visit **www.informaworld.com/alerting**

 updates
Taylor & Francis Group

Register your email address at **www.tandf.co.uk/journals/eupdates.asp** to receive information on books, journals and other news within your areas of interest.

Powered by
informaworld

For further information please contact Customer Services at either:
Routledge Customer Services, T&F Informa UK Ltd, Sheepen Place, Colchester, Essex CO3 3LP, UK
Tel: +44 (0) 20 7017 5544 Fax: +44 (0) 20 7017 5198
Email: subscriptions@tandf.co.uk

Routledge Customer Services, Taylor & Francis Inc, 325 Chestnut Street, 8th Floor, Philadelphia, PA 19106, USA
Tel: +1 800 354 1420 (toll-free calls from within the US)
or +1 215 625 8900 (calls from overseas) Fax: +1 215 625 2940
Email: customerservice@taylorandfrancis.com

When ordering, please quote: XC12301A

View an online sample issue at:
www.tandf.co.uk/journals/ceth